ENDORSEMENTS

"One of the marks of a good Christian is having deeds that match your words. Pastor Jerome has not just written on prayer, but he is a living example of a praying life. In an attempt to cope with the rapidly changing world, men are always in search of methods but God is still looking for praying men. Men who will understand the dynamics of prayer and will stand in the gap to connect heaven with the earth. This book *90 keys to Effective Praying* will definitely challenge and spur our generation back to standing in the gap again for the manifestations of God's plan on the earth".

Dr. Festus Adeyeye,
Senior Pastor, Abundant Life Christian Centre Worldwide, USA

In this powerful book, Pastor Jerome Obode takes the modern day Christian and believer through the various ramifications of a praying life. Scholarly and thought-provoking, it is a no-holds-barred training manual of how to use the greatest weapon on earth. That nuclear weapon is prayer. It is the power to conquer on our knees.

Dapo Ogunwusi,
Former Editor, Nigerian Tribune.

The place of prayer is where humanity meets with divinity. After reading the manuscript, and considered the life of the author whom I have known for many years as a man of prayer and a man after God's heart,…I recommend this book to church leaders as a manual to be used to lift the dying state of prayer in the body of Christ; all Christians need to have a copy. Don't just read this book and keep in the book shelf, give it to someone else and let us change our world.

God bless you.

Rev. Fola Achudume.
Senior Pastor, Victory Life Bible Church, Abeokuta, Nigeria

In my decades of relationship with Pastor Jerome, I have known him to be a man of prayer. He talks the talk and walks the walk. It brings joy to my heart, therefore, to see him sharing his experience of prayer in this book. This book gives simple and practical principles for effective prayer. I strongly recommend it.

Dr Ezekiel Olusegun Alawale
- Senior Pastor, God's Vineyard Ministries, United Kingdom

The activity of praying is one that is much talked and taught about but least indulged in. Pastor Jerome Obode, in '90 keys to effective praying' has written with the spirit of a great praying Saint and effective Intercessor. He reflects the simple, yet deep prayer life of a man of profound and intense prayer indulgences. The great subject of prayer is presented in a way that the message contained therein is simple, easily understood and remembered with ease while at the same time, spontaneously, provoking hunger and desire for prayer. This book is not just about prayer but a praying manual in itself.

Bishop Barth Orji
Coordinator, Praying Generals Network, United Kingdom

In nearly thirty years of Ministry and relationship I am yet to meet another man of God that so richly maximizes both the Privilege and Responsibility of praying. Pastor Jerome enjoys praying; he as well carries around a genuine burden of prayer for the least member of the Body of Christ

Rev. Patrick Odigie, Senior Minister, Prophetic Powerhouse, New York, USA

90 KEYS TO EFFECTIVE PRAYING

90 KEYS TO EFFECTIVE PRAYING

PRAYER A-Z ARRANGED IN ALPHABETICAL ORDER

JEROME O. OBODE

DEDICATION

This book is dedicated to the most-high God. Father, take all the glory for leading and helping me to bring forth this book- the very first of many to come. It is all by your grace.

Contents

FOREWORD

Prayer is a vast subject in the Bible and perhaps one of the most solemn privileges any mortal can be trusted to exercise on the earth. This is because prayer directly draws on the grace of God and grace is the highest power any created being can exercise under creation. The grace of God makes available to His Children, all the potential capabilities of the unlimited God. The privilege of prayer uniquely positions us to draw on that grace and for this reason, the word of God invites us to come boldly to the throne of grace and of course, this is possible only through the privilege and power of believing prayer.

Then of course is the Responsibility and Burden of prayer. Truth is we all must pray and we generally do this to one degree or the other but only a few practically take the responsibility of prayer serious enough to know the meaning of the Burden of prayer. In nearly thirty years of Ministry and relationship I am yet to meet another man of God that so richly maximizes both the Privilege and Responsibility of praying. Pastor Jerome enjoys praying; he as well carries around a genuine burden of prayer for the least member of the Body of Christ. His favourite quote is, *"... so labouring, we ought to support the weak..."* (Acts 20:35).

We are commanded in the scriptures to pray always and without ceasing. In order to progress from the mere duty of prayer to experience the privilege of praying to a serious impactful measure, we must come to know something of the Spirit of prayer. The Bible says Elijah was a man subject to like passion as we are and he prayed earnestly for the space of three years with tremendous results. The question is how did a weak man like him find the tenacity to engage in such soul travail without losing heart? The only answer is that the spirit of prayer rested upon him. God has greatly endowed the author with a rich spirit of prayer.

In close to thirty years of relationship, my very life and those of others have been greatly enriched and helped by the prayer grace on the Servant of God. I will here lift the curtain to help the reader aspire for what I personally consider the authors major and most important contribution to the body of Christ. I somehow trust God that reading a book on prayer by Pastor Jerome Obode, the genuine seeker will come into contact with and be imparted with the Spirit of prayer upon him. I have seen Pastor Jerome get on his knees and in a short time, whole mission begin to get infected with a generous soul-full spirit of prayer.

This particular grace to pray up others into praying, I personally believe forms the basis of the author's highest calling to the body of Christ in this hour. I whole-heartedly commend this book to the body of Christ, and trust that by reading you will be ushered into a new level in the 'school' of prayer.

Dr. Patrick Odigie

PREFACE

The decision to write this book is born out of a desire to write from my personal experience and perspective on the subject of prayer. Like many Christians, when I first gave my life to Christ in 1982, I was strongly drawn to and curious about the subject of prayer. In particular, I was so blessed and spurred by the examples of some older Christians that I craved to know more about prayer within the first few weeks of being born again. Within the first few months of giving my life to Christ, I was so hungry for God that I embarked on a three-day fast without food, and without anyone asking or encouraging me to do so.

Shortly after I received Christ into my life I would be on my knees for several hours in prayers, because I really wanted to be in God's presence. I was consumed by the passion for His presence. Over the years, this has grown into deeper experiences and understanding of prayer that I thought I should add my own story to the several thousands of prayer stories written by God's children.

I felt the need to address the subject in a completely different way which I hope will be a useful addition to the existing volumes. Prayer takes you beyond the confines of humanity into the dimension of divinity, enabling you to overcome every limitation. Through prayers, you can break boundaries, take over territories and reclaim everything that has been stolen by the enemy. If God can do a thing at all, then prayer can do the same, because prayer replaces human ability with God's ability. It sets the forces of success in motion, removes the friction from your efforts and preserves the gains of your labour. No one can be too strong to pray, and no one should be too weak or discouraged to pray. No one should ever give up without praying enough to experience God's power in their situation.

I encourage you to read through these pages with an open heart and mind, pray about and practice whatever insights the Holy Spirit brings to your heart. May you truly be blessed as you read through these pages.

Pastor Jerome Obode

ACKNOWLEDGEMENTS

This book has come to light because of the support and contributions in several ways, by many people to whom I am immensely grateful. I am deeply indebted to:

My Wife: Bola Obode for your love, sacrifices and commitment to me these past years. I cannot find enough words to express my gratitude to you; you have being a great source of strength and encouragement to me generally, and especially, in making this book a reality. Thank you.

My Children: Prince, Bernadette, Samuel and Zoe. It has been a great pleasure to have you as my children, I will always treasure you.

My Church Family: Thanks to you all, every member of Global Impact Tabernacle- you have been such a wonderful team to serve, it has been a joy to relate with you as God's precious gifts to my family. Your support and contributions are highly appreciated.

My Friends: Your list is so long I cannot name you all here; your absence here does not equate your absence from my heart. I am particularly indebted to Rev. Patrick and Pastor Mabel Odigie for being always there these many years. Dr Ezekiel Alawale, your friendship is immeasurable and I will always appreciate you. Special gratitude to Ruth and Tony Ufuah, and Stephen Hammond for your friendship and support over the years. Many thanks to Pastors Sylvester Ojobo, Shola Mene, Gabriel Diya, Tony and Dupe Obayori, Bishop Bartholomew Orji, Matthias

Basil and Dapo Aiyetigbo- you have been very wonderful and reliable colleagues. You are highly appreciated.

Many thanks to Dapo Ogunwusi, former Editor, Nigerian Tribune- your editorial contributions to this book are highly valued. Special thanks also to Esther Joseph, Kenny Arusuraire, Samuel Obode and Bernadette Obode for helping to type the manuscripts for this book. Stay blessed.

Finally, my deepest gratitude goes to the Almighty God- thank you Lord, for your love and calling. Thank you Father for bringing me out of the miry clay, setting my feet on the Rock to stay and putting a song in mouth today. I will forever praise your Name. Thank you once again, Daddy.

INTRODUCTION

You may have been drawn to this book because the title has aroused your curiosity; it may be that you attach so much importance to prayer that you sincerely wanted to know more. It could be that you have a relationship with the author and thought, 'let me have a quick glance at his book'. Many people reading this book will be Christians who believe in the power of prayer; their love for God and interest in the subject may be the singular reason why this work has found its way into their hands. There are several hundreds of books all over the world written about prayer, and many more are yet to be published, but there is something different about each author and their work.

This book addresses many areas already popular with several authors and countless numbers of God's children. The difference I hope, these pages will make is that they will address aspects which are rarely considered as relevant to the subject of prayer. Prayer is too vast a subject to be covered in any single book, because it has to do directly with God Himself. This book will shed plenty of light on some areas taken for granted by God's children as they pray daily. I have addressed several aspects of prayer that are not readily found in many prayer manuals.

The book begins with the need and how to create time for God in prayer. Specific times and places are crucial to a successful prayer life, just like keeping appointments with doctors and business partners are critical to our personal and economic well-being. Some people pray without specific aims, without clearly defining what their prayer objectives are;

this makes their praying undefined, uncoordinated and unfocused. This book offers useful advice on how to overcome this problem and avoid the pain and discouragement that could result from unanswered prayers.

The book also discusses the role of angels in prayers- angelic beings play a critical part in how God delivers prayer answers to His people, yet many of us are not constantly aware of the usefulness of angels to the praying Christian. So much of this book has also focused on the need to develop a personal relationship with God. Prayer is not magical; it is spiritual, and unless you are in a tightly-knit relationship with the Trinity, it will be difficult for you to enjoy a thriving prayer life. God is the source of all prayer energy, He is the only one that can answer your prayer, and without Him you cannot preserve your prayer gains. Prayer can only be as effective as your personal relationship with your heavenly Father. The closer you are to God the quicker you can enjoy the blessings of answered prayers.

Failure is not an option in prayer because everyone who approaches God in prayer often has serious reasons for doing so. This book addresses the reasons why many prayers do not get answered and how you can overcome these barriers. People give up praying because they do not receive answers to their prayers. God has invited us to bring our burdens to Him, but He never intended for prayer to be boring or burdensome. I have written about these as much as possible within the book. I have also discussed how to bring intensity into your praying- weak, lukewarm and passive praying will hardly give you the victory you desire; this book sheds more light on how you can pray with intensity and tenacity, and expedite the answers to your prayer.

One of the most difficult aspects of prayer is how to develop and sustain the habit of praying. Success or failure in any aspect of life is dependent upon the habits we have formed around those areas. Habits affect our health, education, jobs, businesses, family life and much more. As in everything else the habit of prayer has to be cultivated from the point we gave our lives to Christ. You will find here some useful advice on how to gradually develop the habit of prayer by taking little daily steps that can alter your entire prayer life.

I have highlighted the need for discipline as a necessary ingredient to effective praying, and how you can trust God to help you develop a more disciplined life for productive prayer times. You will learn how to never miss your prayer times again, how to keep the prayer fire burning so you never run out of prayer fuel. You will also learn how to keep praying even when you are too down and demotivated to pray.

The easy-to-read chapters of this book have been arranged in alphabetical order from A-Z; they are carefully written to examine a huge number of issues not commonly addressed in prayer books. It is my honest belief that reading this book from cover to cover will take anyone's prayer life to another level. For some people, many of the truths revealed here will be new, but for many others the book will simply serve as a reminder of things they already know, or which they ought to remember or practice. Either way, I believe there is something for everyone who takes the time to read through these pages- in part or in whole. I sincerely hope that your journey through this book will usher you into a new era in your prayer life. Enjoy your reading.

1

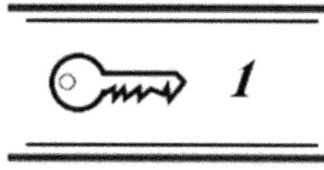

APPOINTMENT WITH GOD

Keep your appointments with God. This is the number one key to effective praying and a successful Christian life. Set aside specific times at which you meet with God; also have a specific place where you are alone with God. People have all sorts of reasons why they cannot find enough time to pray. Prayer is one of the most essential activities any Christian can engage in, and you must do everything to protect your prayer time against every form of interference.

Why Make and Keep Appointments with God

Think about a life, a day or an organization where appointments are neither made nor kept. You will have a picture of confusion, chaos and inefficiency. To enjoy a steady, fruitful and reliable prayer life, you need to make and keep regular prayer appointments with your heavenly Father. Prayer must be deliberate and not left to the mercy of other activities. Appointments with doctors help their practice to run smoothly. It also helps to achieve goals and objectives. Well scheduled activities help make businesses effective and productive. A life where anything goes will never achieve maximum potential.

Scheduled times of prayer indicate to God that your prayer life can be taken seriously. It also portrays you as a person God can depend upon to carry out the ministry of prayer or intercession. God can embark on a prayer project with you and trust that it will be completed with minimal interruption and uncertainty. A planned prayer life teaches you to develop discipline. It is less likely that Christians who do not have specific plan for prayers will have definite plans for other areas of life. Not keeping business or work appointments can cost us and other stake holders a lot. Failing to keep prayer appointments can also have similar consequences because a missed prayer appointment could have a ripple effect on other aspects of life.

Having specific times and places of prayers demonstrate to God that you are reliable. There are times when God really needs someone to carry out a particular prayer assignment. He would rely on you – because He knows He can depend on you to arrive at the right time and the right place for prayers. Anyone who is really serious about prayers must begin here: regular appointments with God.

Why People Do Not Keep Prayer Appointments with God

Prayer is spiritual capital. It is the spiritual air we breathe. It is the foundation for successful Christian living, yet it is easy to give it little attention. Good prayer will lead to good results. Great prayers will facilitate great success. Prayer alone will not achieve much in life, but too little or irregular praying can lead to personal or group failure. There are many reasons why people do not pray enough.

Too Busy to Pray

Too many people are just too busy to create time for quality prayer; they wait to be forced into praying by some undesirable circumstances. Prayer is not primarily for emergencies; prayer is easier in 'peace times' than in 'war times', because then you can pray with greater sanity and stability rather than fire-fight with prayers. Why wait to pray under duress when you can do it without stress? Truth is, the busier we are, the more of God's grace we need. Prayer will reduce your stress; 'lubricate' the 'friction points' of a busy day and put God in charge of everything. I have seen this happen several times in my life. The more I pray, the less I stress. The less I pray the more I am pressed. A divine equation that never changes.

> *"Trust in the LORD with all your heart; and lean not on your*
> *own understanding; in all your ways acknowledge Him, And*
> *He shall direct your paths"* (Proverbs 3:5-6).

No matter how busy you are, finding quality time for prayer will always pay off. Things will not run smoothly until you give God the central place in your life.

Too Disappointed to Pray.

Experience of unanswered prayers is another reason why many people fail to give prayer its rightful place. Nobody wants to be ignored, and there are times when it seems like God has ignored your request. God never ignores His children. In fact, He takes pleasure in our prayer. The answer to your prayer may seem delayed, but God never denies His children their blessings. Just because your prayer has not been answered does not mean that God has forgotten you. Do not give up, do not be disappointed. Make prayer your priority, do it with intensity and consistency. God will never fail you.

Too Blessed to Pray

Christians in poor countries tend to pray a lot more than those in richer ones. The reason is obvious – they have more needs for which they have to depend on God. Are you too blessed to pray? There is always something to pray about, if it is not about you or your loved ones, then there are numerous people and issues needing prayer all over the globe. Find something to pray about if you are too blessed to pray for yourself. Prayer is not always about your personal needs. It is also about a relationship with God in which fellowship is the cardinal objective. Having enough or more than enough should not keep anyone from communing with God. You can spend more time thanking God and interceding on behalf of others.

Too Lazy to Pray

Successful prayer can be hard work. It requires time, discipline and tenacity. Many people find the discipline of prayer too tasking to cope with. It takes energy (spiritual, physical and mental) to maintain a productive prayer life. Incidentally, a lot of very disciplined, hard-working and successful people find prayer an arduous task. Prayer is a discipline that can, and should be learned. It requires some simple daily routine, but might also involve some physical and emotional energy. Any one who wants to enjoy the uncommon benefits of prayer ought to learn the act and discipline of payer. Like everything else of value, success in prayer demands all of your our efforts.

Too Ignorant to Pray.

During His earthly ministry Jesus demonstrated the importance of prayer to a successful walk with God. He knew the power of prayer, so He prayed both day and night. He prayed till the last minute of His life on earth. Ignorance of the possibilities of prayer robs people of its potential benefits. Many of us are like little children who have no ability to know certain things, but the closer you come to God, the more you will discover about the power of prayer. You can know more about prayer through your personal experience or through the experiences of other people. Too many Christians cannot be bothered to learn from others about prayer because everyone thinks they already know how to pray. Read more about prayer. Learn more from, and observe others pray, and your prayer life will continue to grow.

Too Independent to Pray.

Natural abilities can sometimes work to our disadvantage. It can lead to overconfidence and unhealthy independence. People can be so smart and talented they think they do not need God. One can be such a star in his own eyes that he does not see the need to pray. Prayer can avert disaster, activate progress and accelerate success. The smartest thing to do is to make prayer the key to victory in personal and professional undertakings.

Nothing is more crucial than keeping your appointment with God. Create a definite time and place to pray on a daily basis. Your time with God is more important than time spent on anything else. When you draw strength from God you will give Him the chance to eliminate stress from your life, whatever you do. It should be God first; everything else should follow.

2

AIM AT A TARGET

Prayer should be laser focused and razor sharp. Before setting out to pray, take time to define what you want to pray about and possibly put it in writing. Praying without defined aims is to pray without expectations. Write out your requests, deadlines and the amount of time you wish to invest in each prayer item. When a team of footballers set out to play in a tournament, they must first establish their aim – to score goals and win within a time frame. They also create a game plan. They stick to the plan, only making adjustments when necessary. Prayer works in the same way. Paul said,

> *"I therefore so run, not as uncertainly; so fight I, not as one that beateth the air"* (I Corinthians 9:26).

A lot of people pray without clear cut aims- not being specific, and therefore either have no results to celebrate, or are unable to know when their prayers are answered. Setting out your prayer goals helps to clarify direction, create focus, eliminate confusion and increase motivation.

Focus

I have been in prayer meetings where people failed to determine what they wanted before they commenced praying. This always leads to a waste of precious time and lack of sustained motivation. Know what you want before you set out to pray. Failing to plan makes prayer both nebulous and ineffective.

A Boost to Faith

Well defined prayers can lead to greater concentration, and enhancement of faith. When you focus your prayers on specific issues, your faith will be stimulated because your prayers will be more directed on intentional targets. Clearly defined prayers in a group means everyone is singing from the same page. When the results manifest everyone can identify the answers and celebrate together. Well thought out, clearly written prayer aims will boost intensity, tenacity and make prayer something worthwhile.

Elimination of Confusion

When faced with difficult situations, many people find prayer arduous and daunting, and often do not know how to channel their prayers. The solution is to calm down and plan your prayers; if possible write them into a list. I get bewildered when I observe people pray, and all they do is just keep praying endlessly in tongues and without co-ordination. I am a strong believer in speaking in tongues but I also believe that God wants us to be specific in our prayers. Of course, the Holy Spirit will interrupt you sometimes, and at other times, you may run out of words or spiritual energy and the only way to stay effective and energised might be to pray in tongues.

Performance Enhancement

As mentioned earlier you are likely to achieve enormous results in prayer when it is well planned and targeted. The plan should include what to pray about, and how much time to invest in prayer (the Holy Spirit can overrule this). Imprecise and ill-defined prayer can sap you of spiritual energy, especially for prayers that require continuity in the medium and long term. If prayer is not well aimed and focused, you will be stabbing the air.

Performance Measurement

This will be addressed in greater detail later in the book. What gets measured gets done, monitored and accounted for. How can one truly account for their prayer lives unless prayer goals are expressly stated? Set daily, weekly, monthly, quarterly and yearly prayer goals. Do not just pray; know the number of prayer items you must pray about daily, allocate time to each. It may not always end up smoothly, but you will be able to look back and assess your prayer success. Also make room for unplanned prayer activities because life does not always go according to plan. The Holy Spirit may also occasionally put aside your prayer plan and present God's plan to you.

Before commencing prayer, it is always important to ask, 'what is the purpose or aim of my prayer?' Be precise about this. Put into writing in as few words as possible, what exactly you are asking God to do. Praying should be done as specifically as possible with minimum ambiguity and fuzz.

3

ADVANCE IN ADVERSITY

To advance is to make progress, accelerate, improve or increase. The true test of a mature Christian is the ability to trust God when the chips are down and the going gets tough. When Satan throws everything at you and you become overwhelmed with crisis, that is the time to prove the 'stuff' you are made of as a Christian. In the day of adversity God wants you to turn your stumbling blocks into building blocks and move to the next level of your life. Only a very small percentage of Christians really pray when faced with major obstacles. Some turn away from God. Others seek alternative solutions to God at a time when they need God the most.

Weak and Weary Ways

There will be seasons when you become weak and weary. God sees those moments and expects you to turn everything over to Him in prayer. He will ensure that you come out of the situation a shinning star. Trials and testing are inevitable parts of the Christian life. You cannot avoid them. Your response to them however, will either make or mar you as a child of God. The lessons to learn from the experience and testimony of Job is that God knows everything; and that after all said and done you shall come out purified as gold if you hold fast to the end. Every challenge or obstacle have opportunities and blessings concealed in them, which are as precious as gold. In turbulent times, many people unfortunately abandon God and seek for alternatives to God.

1. In the midst of suffering do not blame God or people. Remember the cataclysmic events that happened in the life of Job. Yet, *"In all this, Job sinned not, nor charged God foolishly."* (Job 1:22). Keep praying; stop blaming; pray until you are out of the woods. Learn the lessons and move on. There is always a lesson to learn, something to 'take away'. Jesus says, "Come unto me, all ye that labour and are heavy laden, and I will give you rest" (Matthew 11:28). Take it to Jesus in prayers.

2. Maintain a positive attitude in crisis. If your attitude to difficult times is wrong, nearly every step you take at the time could go wrong. Habakkuk teaches us how to respond to trying times: *"Although the fig tree shall not blossom, neither shall fruit be in the vines; the labour of the olives shall fail … yet I will rejoice in the LORD, I will joy in the God of my salvation."* (Habakkuk 3:17-18) Be determined to stay happy and steadfast to the end. God will honour your prayer of faith and come to your rescue from every storm of life.

3. Protect your mind. The mind is the biggest battlefield in life. It is the most important theatre of war. The battle is either won or lost in the mind. Satan knows this, and will do everything to conquer you in this arena. If you lose the battle of the mind, you are most likely to live in defeat. Protect your mind at all costs by meditating upon God's word and using every spiritual weapon available to you to overcome the enemy. The more room you give to negative thought, the more likely you are to speak, act and end up negative and defeated. This will weaken your ability to pray, as the time you need prayer the most is when you face the wind of adversity. It is not a time to quit, but a time to fight; and more importantly, fight and win.

When you stop praying and believing God, you keep God out of your problem. The devil becomes emboldened. You must pray when things are going well and when they are not. Stay on top of your problems and encourage yourself like David did when his wives and property were taken away by the Amalekites. Find a reason to be happy, prayerful and optimistic. Stay around people who can inspire and encourage you. Solicit the prayers of others when it gets too tough for you. Believe that you can, as no one can do the believing on your behalf. Remember to ask God for a way out of or around the crisis because He has promised to make a way even in the wilderness and where there seems to be no way. Never fail to look for the hidden opportunity within your challenges as there is always at least one.

The Lord knows that sometimes you feel you have had enough and can no longer continue. The bible says, *"...they that wait upon the LORD shall renew their strength; they shall mount up with wings as the eagle. They shall run, and not be weary; and they shall walk, and not faint"* (Isaiah 40:31).

Waiting upon the Lord is an active rather than a passive state. When the children of Israel were faced with the danger of extinction at the Red Sea, they remained motionless and hopeless in the face of disaster. God said to them to go forward. They simply obeyed. They went forward, God went with them and the rest is history. You must advance in adversity. Take things to the Lord in prayer. Do not accept defeat, even for once. Get into prayer action. Fast, pray and study God's word. Do not stay there waiting for something to happen. You must make it happen in prayer and by every other godly means at your disposal. The worst time not to pray is when you find yourself in crisis. And guess what? Anyone- just anyone, can find themselves there. It is a point when you do not feel like praying, when you do not want to pray, and when you wish everything would just happen the way you wanted without lifting a finger.

4

ALERT BUT NOT ALARMED

A victorious Christian life requires watchfulness and battle readiness. The enemy is very deceptive. He operates in total disguise and attacks in all forms and shapes, many of which may never reveal him as the source. If you knew the devil was the origin of a particular problem you would definitely fight back in every conceivable way. But this is not always the case. Satan is out there to harass God's people, and he conceals himself in things and people that are actually orchestrated by him to trouble and terrify God's children. You should therefore,

> *"Be sober; be vigilant; because your adversary the devil walks about like a roaring lion, seeking whom he may devour. Resist him steadfastly in the faith, knowing that the same sufferings are experienced by your brotherhood in the world"* (1Peter 5:8).

God does not want His children to be careless and be taken unawares by evil. God's Word tells us that Satan is all over the place, always seeking an opportunity to attack. The answer to his threat and craftiness is to watch and pray. This means to:

- Avoid spiritual slumber.
- Be conscious of your environment and the impact it may have on your faith and prayer life.
- Avoid being carried away by the things of the world.
- Be spiritually alert and not be deceived by demonic camouflages.

- Be able to differentiate between the truth as revealed in God's Word and the lies of Satan.
- Examine your spiritual life and take corrective measures to put your Christian life on tract.

Satan is a master at putting up a mask in the form of illness, financial crisis, marital problems, troublesome children, difficult relationships and all sorts of harsh and ungodly activities. Rather than taking to your heels, getting depressed or discouraged, go to God in prayer. It is the most powerful tool in the world. Put God to the test and trust Him for the best. Position yourself for a miracle. If it does not happen today it will happen in the coming days. Know the facts, but use the facts to fight a good fight. Never let your problem (or your knowledge of the facts), rob you of your willpower to pray because many things you worry about will never happen the way they first appear. Stay calm and refuse to panic.

Never allow Satan to cripple, taunt or threaten you through the negative events that take place in your life. Satan would like to use them as a tool to incapacitate you but God wants to use them as a tool to manifest His power in you. Worrying, moaning and complaining will never change your situation. Brace up and put yourself together. Different types of sicknesses require varying levels of concentration, quantity and duration of medication. All medical conditions do not require the same type and levels of treatment. Similarly, different dimensions of problem demand different levels of prayer warfare. In the days of adversity you must never be found weak and worn out. It is the time you must gird yourself with divine strength and overcome the enemy.

There is nothing new about Satan's schemes; it is the same old devil. Never back off when Satan barks at you. Turning your back will feed the enemy's pride. Fighting back will constrain him, elevate you and give you something to celebrate.

5

ANOINTED FOR CONQUEST

Victory in spiritual warfare cannot be achieved without the power of the Holy Spirit. The anointing of the Holy Spirit empowers you and guarantees your success in prayer. To anoint means to smear or rub with oil. It also means to consecrate to an office or ministry. To enjoy the fullness of God's presence and the power of God in prayer, every Christian needs to be baptised in the Holy Spirit with the evidence of Speaking in tongues. The anointing is the grease on your gear, the wind in your sails and the spring in your heel when it comes to prayer and every Christian work.

Not By Power, Not By Might

Prayer is a spiritual exercise, and one that can only be made effective by divine assistance. Your personal strength will not take you far enough. In fact, your prayer life could sometimes end up in frustration if you depend on personal ability and wisdom. Personal stamina, experience and knowledge are all important to prayer, but more crucial than these, the power of the Holy Spirit is the secret behind every successful prayer life. Romans 8:28 sheds light on the part played by the Holy Spirit in our prayers:

> *"Likewise the Spirit also helpeth our infirmities; for we know not what we should pray for as we ought: but the Spirit itself*

maketh Pintercession for us with groaning which cannot be uttered" (Romans 8:26).

This passage says the Spirit 'helps' our infirmities or weakness. The word 'help' in this passage originates from the Greek word 'paraclete' – which means the following:

- Advocate or help.
- One who consoles or helps.
- One who encourages or uplifts.
- One who refreshes.
- One who intercedes on behalf of another.
- Comforter.

The Holy Spirit performs these roles in your prayer life. Barrier breaking, life changing and result oriented prayers are those which carry the touch of the Holy Spirit. Your prayer life will be extremely successful if you are baptised in the Holy Spirit, and allow the Spirit to continually take charge of your entire life.

Teaching Us to Pray

The greatest teacher of all times – the Holy Spirit is ever present to teach us to pray. The disciples frequently witnessed Jesus praying, and on one occasion one of them requested from Jesus at the end of His prayers,

> *"... Lord, teach us to pray, as John also taught his disciples"* (Luke 11:1).

The Holy Spirit can also teach us through books and conferences produced or organised by other Christians. It will take some humility and willingness to learn from these people. Jesus did surely answer the disciple's request, and hence the model prayer commonly referred to today as the Lord's Prayer. The Spirit teaches us the right words to use when we pray, the prayer duration, what and who to pray for.

The Spirit also teaches us when to know our prayer is answered, how God speaks and how to listen to His voice when we pray. He will tell you when to change prayer direction, how to know whether your prayer is on target, or whether to simply worship God on a particular occasion rather than presenting Him with a list. People void of the presence of the Holy Spirit will lack prayer fire power.

Strength to Pray

The power of the Holy Spirit working in us gives us strength, faith and tenacity to press through our prayers. You will never fully enjoy all that God has for you in prayer unless you pray in the power of the Holy Spirit. The Spirit gives you strength in the inner man. The Spirit helps you bear the burden of prayer to the very end, by helping your infirmity or weaknesses.

Many times you do not have the strength, or see the need to pray. All you need at such times is to go ahead anyway, and ask for the enablement of the Spirit. In my personal experience I have never been disappointed by the Holy Spirit. All I needed to do each time was to take a step of faith and go before God in payer, and His power will be released. The Holy Spirit assists our prayer life in many ways:

1. He empowers us to pray.
    Jesus promised that we will receive power after receiving the Holy Spirit (Acts 2:8).

2. The prophet Micah said 'I am full of power by the Spirit of the Lord…' (Micah 3:8).
3. He gives us spiritual liberty in prayer
    The anointing of the Holy Spirit, gives liberty or freedom in prayers (2 Corinthians 3:17).
4. The Spirit makes intercession for us (Romans 8:23, 26).
5. The Spirit burdens us to pray.

6. The Spirit gives us direction and discretion in prayer (Romans 8:26, 27).

7. The Holy Spirit gives us boldness to access God's throne (Hebrews 4:16).

8. The Holy Spirit enables believers to pray in line with our Father's will (Romans 8:27).

9. The Spirit gives us assurance that our prayers are answered – by impressing this on our heart.

One of the greatest problems with Christians is that everyone thinks they are very good at praying; everyone pretends that their prayers always yield results. There is not a single Christian out there who can claim they know all about prayer, yet only new believers in many cases, desire to learn or study how to develop their prayer lives. Without the Holy Spirit you will never get the best out of prayer. The anointing of the Spirit is the fuel that powers your prayer engine. If you are not yet baptised in the Holy Spirit, pray for this to happen- get all the support and help you need to receive this precious gift. If you have already received the Holy Ghost baptism, more prayers means more power. Fasting, worship and bible study can help activate and sustain the power of the Spirit in you. If you do not pray with power, Satan will know this and continue to take you for granted.

6

Angels on your assignment

The bible explicitly teaches the existence and activities of Angels. There are demonic as well as godly angels, but the focus of this section is on heavenly and godly angels. Evil angels are referred to as demons. Angelic relationship with us and our prayer is so important that it deserves some treatment in this book. Angels perform various roles such as carrying God's messages, protection of believers, provision, and worshipping God. In many cases God deploys angels in response to the believer's prayers. Their mission is to minister to the needs of the saints as God deems fit, especially after we have prayed.

Angels are very powerful beings. Only one angel slew 185,000 Assyrians on behalf of Israel in one night in the days of King Hezekiah (11Kings 19:35). They can understand or speak any language due to their divine ability (1Corinthians 13:1). Angels are God's own army – the hosts of God (Psalm 103:21; Nehemiah 9:6). So, when you pray expect angels (we do not pray to them) to be used by God to convey the answers as God choses. Most spiritual battles we win are fought by angels on our behalf in answer to prayers.

Jesus and Angels

An interesting passage in Hebrews says,

> *"Are they not all ministering spirits, sent forth to minister for them who shall be heirs of salvation?"* (Hebrews 1:14).

Jesus is much superior to angels (Hebrews 1:4) and they are created to worship Him (Hebrews 1:6). Jesus is king and angels are His servants. Jesus is the head of the Church and angels carry out His orders on behalf of the redeemed.

Angels and the Believer's Prayers

God can use angels to supply our spiritual, emotional and physical needs. Whilst we should not pray directly to angels, there are numerous examples of how God uses these beings to meet the needs of His people.

Strength for the Weary

First Kings gives an account of how Elijah had killed all the prophets of Baal during the idolatrous and evil reign of King Ahab. Ahab's wife, Jezebel, vowed to kill Elijah with the sword in revenge for killing the prophets of Baal. Elijah absconded into the desert for fear of his life. As he sat under a tree, discouraged, complaining and exhausted, an angel delivered to him food and water which sustained him for another forty days and forty nights during his flight from Jezebel (1Kings 19:5-6).

Another example is when Daniel fasted for three weeks for the nation of Israel and was fatigued from fasting and praying. Daniel stated, *"...I had no strength left, my face turned deathly pale and I was helpless"* (Daniel 10:10). An angel appeared to Daniel and told him that the answer to his prayer was delayed due to satanic opposition which was eventually overcome by the arch-angel Michael. As Daniel explained that his strength was gone and he could hardly breathe, the angel touched

Daniel and asked him to receive strength. Immediately, his strength was fully restored.

Jesus also benefited from several angelic ministrations. During his forty days and forty nights of fasting, He was tempted by the devil to do things that were against the Father's will. At the end of the temptation, Matthew records:

"Then the devil leaveth him, and, behold, angels came and ministered unto him" (Matthew 4:11). The bible's says those who wait on the Lord shall renew their strength, if you are feeling faint pray and ask God for renewed strength. You need strength to be successful in prayers.

Provision and Protection

Often, when we pray for protection angels are assigned the task of protecting us from evil.

- An angel shut up the mouths of the lions when Daniel was thrown into the lions' den. The lions could not harm Him (Daniel 6:1-24).
- On the night before he was to be killed by the Jewish leadership for preaching the gospel, Peter was delivered from the prison cell and his shackles by an angel (Acts 12:5-11) as a result of believers' prayers.
- Two angels delivered Lot out of Sodom from God's judgement that was to come upon the land (Genesis 19:1-24).
- When the king of Syria sent an army with horses and chariots to go and capture Elisha as a punishment for helping the king of Israel (through his prophetic ministry) to avoid Syrian attacks, God opened the eyes of Elisha's servant to see a protective host of angels surrounding Elisha. The angelic host foiled the Syrians' attempt to capture Elisha (11Kings 6:12-18).
- God commands His angels to guard us in all our ways. His angels encamp round about those who fear Him (Psalm 91:11; Psalm 34:7).

I am not convinced it is necessary to ask God to send His angels to protect us (He will do it with or without our asking), neither am I saying it is wrong to make the request. When you pray for protection or provision God will send His angels if He chooses. On several occasions He sent His angels to deliver the answers to His children's prayers.

A lot of people have never seen an angel; (it is baseless to pray to see one) what is crucial is that you are aware that angels may be used by God as a means of protection and deliverance from evil in answer to our prayers. They are at your service. You can expect God to scramble them when you desperately need protection. Pray for your own protection and that of your loved ones; never imagine for once how it would happen; if God chooses to, He will use one of them – just one is enough for you in the most critical or dangerous situation.

Put your angel to work today. Angels are ever ready for your assignment! Angels are at your service when you pray.

7

ARMOUR OF PROTECTION

Prayer is the perfect place where every child of God can perform their role as a soldier of Christ. Through prayer we wage endless warfare against the devil and his demons. As soldiers in the frontline not only do you need to be fully armed, you also need to be fully protected by wearing the complete armour of God. This way, you can be confident that as the battle rages you are well shielded from the enemy's arsenal. Too many great and small Christians are falling easily and unexpectedly because of exposure to enemy weapons. These incidences have nothing to do with how long you have been a Christian- very experienced and inexperienced soldiers can both fall by the sword of the enemy if they are not full-proofed from attacks. The bible warns that we should: *"Put on the whole armour of God that ye may be able to stand against the wiles of the devil"* (Ephesians 6:11).

The Difference between an Armour and a Weapon

An armour is a protective covering worn to protect the body in a battle. There are different types of armours which include body and vehicle armours. Vehicle armour is designed to protect a military vehicle or ship from external attacks. Every one of us needs the full armour of God to protect us from spiritual damage during combats. Remember, whether you are actively engaged or not in hostilities, the mere fact that you have enlisted in the army means you are an automatic target of the enemy's forces. Being fully cladded with your spiritual armour is the only guarantee that the enemy's weapons will be ineffective on you.

A weapon is fashioned for inflicting physical injury; it is aimed at attacking and crippling the opponent and causing them debilitating harm. Some weapons can both be used for attack and defensive purposes- an example is a sword; and in the spiritual sense, God's word is a sword, and it can play the dual role of attack and defence.

Put on the Whole Armour

Worldly soldiers not only equip themselves with weapons of attack, politicians and military leaders have a responsibility to ensure adequate supply of body and other armours to their country's military. In the same way God has provided us with whole armour needed to preserve us from the attacks of opposing forces. It is the responsibility of every Christian to ensure they are completely protected with the full armour provided by God.

Belt of Truth

In Paul's day a soldier would fasten a leather girdle around his waist, both as a protection for their loins and to help carry weapons. The girdle also helped the soldier to hold their tunic properly in place and to prevent sagging, discomfort and distraction.

For the Christian this is symbolic of truth, which helps to hold the centre together; God desires truth in our inward parts. Insincerity and dishonesty will both expose and make the believer vulnerable in spiritual warfare. The devil roams about looking for whom to devour and the most secure place for the believer is the arena of the truth. Praying big and prolonged prayers will be useless unless a child of God lives continually in the truth. That is what makes us different from the devil- the father of lies.

The Breastplate of Righteousness

The vital organs of the body are in the breast or chest region. In bible times a soldier's breastplate was made of physical, hard-to-pierce materials. For the Christian, staying spiritually fit and protected entails staying away from (fleeing) all forms of lust and filthiness. This includes keeping away from videos and movies that defile the heart. The first target of Satan is the believer's heart- that is one of the easiest places to kill an individual. Maintaining a pure heart makes you ever battle ready, and able to ward off every fiery dart of the wicked one. Things easily get into and settled in the heart because the heart is a very tender organ of the body. Protect your heart by constantly feeding it with the word of God and always asking the Lord to renew your heart; failing to guard the heart can easily make an individual a spiritual casualty.

Gospel Shoes of Peace

The Roman soldier needed solid footing and flexible movements. Good shoes with cleats, like those worn by footballers, was key to their victory. This acted in similar manner as the horse shoes which can determine victory in a race. Symbolically, it represents the gospel; a solid or sound Christian life must include the preaching of the gospel of peace. Salvation is at the heart of spiritual warfare; to stay victorious a child of God must stay assured of their salvation, preach the gospel and keep their peace. When the gospel of peace is preached and received the devil loses the fight over the souls of people. When you preach the gospel, you will set them free from the chains of darkness, when you keep your assurance of salvation and the peace that goes with it, you will seal up every loophole the devil could possibly exploit against you. The preaching of the gospel gives you sound footing and stability in warfare. It is written,

> "How beautiful upon the mountains are the feet of him that bringeth good tidings, that publisheth peace; that bringeth good tidings of good [things] that publisheth salvation" (Isaiah 52:7).

This also means that we must constantly march into the territory of the devil- beware though that Satan has got booby traps. If you are well equipped with the truth and message of the gospel, Satan's obstacles on the way will not deter you as you are aware that the preaching of the gospel is the only way to establish peace between God and man. Preaching the gospel places you at the centre of God's will, and being at the centre of God's will removes the struggle from your prayer.

The Shield of Faith

In ancient times soldiers used shields for protection against spears, swords and arrows- in fact, from anything that pierces or can cause bodily harm. Shields protected soldiers from all the darts and arrows of the enemy. As we fight spiritual warfare Satan will continue to fire flaming shots at us to cause doubts and discouragement which are capable of destabilising and exposing us to further enemy attacks. You must keep the enemy perpetually on the run by feeding and maintaining your faith with the word of God. You cannot win the prayer war without living consistently in faith.

The Helmet of Salvation

Helmets are useful for protecting the head. The head is the seat of all thoughts and knowledge. Satan never fails to go for the head; that is why the bible says:

> *"Casting down imaginations, and every high thing that exhalteth itself against the knowledge of God, and bringing into captivity every thought to the obedience of Christ"* (2Corinthians 10:5).

Soldiers take their helmets very seriously because any shot at the head can result quickly in fatality. For the Christian the helmet is a symbol of the knowledge of God's word, it also signifies salvation (1Thessalonians 5:8). It is critical you do not allow the devil to go on rampage in your mind, never allow anything to compromise your salvation if you do not want to lose the fight to Satan.

The Sword of the Spirit

The sword of the spirit is the word of God- a primary weapon of offense which can also be used for defending yourself in a battle. Always keep your sword sharpened and within easy reach. Let the word of Christ dwell richly in your heart. God's word within you will continue to protect, purify and empower you for victorious living. Many of God's people conceal rather that unsheathe their sword when the enemy attacks. Speak God's word confidently against every negative situation-there is power, healing and victory in the word.

Friendly Fire Kills a Comrade

The guardian (August 1, 2006), reported the findings of an inquiry into the death of a British soldier from gun injuries sustained from his own colleagues. The army sergeant was killed when his comrades fired gunshots in an attempt to protect him from attacks from a "stone-throwing protester at a vehicle checkpoint". The colleagues accidentally killed him because their guns were inaccurate at short range. The inquiry concluded that this soldier *"killed by friendly fire in Iraq would have survived if he had been wearing body armour."*

This report highlights the seriousness of not having your body armour on in the midst of warfare. The complete armour discussed above is an imperative for every child of God. We must be ever ready for the worse from the enemy. Unfortunately, in this case it was 'friendly fire' that killed this brave soldier who was out there on the service of his country. In spiritual warfare anything can happen any day or time. Put on the whole armour of God because any exposed part will be swiftly targeted by the enemy. (www.theguardian.com/uk/2006)

8

BURDEN FOR PRAYERS

The dictionary definition of burden include: care, worry, weight and load. Burden for prayer is fundamental to successful praying. Unless you have passion for prayers you may not always experience the power and motivation to pray. For everything we do we need to have a drive. The good thing about prayer, unlike many other things is that even if you do not have the drive, the Holy Spirit can always impart you with the burden to pray if you ask Him for it. It is in the interest of God's work, and our spiritual development, that we are able to pray with consistency and results. You need that ongoing hunger and desire which can make you restless until you pray.

Also you need to arrive at a point whereby prayer becomes literally (even physically) a task that you enjoy. This will manifest in the quantity and quality of your prayers, as well as in your prayer coverage. Paul's Letter to the Galatians suggests that he carried a prayer burden for them:

> *"My little children, of whom I travail in birth again until Christ be formed in you..."* (Galatians 4:21).

Prayer burden is similar in some ways to the weight of pregnancy. When you are pregnant you know it; you feel it. A pregnant woman's life is completely different from that of a woman who is not carrying a baby in the womb. When you carry a prayer weight in your heart like a pregnant woman, you will naturally deliver prayer results. The burden (intense inner feeling) can be spontaneous or progressive. After you have prayed sufficiently about the weight in your heart, you will feel like you have had a delivery– the answer to your prayer. Let us examine great examples of people who were saddled with the cares of divine assignments.

- **David**

  "I will not give sleep to mine eyes, or slumber to my eyelids, until I find out a place for the LORD, an habitation for the mighty God of Jacob" (Psalm 132:4-5). David was encumbered with building God a house. He was consumed with this passion. Nothing and nobody would stop him in his bid to do this. He lived and breathed this. Only God could say no to David by giving the responsibility to someone else.

- **Isaiah**

  "For Zion's sake will I not hold my peace, and for Jerusalem's sake I will not rest, until the righteousness thereof go forth as brightness and the salvation go forth as lamp that burneth" (Isaiah 62:1). Isaiah wanted God's visitation upon Israel and would not rest until this happened. He was overwhelmed with this feeling. Prayer burden is a restlessness in your heart to pray either routinely or in response to a known or an unknown need.

- **Jeremiah**

  "Then I said I will not make mention of him, nor speak any more in His name. But His word was in mine heart as a burning fire shut up in my bones, and I was weary with forbearing, and I could not stay" (Jeremiah 20:9). Here again, we see Jeremiah carrying a burden to speak God's word; he wanted to resist the urge, but the weight was too much until he did the right thing – speak the word of God. This was a spiritual burden at work – when you carry prayer in your heart, just like that, you will bring forth the answer. Nothing will be able to stop you. You will get better results in prayer when you are pregnant with prayer!

- **Paul**

  "Now while Paul waited for them at Athens, his spirit was stirred in him, when he saw the city wholly given to idolatory" (Acts 17:1). A prayer burden or any spiritual burden for that matter, could express itself in the form of a holy anger or vexation in your spirit that drives you to do something about a situation that requires prayer.

- **Jesus Christ**

  "Jesus saith unto them, my meat is to do the will of Him that sent me, and to finish His work" (John 4:34). Jesus lost His appetite for physical food because He carried a heavy burden for the salvation and deliverance of humanity. When you bear a prayer burden everything else becomes temporarily irrelevant, until you deliver the prayer 'baby' you are carrying. You do not always have to feel this way before you pray; prayer is one of those things that have to be planned and followed through. You may never have the strong urge to pray, so do not wait for it.

You have to pray to meet the needs of the hour or the times. If you lack the burden to pray, just look around you and you will find enough reasons to pray. When you measure your family, society and people around you by the standard of God you will find every reason while you must pray regularly and consistently.

What do you do when the Holy Spirit places the weight of somebody else's problem upon your heart to pray for them? You must be quick to obey. God may wake you up in the middle of the night, may ask you to pull up whilst driving, or divert you from your regular prayer points- asking you to pray about something for which you have no idea and no plan to pray. Your total and prompt obedience is the only thing that will save the situation. Be it for yourself, loved ones, somebody or something else, whenever God lays upon you to pray do so very quickly because God will be relying on you at that time to save the situation.

Responding swiftly to the urge to pray will save you or someone else from impending crisis.

The Holy Spirit may place a strain in your heart to pray when you feel unwilling or unable to pray; you may even be unaware of the need to pray. He creates in you a desire to fellowship or commune with God. As a Christian that is what you are created to do. The eagerness and urgency to pray laid upon your heart by the Spirit is usually for some serious reasons, and must therefore never be ignored.

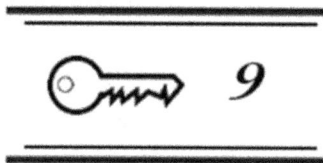

BREAK DOWN BARRIERS

Anything that has the potential to stop or interrupt you from achieving an objective is a barrier. It is very easy to allow obstacles in our way of progress. Some roadblocks to success are self-made while many originate from Satan and other sources. Satan cannot effectively stop you from praying without your permission. You need to identify the enemy's obstructions to your prayer life and put up a strong resistance against them.

The Barrier of Sin

This is by far the most serious hindrance to prayer. Sin is no respecter of any Christian, whatever your spiritual status. Everyone can pray or at least pretend to be praying, but not all prayers get results. Nothing weakens the power to pray more easily than sin; and very many Christians harbour secret sins and still expect their prayer life to blossom. Unconfessed sins will block the flow of God's power into a person's life, cripple them spiritually and neutralise their prayer efforts.

Idols in the Heart

Too many Christians go before God to pray with 'idols' in their hearts. They have made up their minds what they will do before going to God in prayers. This is an idol in the heart. God says He will answer such people according to the idol in their hearts. Whenever God answered people according to the idol in their hearts, they always got into trouble. God once told the prophet Ezekiel regarding Israel,

> *"Therefore speak to them, and say to them, Thus says the Lord God: Every one of the house of Israel who sets up his idols in his heart, and puts before him what causes him to stumble into iniquity, and then comes to the prophet, I the LORD will answer him who comes, according to the multitude of his idols, …"* (Ezekiel 14:4).

To go before God with a dishonest heart and expect a positive response from Him makes a mockery of spiritual things. It is ridiculous for people to make up their mind about something and simply expect God to sanction it. God never works that way.

He knows our innermost being, but sometimes plays along with the deception in the heart. However, He will always give room for repentance. It pays better to come before God with an open mind, and leave things in His hands. When it comes to God honesty is the only policy.

Un-forgiveness

Jesus tells us in the bible,

> *"… if ye forgive men their trespasses, your heavenly Father will also forgive you: but if ye forgive not men their trespasses, neither will your heavenly Father forgive your trespasses"* (Matthew 6:14-15).

Un-forgiveness is one of Satan's most powerful tools against believers. Un-forgiveness is a poison and the one that suffers the most from it is the person who fails to forgive. It manifests in many forms including pain, bitterness, hate, slander, gossip and discomfort towards the thing or person. Vengeance belongs to God, so leave the person with Him. An un-forgiving spirit is a losing spirit, and a person who refuses to forgive should not bother coming into God's presence to pray. The quicker you can forgive the better, and the more effective your prayer will be. Christianity is founded on forgiveness and God is saddened when His people fail to forgive. Any person who holds someone else in their heart should not expect God to answer their prayers.

Withholding From God

If a person withholds or keeps that which belongs to God, their prayer can be affected. The tithe of your earnings belongs to God. God desires a generous proportion of your time, talents and resources. Pay your tithes, give your offerings, and be generous at supporting God's work and good courses with your resources. When you give you receive. As you keep giving you will keep receiving (Malachi 3:8-10). If you violate the principle of sowing and reaping, prayer cannot turn situations around.

Marital or Family Discord

The bible clearly teaches on the implications of relational crisis in marriage. Not only does the enemy exploit them, unresolved marital or relational problems can stand in *the way of receiving answers to prayers, hence the bible says,*

> "Husbands, likewise, dwell with them (wives) with understanding, that your prayers may not be hindered" (1Peter 3:7 emphasis added).

Disobedience and Self Will

When King Saul of Israel failed to obey God's instructions to destroy God's enemy, the Prophet Samuel said to the king that God is more interested in obedience than in sacrifice. Saul lost favour and much more, with God. Disobedience to God's word will hinder the move of God in the life of any person. If anyone deliberately fails to do what God says, God would pay no attention to their prayers. God requires total submission to His word.

10

BALANCE YOUR PRAYER TYPES

Our heavenly father is a God of variety and He honours all types of prayers. Everything works better when there is balance – balanced diets, balanced lifestyles and business portfolios are great for the smooth running of life and businesses. It is unlikely that anyone will embark in all prayer types regularly or at any given time, but understanding them is paramount to a thriving prayer life. Your daily prayer focus should not be limited to one subject or to your personal needs. In Ephesians 6:18, God says we should:

> *"…pray always with all prayer and supplication in the spirit, and watching thereunto with perseverance and supplication for all saints."*

It is commonly said that 'variety is the spice of life'. Prayer can easily turn to boredom and a rut if we become selfish or get stuck in the circle of repeating one form of prayer. Let us examine a few types of prayer.

Adoration

To adore means to honour and worship. When you commence prayer with adoration, you are telling God how much you cherish and treasure Him. Through words you express your love and admiration for God. The bedrock of prayer is relationship, and when you begin by expressing your love and appreciation for God you set the stage for a blissful time of communion between you and your heavenly father. He is your friend, your Lord and your God. It is a time you revere and tell God how much He means to you – He is priceless to you. You let your thought, actions and words greatly exalt and esteem God, giving Him the glory that He alone deserves. (Isaiah 6:1-4; Revelation 4:11). Adoration can take the form of praise, worship, thanksgiving or simply meditating and appreciating God for His awesomeness and who He is.

Confession

Confession should be a central part of the prayer time. You do not need to be sin conscious. You do not need to be self righteous either- some Christians believe that we must never talk about sin at all. I think this is hypocritical as these same people know their daily battles with sin. Sin must not have dominion over God's people but there is nothing wrong in humbly going before the Lord and asking Him to search you just in case there is anything standing in the way between you and Him. No child of God can claim to be perfect, yet no child of God should think of themselves as a wretched sinner. It is a safe thing to ask God to search you for any wrong doing which you may or may not be aware of.

Confessing and forsaking your sins puts you in a better standing to talk to God and maintain an audience with Him. Needless to say that in an emergency you may not have sufficient to do your praying let alone confess sins, yet God's love and mercy will prevail on your behalf. He never forsakes His children, but no child of God should continue in sin and expect God's grace to abound. Sinning will stop anyone from praying.

Petition

To petition means to appeal, address, request, beseech or entreat. This is the most common form of prayer. A lot of people go before God with a long list before they have time to thank Him for what He has already done. When we petition God, we are making a request – may be for ourselves or on behalf of someone else. This is often the main focus of many prayers. Prayer that does not go beyond this dimension is incomplete, childish and may be, selfish. Our heavenly father wants us to grow beyond presenting Him with a shopping list.

Intercession

Intercession means to mediate, intervene, arbitrate or advocate. This is one of the most refreshing and rewarding type of prayer. It is a selfless form of prayer which places the focus on others. Many of the greatest men and women of prayers are great intercessors. Jesus is interceding for us daily in heaven; you will never get into certain realms of prayers and communion with God until intercession becomes a key part of your prayer life.

God wants us to intercede for those in authority (Timothy 2:2); ministers of the gospel (Ephesians 6:19-20); God's kingdom to come, and His will to be done on earth (Matthew 5:9-13). He also wants us to pray for sinners (Luke 23:34); those who are new to the Christian faith (1Thessalonians 1:11); haters of the gospel (Matthew 5:44); the sick and people with other types of needs (James 5:13-16). The intercessor also assumes responsibility for praying for backsliders (1John 5:16); workers to be available for God's work; their country of residence, the nation of Israel and the world at large.

The role of the intercessor is a privileged one, and is highly esteemed by God. It is an awesome spiritual position and every Christian has been called into this noble office. Only those who obediently operate in this office can really tell what a benefit and blessing it is to be an intercessor. To me it is the best form of prayer and I count it a great honour to be enlisted into God's army of intercessors. If you want to get deep into the heart of God, intercessory prayer is the place to start.

Praying in Tongues

Praying in tongues carries several benefits and every child of God should take advantage of this weapon. My position is that speaking in tongues is the initial visible proof of the Holy Spirit's baptism in the life of a Christian (Acts 2:4; Acts 10:46). This does not imply that people who do not speak in tongues do not have the Holy Spirit – yes they do, if they have given their lives to Christ and have been saved from their sins. The baptism in the Holy Spirit takes the Christian experience to a higher level.

Speaking in tongues gives you personal spiritual edification (1Corinthians 14:4). Speaking in tongues establishes a consciousness of the Spirit's indwelling (John 14:16-17). When you speak in tongues at the time of prayer, you are able to stay in line with God's will (Romans 8:26). Your faith is stimulated when you pray in tongues (Jude 20). The Spirit helps you to pray for the unknown when you pray in tongues. Tongues can be used as a language for giving thanks to God (1Corinthians 14:15-17). It can also can be a supernatural sign to unbelievers (1Corinthians 14:22).

God wants you pray in tongues (1Corinthians 14:5); it will add vigour, speed and accuracy to your prayer, but praying in tongues does not always mean a person is praying under the full control of the Spirit. Someone with a sinful lifestyle may pray in tongues, yet the payer can be pathetically devoid of the power of the Spirit.

The Prayer of Consecration

An example of the prayer of consecration can be seen in Adelaide Pollard's (1907), beautiful song:

> *Have Thine own way, Lord! Have Thine own way!*
> *Thou art the potter, I am the clay,*
> *Mold me and make me after Thy will*
> *While I am waiting yielded and still*

In a prayer of consecration you ask the Lord to help you live the crucified, broken and surrendered life. Abraham laid all on the altar. Jesus did the same. Present your body a living sacrifice to the Lord; let go of things that should go, and let God take centre stage in your life. It is a time when you pray to seek first the kingdom of God (Matthew 6:33), take up your cross and follow the master (Matthew 10:38) and give up your life so you can save it (John 12:25). During this time you are praying never to live again to yourself, but to the one who died and gave Himself for you (2Corinthians 5:15).

The Prayer of Agreement

Nothing can stop any two or more people who agree to do something and stick together with it till the very end. When two or more Christians come together, united in spirit and soul to pray about anything, Jesus promises to be in their midst, and to do whatever they ask of Him (Matthew 18:19-20).

The Prayer of Binding and Loosing

Binding and loosing is taught by Jesus in Matthew 18:18-19:

> *"Assuredly, I say to you, whatsoever you bind on earth will be bound in heaven, and whatsoever you loose on earth shall be loosed in heaven."*

God has delegated His authority to believers to permit anything on earth, and He will authorise it in heaven, and disallow anything on earth, and He will disallow it in heaven. You have authority to bind demons, or loose God's blessings on earth and your actions will receive God's stamp of approval. This is part of your prayer duty.

11

BLOODSTAINED BANNER

Holding up the blood stained banner of Christ is something the devil can neither comprehend nor counteract. A banner is a flag or other piece of cloth exhibiting a symbol, logo, slogan or any similar message. A banner represents an official proclamation prohibiting some form of action or activity by an enemy or other people. When you raise the blood stained banner or plead the blood of Christ you are prohibiting the devil from touching you and your loved ones. Victory in prayer is on the platform of the blood.

When you confront the devil with the blood of Christ, you are invoking the realities, presence and protection of the blood. You are calling upon Jesus and the power in His blood to come through for you. You are hiding behind the most powerful cleansing and protective agent, for your justification and insulation.

Victory through the Blood

In biological terms blood is a fluid that circulates all through the vertebrate body and transports food and oxygen to the body tissues. It also removes waste and carbon dioxide from the body system. In the Old Testament the blood of animals was used for purification from sin by God's people (Leviticus 16:18-19). The blood of animals was also placed at the door posts of the Jewish people to restrain the angel of death, and preclude God's people from His judgement against the Egyptian oppressors (Exodus 12:1-7, 12-13). This typifies the blood of Christ which was shed on the cross at Calvary, with which we overcome the devil. Jesus shed His blood in seven main places and each has great symbolism for the believer. Understanding their significance can be a game changer to your faith and prayer life.

Nail Pierced Hands: Material and Financial Victory

When Jesus died on the cross His blood flowed out from the nailed pierced hands. Hands in the bible represent authority and prosperity. The Israelites saw the mighty hand of the Lord against the Egyptians (Deuteronomy 34:12). God promises that those who obey His word are like trees planted by the river bank, and whatever they do will prosper (Psalm 1:3).God wants His people to profit in labour (Proverbs 14:23); God wants you to eat the fruit of the labour of your hands (Psalm 128:2). When you know and acknowledge this in your prayers, you will be praying in line with God's word. Plead the blood over your finances and over every work of your hands. Stand on the authority and power of the blood and declare your material and financial blessings.

Dominion over the Enemy

The feet of Jesus were nailed to the cross, again with blood flowing out of them. Feet represent dominion. God told Joshua, *"Every place that the sole of your feet shall tread upon, that have I given unto you, as I said unto Moses."* (Joshua 1:3). As a result of the pierced feet of Jesus, our dominion has been restored. You should not simply pray, you must break new grounds by prayer; walk in dominion and impose God's will and desire on everywhere you find yourself. The blood from the feet of Jesus means that you are unstoppable. Taking dominion means you should be a force to be reckoned with in your office, industry and ministry.

The devil and his host must fall under your feet. You must tread upon serpents and scorpions; their ability to hurt you have been neutralised by the blood of Jesus. You can enforce all these by prayer with the knowledge that Jesus finished it all when He shed His blood on the Cross.

Salvation and Emotional Healing

When the soldiers pierced the side of Jesus with a sword, blood flowed out. He died of a broken heart. This obtained heart cleansing for the sinner and emotional healing for everyone who comes to Jesus with emotional challenges (Zechariah 12:10); (John 19:32-35). Whenever you pray for emotional healing or present a broken heart to God, remember that His heart was broken in order to mend yours. Raise the banner of the blood against discouragement, depression, and every form of emotional trouble. The blood of Christ purchased your peace, so do not let your heart be troubled. Take it all to the Lord in prayer through the blood of Jesus.

Deliverance from Infirmity and Afflictions

Jesus was beaten with scourges up to the maximum 39 stripes allowed by the law, inflicting wounds and tears of the most horrendous proportion on his bare body. This was for the healing of the bodies of those who come to Him. You will pray more effectively and with less friction when you truly understand and accept that Jesus finished the work of your healing. It no longer requires endless prayer to get your healing. You can simply confess, appropriate and walk in your healing. Raise the banner of the blood of Christ over every sickness the enemy has put on your body. There is healing and deliverance in the blood.

> "... He was wounded for our transgressions; He was bruised for our iniquities: the chastisement of our peace was upon Him; and with His stripes we are healed" (Isaiah 53:5).

The Crown of Thorns

Blood flowed down the brow of Jesus when He wore the crown of thorns. This paid the price for your poverty, mental illness and subjection to the god of this world- the devil. (Genesis 3:19). Plead the blood over your mind whenever the devil tries to invade your mind with negative and unbiblical thoughts. Crown represents kingship. Christ has made us kings and priests. You must walk in this and no longer live a beggarly life and at the mercy of the devil. The blood of Jesus shed from the head and brow secures your position as king. The king of kings is your king maker. When you pray or carry out spiritual warfare, speak as a king- with power, authority and confidence, expecting every word you speak to achieve its purpose. Pray with authority, not as an underdog.

You must fully comprehend the power in the blood of Jesus. You must activate this power each time you pray by faith and confession. It is God's great gift to the world, and the believer, in particular. Without the blood of Jesus you will be nowhere near conquering the enemy, and your prayer will fail to have desired impact.

12

BROKENNESS OF HEART

God has great respect for penitence and humility. An arrogant, unbroken and obstinate heart cannot connect with God in prayer. We can definitely not impress God by putting on a grief-stricken, heavy-hearted or miserable appearance. Some people pretend to be sanctimonious, displaying a holier-than-thou attitude. God is not interested in that. Jesus condemned the Pharisees for such a display. God also does not want you to appear deflated and defeated. However He is pleased when His children are unassuming, meek and genuinely humble.

> *"The Lord is nigh unto them that are of a broken heart; and saveth such as be of a contrite spirit."* (Psalm 34:18).

> *"The sacrifices of God are a broken spirit: a broken and a contrite heart O God, thou wilt not despise."* (Psalm 51:17).

God multiplies His grace on people who approach Him with brokenness of heart and contrition of spirit- two imperatives for effective praying. A good percentage of Christians possess great faith in prayer but woefully fall short of the key requirement for approaching God- humbleness of heart. Even if a person knows all there is about prayer, they will still lack real depth in prayer if their heart is not right. The ideal heart of a praying Christian should be one that:

- is malleable and can be easily influenced by God
- is remorseful over personal sins and the sins of others
- is void of rebellion and self
- easily owns up before God and men
- completely displaces self and exalts Christ in all things

No pretending! Prayer is serious business and you need to be plain and pure-hearted before God. If you do not have this kind of heart, your prayer may be grammatically high sounding, colourful, and 'earth-quaking', you will still have limited results. God focuses on one place, and that is the heart. If you do not have the kind of heart we are talking about you can ask God to work on you and make you the person He wants you to be.

Spiritual Revival

If you feel like your heart is growing cold and less spiritually sensitive, go to God in genuine humility and ask Him to visit and revive your heart once again. He will touch you with His fire of revival and renew your heart. God has promised to revive the heart of everyone who comes to Him in humility (Isaiah 57:15).

Divine Visitation

God takes interest in people who approach Him with a humble heart. On the contrary He resists pride and rebellion. *"The LORD is nigh unto them that are of a broken heart, and saveth such as be of a contrite spirit"* (Psalm 34:18). God cannot hang around people whose heart is callous, while they remain unwilling to do something about it. If you want God to continue to bless your prayer times with His presence, keep a watch over the state of your heart.

Abundant Grace and Mercy

True remorse and repentance will release an abundance of God's grace and mercy. The Prophet Joel says,

"… rend your heart, and not your garments, and turn unto the Lord your God: for He is gracious and merciful, slow to anger and of great kindness, and repenteth Him of the evil" (Joel 2:13). Expect an outpouring of God's grace and mercy when you frankly humble yourself at His feet. Result oriented, God-pleasing prayer must come from a contrite heart.

Divine Intervention

God never takes His eyes of people whose heart are right before Him, even when they make mistakes. He looks upon them with mercy because He can see sincerity and honesty within them.

Receiving Jesus into your heart is preliminary to receiving the God-kind of heart. After this you must continually approach God in sincerity, asking Him to reveal yourself to you as you are, tell Him to continually work on you so you can live a life of humility- one that trembles at His word. Be quick to act upon anything that God tells you, and be forever hungry for God and His word. Lack of spiritual hunger or desire is clear indication that you need a touch from God.

Humility of heart has nothing to do with trying to prove moral superiority or self-righteousness. It has to be genuine as God will not accept anything less. A stubborn, unyielding and unbroken heart can never fully enjoy a relationship with the Lord. An insensitive and backslidden heart cannot maximise the benefits of divine fellowship.

13

CONCENTRATE YOUR PRAYERS

In both physical and spiritual warfare, concentration of resources and efforts is vital for victory. Concentration could be a short or medium term approach to warfare. It is aimed at ensuring that the volume of assaults on the enemy is overwhelming and overpowering to force them to surrender. In physical warfare the amount of forces or armoury at your disposal does not always determine your success in combat. Rather, victory in many cases is decided by the mass of resources you concentrate continuously on where it really matters until you win.

When Peter was locked up in prison by King Herod, the church prayed for him ceaselessly until an angel delivered him from the prison. This demonstrates the impact of massive or concentrated intercession, especially if there is so much at stake. This type of effort is known as the Principal of the Mass, in physical warfare. It is like heating an iron continuously to the point when you can make it into whatever shape you want. The prayer of the early church for Peter was concerted, concentrated and continuous. It went on until physical forces succumbed to the superior power of prayer. Then Peter went free out of prison without the permission of the authorities.

The Blitzkrieg (Lightning War)

During World War 11 the Germans adopted a tactic known as Blitzkrieg or "lightning War". In this tactic the Germans would concentrate their tanks, infantry, artillery and air power on a target with such overwhelming force and speed that rendered their opponents impotent. The enemy is thrown into such panic and pandemonium that effectively rendered powerless. They would be left with little or no time to react or regroup as a result of the intensity and velocity of the German attack. The Germans would converge their efforts where it mattered until the enemy's will was broken. (www.britannica.com)

Touch and go or hit and run type of prayer gives the enemy time to recover, regroup and reinvent itself. Casual, non aggressive praying may be enough for some types of problem but in many serious situations it will be insufficient. Spiritual Blitzkrieg might involve fasting and praying, it may simply involve a large number of people praying (as was the case of Peter in prison) for a continuous and intense period of time. It could be for one day, a few hours; several hours or minutes a day for some days. The key is that it must be non-stop and in large enough volume to cripple the enemy. It really works. This way, you could be doing one-year, one-month, or one-week prayer in just one or a few days until the problem gives way, or until you receive unmistakable assurance from the Lord that it is over.

If you are desperate you may need to ask others to supply the prayer input needed to make this happen. It does not matter how the prayer happened or how the victory is won, it is the result that matters. In great wars like the world wars, nations come into alliance to create a joint force especially in the face of a global threat from an evil power or nation.

Decisive Moments and Problems

There are times and places in our lives that will greatly influence our destiny. All fingers are not equal, so also are all problems not equal.

Some problems will either make or break you. You can therefore not approach every prayer the same way. Praying 5 minutes a day for ten days will address some problems. Some other challenges might require praying 15 minutes a day to simply scratch the surface of the matter. Some cases may need praying 30 minutes daily for a few days or weeks to completely resolve the matter.

Massive praying may not always be enough on its own. Massive, rapid and progressive praying helps a lot more in certain circumstances. This book is not for those who do not believe in prayer, or those who believe plenty of prayer is unnecessary. It is for those whose spiritual principles square up with the ones shared in this book, or who are prepared to read with an open mind. Some people believe in little or no prayer. Other people believe in so much prayer and little action, neither of these positions is balanced or spiritually safe.

How the Blitzkrieg Worked

We have so much to learn from the German lightning tactic which can be useful in conducting spiritual warfare. The Germans:

- Concentrated weapons on a specific front using planes, tanks and artillery
- German forces aggressively breached enemy defences
- Armoured tanks easily moved behind enemy lines
- There would be shock, awe and chaos within the enemy's camp
- The Germans will continue to pound the enemy camp by air, degrading their ability to get supplies, redeployment or reinforcements
- Eventually German forces round up their opponents giving them no option but to surrender

All these were done at the speed of 'lightning'. No room for the enemy to regroup or manoeuvre. The opponent is suffocated and stripped of will power and fire power. The scriptures say,

"I have set watchmen upon thy walls, O Jerusalem, which shall never hold their peace day nor night: ye that make mention of the LORD, keep not silence, And give him no rest, till he establish, and till he make Jerusalem a praise in the earth" (Isaiah 62:6-7).

When Joshua and his men fought the Amorites, the sun and moon stood still into the night until Joshua and his army defeated them. They did not have to fight and come back another day. Joshua and his army fought aggressively and continuously until the battle was won. (Joshua 10:12-13) Too many prayers take too long because God's children play too safe. Prayers that lack vigour, guts and speed will be too weak to paralyse opposing forces. A lot of us ramble in our prayer when the enemy is clearly on rampage. God wants you to pray hard, fast and massively until you have completely destroyed the enemy.

14

CHANGE THE WAY YOU PRAY

Change is a fact of life. The only way to make continuous progress in anything is to keeping making necessary changes. That is why organisations spend awful sums of money implementing changes- to systems, structures and resources. Change is the only thing that is constant about life. Whenever change is resisted something will go wrong. In every area of life, failure to make important changes will hinder progress.

Stuck In a Rut

Too many prayers take the form of uninspiring, unproductive and ineffective chores. Some people simply pray for the sake of doing so- no tangible results, no fresh approaches or outcomes, and no new breakthroughs are expected or received. You may need to unlearn or undo old ways of praying which you have adopted for years, and which have not taken you further spiritually. Prayer is an active and fluid undertaking which must constantly turn in results. If the way you pray is not yielding expected results, then something needs changing urgently. Most secular organisations are ceaselessly changing or adjusting things that do not work so their end results would change. The prayer pattern and type that worked yesterday may not work today, or may not work for a different problem or situation. God has many ways of making things work for us, although God is the ancient of days, He is never stuck in old ways.

Long adopted ways of praying may still be working, but not effectively. Some may no longer produce desired victory because darkness is becoming darker, the devil has doubled his efforts, consolidated his tactics and reinvented his schemes. The devil is always remaking himself and God's people must also find new ways to deal with his new threats, otherwise the cutting edge in our prayer may become too blunt for modern challenges. In today's world many sicknesses and diseases have become resistant to long existing medicines, and so scientists are clamouring for the development of new drugs to combat these diseases. Old, familiar or popular ways of doing things do not always work forever. Neither is there any guarantee that the prayer type and style that gave you victory yesterday will be enough to defeat Satan's more sophisticated tactics and antics of today.

Build On What Works

Build on what works and discard with what does not. If the way you pray continues to yield maximum results, then keep it up; build on it, and continue to refine it. Increase the hours; couple it with fasting to multiply its potency. For example, if praying in the early hours of the day gives you best results, stay with it. If praying later in the day is your best chance of success, stick with and increase the hours. If long periods of fasting have been critical to your payer success, never take that for granted, because if you do, you will be disappointed by what you get. If as you grow older and become busier, long fasting is no longer attractive or effective, you may then need shorter, smarter and may be, fewer periods of fasting.

Discard with what no longer works. If you have to adjust your prayer times, prayer hours and location to make you more productive, do not hesitate to change. Your prayer life is important to your entire life. There will be no point holding onto the old ways just because they are convenient, less tasking and less threatening to your comfort. If you have always prayed for long hours (like I used to do), but age and current commitments no longer permit, why not try shorter but more frequent amounts of time.

You can glean some minutes from your break, driving and waiting times. You can also chose to deliberately walk 10 or 20 minutes of your commuting time to and from work, if you use public means of transportation. Every few minutes will add up. If you need a change in location, why not? If your usual place has become too noisy, or you can no longer enjoy the privacy you crave, you may have to take a walk away from home or find somewhere that will give you the quietness you need. You need to constantly find ways to make your prayer more effective, whatever the cost.

Many things in life work for a while, some for a very short while, and some for much longer, but nothing ever really works for ever. Most procedures and methods need constant change for them to stay fit for purpose. Hardly is there anything in life that will function uninterrupted without needing adjustments or improvements at some point. If it applies to everything else, the natural thing is that prayer cannot be an exception.

Find fresh and more successful ways to pray. Change what needs to be changed. Attempt that new prayer challenge. Make that new prayer journey. Do what you have never done before when it comes to prayer. Give God a chance to do something new in you today. There is a new level that God wants you to attain in prayer, finding new ways is the only way to finding that blessing.

15

CLEAR CONSCIENCE

The conscience is that part of you which makes you aware of your actions as being morally wrong or right. It is the faculty within that judges whether something you do is lawful or unlawful, the self-judge that blames or accepts a particular conduct or intention. A good conscience will prevent you from doing what is wrong, a clear conscience will promote faith and assurance to pray. A guilt laden conscience will find no peace and confidence in praying to God.

If your conscience does not condemn you, you will never be afraid or ashamed when you go to God's throne room- there is an assurance that prevails in the closet when there are no skeletons in the cupboard because, *"There is therefore now no condemnation to them which are in Christ Jesus, who walk not after the flesh, but after the Spirit"* (Romans 8:1). You need a good and clear conscience to stand confident in front of God's throne. Our conscience either approves or condemns our actions. A guilty conscience cannot have boldness in approaching God. The bible says we should have a good conscience, *"... that whereas they speak evil of you, as of evil doers, they may be ashamed that falsely accuse your good conversation in Christ"* (1Peter 3:16).

Everyone came into this world naturally with a conscience, and the nature of each person's conscience is conditioned by the values they hold dear for years – what they consider to be good or bad, wrong or right. This will determine whether their conscience pricks or frees them when they take certain actions. Therefore an individual may feel justified doing certain things due to their own values and principles; this does not mean they are right in the sight of God. Just because there were no alarm bells ringing in your heart when you took a certain step, does not necessarily make you right. What justify you are God's word and the standard of heaven. When some people say, 'my conscience is free', they may be right in their own eyes but not in the sight of God. The question is 'by whose standard do you condition your conscience'?

The Christian Conscience

When a person gives their life to Christ, their spirit becomes regenerated by the Holy Spirit and the Word of God. Their conscience become enlivened by the life of God, then they will begin to live or act by the standard of God's word until such a time that they hinder the work of the spirit in their heart.

A born again conscience should be tender and sensitive. A non-regenerated heart may not be as sensitive to divine influence as the one that has encountered God. A saved conscience easily picks up warning signals before, or if they do any wrong.

Prayer and a Good Conscience

A bad conscience makes you fearful and lacking boldness in God's presence. It is difficult to have an exciting, guiltless and confident prayer life if your conscience is saddled with the burden of wrong doing. Some things are not blatant sin, but because they are not quite right they have the tendency to create a gap in a person's relationship with God. There are many benefits that result from a heart that is free from accusations. Some of these are:

1. **Self-Pride**

   A free conscience gives you self-pride, a feeling of self-respect- a strong factor in a relaxed fellowship with God. Although we do not approach God on the ground of personal worth, if your conscience accuses you and make you unworthy, it can have adverse consequences to your faith.

2. **Peace and Joy**

   A conscience that has nothing to worry about is a happy and free one in contrast to the one burdened by guilt and self-imprisonment which cannot truly enjoy the peace that Jesus gives. If your conscience is free you are truly free, if it is not, then you are in bondage. If you face external troubles you can run to God for help and safety, but if you inflict wounds on your own conscience, you will have to help yourself out.

3. **Boldness before God**

   "Let us draw near with a true heart in full assurance of faith, having our hearts sprinkled from an evil conscience, and our bodies washed with pure water" (Hebrews 10:22). You need peace in your inner being to have peace before God. When you go to God you do not need to carry in your heart things you could do without. You do not need to wonder whether God will welcome you or not.

"Follow Your Conscience"

People are often advised to follow their conscience; many things will end up the right way for a lot of people when they follow their conscience. However, for some people the opposite happens because most people control their conscience, instead of letting their conscience guide them. I have heard many people say "my conscience is free and I have nothing to worry about.", when they are clearing in the wrong in a relationship or in taking certain steps. The reason, I suppose, is because they have not really yielded their conscience to God and His word, or because they have a set of values by which they judge their conscience other than God's word. The question is, 'can you really follow your conscience?' I think you can- only if you have completely submitted your conscience to the influence of the Holy Spirit; then you may confidently follow your conscience.

Is your conscience too strong for God? A conscience that is too strong for God to control is in serious trouble. We can all enjoy a free conscience, but everyone must first examine whether their conscience has been hardened overtime by disobedience or wrong values, or whether it has been surrendered completely to God before they can claim to have a clear conscience. Never let your internal thermometer run out of batteries. Never come close to a point when your inner 'sensor' stops working. Your heart need to be constantly connected with God- to do this, it must always remain tender. The bible says we should:

1. Act honourably in all things (Hebrews 13:18)
2. Keep our heart with all diligence (Proverbs 4:23)
3. Exercise faith with a good conscience (Romans 4:23)
4. Not let our hearts condemn us (1 John 3:19-21)
5. Maintain a conscience void of offence (2 Corinthians 1:12)
6. Not make a shipwreck of our faith by ignoring our conscience (1 Timothy 1:19)
7. Come into God's presence with boldness (Hebrews 14:16)

A clear conscience is powerful, confident and free; without it you can feel timid and agitated before God. This can affect your faith and ability to receive from God when you go before Him in prayer. If you have a problem conscience though, do not run away from your heavenly father. Go before Him, repent (if you need to) and ask Him to revive your conscience again. You need a completely free spirit for a hitch free prayer time.

16

CONSISTENCY

If you have a prayer goal it is important you steadily pursue it no matter the odds. We all struggle in one form or the other to stay consistent- whether it is in exercising, business, study, relationship or anything else. Steadfastness is the key to achieving any goal in life.

Nowhere is consistency more a factor than in our prayer lives. Praying is like cultivating a piece of land. You plant your crop and hope they will grow to maturity, and until harvest. Then come the weed, springing up and threatening to choke the life out of your precious possession. If you are determined to see your crop reach the time of harvest, you must keep eradicating the weed on a regular basis. If you are not consistent at weeding out unwanted plants from your farm at the right time, they will spring up again before you realise it. Prayer works just the same way. Every time you cool off, or leave a gap the enemy steps in. So, you need to pray steadfastly about an issue until you can actually tick it off your list.

Keep the Fire Burning on the Altar

The reason many Christians never reap the fruit of their prayer is because they pause or give up before they get a breakthrough. Jesus taught that,

"...men ought always to pray and not to faint" (Luke 18:1). Many people start their prayers with great enthusiasm and sometimes, desperation; then they get side-tracked, frustrated and lose focus. The prayer process gets derailed, momentum is lost and the devil steps in again. To experience great results in prayers you need to keep the fire burning like God told His people in Leviticus:

> *"And the fires on the altar shall be kept burning on it; it shall not be put out. And the priest shall burn wood on it every morning, and lay the burnt offering in order on it; and he shall burn on it the fat of the peace offerings."* (Leviticus 6:12).

Keep the fire burning. God wants you to keep the fire of prayer aglow and uninterrupted. Whether it is about personal needs or intercessory praying, the engine of prayer must keep running to generate the power needed for victory. It is better to pray a little bit everyday on certain issues than spend large amounts of time on a one off basis.

Consistency Helps You to Evaluate

Irregular prayer times will undermine your ability to learn necessary prayer lessons. Experience is the best teacher, but how can you evaluate your prayer effectiveness unless you have being consistent enough to learn sufficiently from it? I constantly adjust my prayer design, especially the ones I have been adopted for a long time- some prayers are usually for the long haul. Examples are when you are praying for a revival or the salvation of souls. Until you get the results you do not stop, and if you break the trend, you are likely to interrupt the process of victory.

Consistency Makes You Reliable

Satan has nothing to fear about any Christian who cannot follow through on prayer subjects. God cannot rely on Christians to fight Kingdom battles if their prayer life is unstable and irregular, because when they are needed the most they cannot be trusted to do the job.

God wants His children to be reliable partners in the fight against the enemy. He will be more willing to trust anyone with a greater measure of prayer anointing if He is certain the person will be at his duty post whenever he is needed.

Consistency Speaks For you

When you maintain a steady prayer life, your actions will speak very loud and clear. Your children will get the message that prayer is very important. It will rub off on your spouse. If you are a minister of the gospel your followers will learn prayer from you by default. Other people will get inspired and infected by your prayer life. And, of course the result of your prayers will speak for you. Everybody around you will be fired up by your prayer habit.

> *"Therefore, my beloved brethren, be ye steadfast, unmovable, always abounding in the work of the Lord, for as much as ye know that your labour is not in vain in the Lord."* (1Corinthians 15:58).

The right thing to do is to stick to your prayer subject consistently, regularly until you achieve your prayer goal. Keep the power supply running. Keep your finger on the trigger until you see the enemy fallen on his face.

17

CONFESS your SINS

The greatest obstacle to prayer is unconfessed sin. Sin stands in the way between God and His people. Sin has to be completely out of the way to give room for God to move in your prayer life. Many Christians argue that it is wrong to talk about sin at all because you are born again. The most important subject in the bible is redemption from sin. Sin cripples and corrupts, and must be dealt with in its slightest form to enjoy a buoyant relationship with God. A person's prayer life will only be as healthy as their spiritual life. Sin is a spiritual sickness. Sin and prayer are incompatible, and God can not stand any form of unrighteousness.

If We Confess Our Sins

The bible encourages God's children to confess and forsake their sins. This advice is not only for unsaved people. Things do go wrong sometimes, and those times are enough to create a relationship problem between you and your heavenly father.

"If we confess our sins, He is faithful and just to forgive us, and to cleanse us from all unrighteousness" (1John 1:9). Obviously, a child of God must not be bogged down by sin consciousness. Christ forgave all your sins when you turned your life to and accepted Him; a sinful life is therefore not an option. God has given all His children the power to live above sin. Temptations are no sins, so being tempted to do something should not

lead to confession of sins. If however, you fall short of God's standard, as many Christians will do during the course of their lives, (including those who claim it is an abomination to talk about sin) you must do something about it very quickly.

John was clearly talking to believers here; to think otherwise will be pretentious. That said, God does not want His children to be servants to sin. Sin should not have dominion over God's people because the one in us is greater than the enemy and the challenges outside of us. (1John 4:4). Anyone who wants uninhibited fellowship with God must keep away from sin- better not to commit than to confess sins.

Do It Now

Do not hold yourself back from God's blessings by postponing repentance. The moment something goes wrong put it right with God straight away. Some sins may not be obvious; it could be wrong attitude, unbelief, spoken words, wrong thoughts or even intentions not yet acted out. God may have given you a rebuke, conviction, reproof, burden of guilt or just an awareness that you need to put something right. It all adds up. Unrepented sins can stifle your prayer life and disrupt your relationship with God. A life of sin is a spiritual death sentence. The longer a person stays in sin, the longer and stronger they are bound to the devil.

Hindrances to Repentance

One strong barrier to repentance is procrastination – wanting to do it later. This will mean postponing the blessings of repentance. Your best bet is to always do it immediately. Some people feel they are too bad to be forgiven. No sin is too great for God to forgive. Jesus came to die for the sins of humanity, He is ever ready to forgive and cleanse – whether you are an unsaved sinner coming to Him for the first time or a believer who has just made a mistake and wants to put things right with God.

God never remembers our sins. Place them before Him, leave them with Him and move on. Never let your feelings stand in the way of what God has done in your life. Just make sure you do not take God for granted and keep going back to the same sin repeatedly.

Benefits of Confession and Repentance

Psalm 51:7-19 points out several benefits that come with repentance:

- Spiritual cleansing. vs. 7,9
- Joy and gladness. v. 8
- Renewal and revival. v. 10
- Audience with God; anointing of the Holy Spirit. v.11
- Salvation and divine sustenance. v. 12
- Divine acceptance. vs. 16-17
- God takes pleasure in you. v. 19

Sin leads to spiritual sickness; sin also leads to certain types of physical sicknesses. No wonder the Psalmist prayed:

> "Oh LORD, have mercy on me; heal me, for I have sinned against you." (Psalm 41:4).

This passage does not necessarily state that sin is responsible for every sickness. Nevertheless, sin can open the door to sickness and other demonic influences in the life of a Christian. Definitely sin can stand in the way of anyone who wants to pray. If you want God to show up whenever you pray, keep yourself pure. Living a clean life leads to peace, confidence and power at the place of prayer.

18

COVENANT COMMITMENTS

Our covenant relationship with God provides a strong basis for taming our enemy, living victoriously and enjoying every blessing God has ordained for us as His children. When you pray you do not come to God based on your strength or smartness, but by the richness of God's grace and His covenant provisions.

A covenant is "a solemn agreement between two or more parties, made binding by some sort of oath" (Freeman, 2000) P. 288. In a covenant, the future conduct of one or both of the parties is usually the main issue. A covenant is only viable to the degree that the parties to it remain bonded and loyal. The main emphasis of God's covenant is relationship and intimacy with His people; He tells His covenant people, I will be your God (Genesis 17:7-8); you shall be my people (Exodus 6:7); I will dwell in the midst of you (Exodus 29:45-46). These covenant promises are the platform upon which every act of prayer is carried out, it gives the confident assurance that God is both our God and Father. God confirmed His covenant with us with a promise, an oath and sacrifice (Marshall, 2003) - three elements critical to consolidating the strength of every covenant:

Promise

Promises are meant to be kept, and God is the perfect promise keeper. He assures us that He takes His covenant promises seriously:

> *"Know therefore that the LORD thy God, he is God, the faithful God, which keepeth covenant and mercy with them that love him and keep his commandments to a thousand generations;"* (Deuteronomy 7:9).

Oath

Confirming a promise with an oath makes the maker more accountable for their commitment because they have put their reputation at stake; this was a very serious matter in ancient times, and,

> *"... God, willing more abundantly to shew unto the heirs of promise the immutability of His counsel, confirmed it by an oath:" (Hebrews 6:17); "When God made this promise to Abraham, since there was no one greater for Him to swear by, He swore by Himself, saying, 'I will surely bless you and give you many descendants'."* (Hebrews 6:13-14) NIV.

By this oath God staked His character, holiness and faithfulness as an assurance that He would fulfil His promise. When you appear before God's throne in prayer, you do not even have to remind Him about His promises before He keeps them, He has already bound Himself to fulfilling His word to you. All you need to do is lay claim on these promises when you pray. It is your covenant right.

Sacrifice

Every ancient covenant included a sacrifice which involved the shedding of blood. This symbolises atonement and separation (Hebrews 9:19-20; Jeremiah 31:31-34; Hebrews 9:22; Matthew 26:27-28; Genesis 15:9-10; 17-18). The blood of the covenant covers or washes away our sin, qualifying us to come into God's presence. The blood also signifies the death of the covenant parties, *"For where a testament [is], there must also of necessity be the death of the testator."* (Hebrews 9:16).

God will always keep His part of the covenant. All of God's word (the bible) represent His covenant promises. Prayer will be easier and victory will be a walk over if God's children simply keep to their part of the covenant.

God made covenants with Adam, Noah, Moses, David and generally, with all people (the New covenant). Each covenant has varied and comprehensive details; at the same time they have a unified message- a recurring theme by God saying:

"I will be your God" (Genesis 17:7-8); "You shall be my people" (Exodus 6:7); "I will dwell in the midst of you" (Exodus 29:45-46); "I will walk among you and be your God, and you will be my people." (Leveticus26:12). In what greater way can God assure us that He is closely knitted with us, that we can always count on Him at the time of need? His ears are ever listening to our prayers; He is always touched by the things that affect us.

The Covenant with Abraham- The focus of this was grace (Galatians 3:18) and faith (Romans 4:16-17). So Abraham is called the "father of all who believe." (Romans 4:11).

The Covenant with Moses- The main focus of this covenant was obedience to the terms of the covenant (Exodus 19:5; Psalm 103:17-18).

The Covenant with David- The main emphasis of this was the Kingdom- with the society and the entire creation being under the Kingship of the Messiah – Jesus (Isaiah 9:6-7).

The New Covenant- This is an expansion of the previous covenants. The earlier covenants progressively anchored in the New Covenant. Under the New Covenant, God writes the terms (law of God) of the covenant in the human heart. God's ongoing objectives (relationship) in the previous covenants were finally realised through the shedding of the blood of Christ. The covenants are all about relationship, fellowship and undeterred communion between God and humankind. Prayer is a key aspect of this relationship. In prayer there is a strong communion between God and His people.

The Old and New Covenants point to the same direction, and address the subject of relationship, obedience and the rewards of faith and obedience. Both covenants promise the same blessings which we can claim when we go before God in prayers. Prayer is the major tool for actualising the covenant blessings through faith.

We can definitely stand upon both the Old and New covenant promises each time we go before God to pray. Most of our needs during prayers fall within the above categories provided for in both the old and new covenants. God has asked us to come boldly to the throne of grace. This is what we do when we enter into prayer. Go to God with a strong assurance because you are in a covenant relationship with Him. You have His name, strength, provisions and protection. You have access to everything. We are joint-heirs with Christ, and God will not deny you His blessings. Claim and enjoy your covenant blessings.

Promise	Old Covenant	New Covenant
Spiritual Blessings	Genesis12:3; Deuteronomy 28:3-14;	Ephesians 1:3; Romans 15:29
Material blessings	Deuteronomy 28:8, 11-12	2Corinthians 9:6-15
Healing	Exodus15:26;23:26; Deuteronomy7:15; Isaiah 35:5-6	Matthew 8:16-17

Victory over enemies	Deuteronomy28:7; Isaiah 54:14-17	1John 5:4; 1Corinthians 15:57; Revelation 12:11
Families and children	Deuteronomy28:4; Isaiah 59:21	Acts 2:39; Mark 10:14

19

DISCIPLINE

Key words for discipline are control, willpower, self-mastery and strength of mind. A disciplined life exhibits all of these and more. Discipline is central to a fruitful prayer life. Lack of it is a major cause of failure in prayer. Irregular, inconsistent and ineffective prayer habits are the result of indiscipline. In fact a lot of people who are able to follow routine, and exercise great self control in many areas frequently fail to follow through with a regular or rigid prayer life.

It Is Every Where

Successful athletes have success stories because they discipline themselves to train for countless numbers of hours. Successful mountaineers are extremely disciplined, so they make and break records. Successful business people have very strict routines that keep them at the top and separate them from their competitors. Successful academics go through agonising self-denial and rigour before they reach the pinnacle of their professions. Actors and actresses repeatedly go through painful moments of training- sometimes for months and even years before they make that movie that brings them to limelight.

Indiscipline is an arch enemy to peak performance. It takes discipline to get out of bed with or without the alarm clock. Moderation in eating, talking, sex, watching television is possible only for the self-controlled individual. Keeping to the times and places earmarked for prayer will remain as mere intentions unless you have the will power and strength of mind needed to make it happen. Self-discipline is an inevitable part of a successful prayer life.

> "Now no chastening for the present seemeth to be joyous, but grievous: nevertheless afterward it yieldeth the peaceable fruit of righteousness unto them which are exercised thereby" (Hebrews 12:11). The bible also tells us that "Like a city whose walls are broken down is a man who lacks self-control" (Proverbs 25:28).

The commonest complaint about prayer is lack of time. We all create time for things that are important to us. If you consider prayer to be the hinge upon which you rest your spiritual and physical success, you will restrain yourself from anything that distracts you from praying. Common and very harmful habits to prayer include failure to keep to prayer plans, laziness, sleeping late, unhealthy diet, talkativeness, poor time management and sin. It takes discipline to overcome these as they can weigh seriously on your prayer life.

Discipline in Devotional Life

Your attitude towards your daily times with God will influence your ability to pray. Regular study of God's Word, for example will give you inspiration and refreshing which are critical to quality prayer times. Prayer cannot stand on its own – you need to have regular periods of studying God's word, worship and meditation, and other spiritual activities that will enrich your times with God.

Train Your Mind

The mind needs to be trained (tamed?) to stay on course when praying and when you are not praying. What you do with your mind can have serious repercussions for your prayer life. Allowing negative materials into your mind can stop you from praying in the first case. During your prayer times, permitting unnecessary information into your mind can make you lose focus. It is therefore crucial that you protect your mind at all times. Freeing your mind will give you the freedom to enjoy regular communion with God.

Trade Something for Your Prayer Life Today

What are you prepared to trade for your prayer life? To get anything we must give away something else. Self-control may be somewhat difficult to achieve but in the long run, the benefits far outweigh the alternative-intemperance. Self-mastery cuts across every aspect of life, as a Christian it will:

Help you integrate regular and consistent prayer times into your busy lifestyle.

Enable you generate and maintain prayer momentum.

Help you conquer any undesirable habits that may contend with the time you need with your heavenly father.

Help you combat procrastination – a major cause of failure to pray.

In the summer Olympics of 1936, a black American named Jesse Owens won four separate gold medals in 4 track and field events, in sprints and long jump- at a time when racism was at its highest and blacks were hardly given opportunities. He simply believed in his dream and let nothing stand in his way. He had put in all the dedication, discipline and determination needed to get him to his destination.

Trade something for your prayer life today. Nothing else you do is more crucial than your time alone with God. Eliminate every distraction and create time for regular fellowship with God.

20

DECLARATIONS

Wars are started with words, fought with words and ended with words. Your declarations will determine your destination. When you make a declaration you are stating openly what you believe, know or want a situation to be. In most cases you do not get what you pray for, you get what you speak forth. It is alright to pray but after praying many people annul their prayers by the things they proclaim. Proverbs 6:1-2 makes clear that,

"… Thou art snared with the words of thy mouth."

It makes no difference what you pray about, what you say is what you will receive. If you pray for prosperity and speak poverty, you will get penury. If you pray for good health and persistently speak ill health, you will reap bad health.

Speak God's Word Only

What you say reveals your level of faith, and without faith it is impossible to receive from God. God even tells us that whatsoever is not of faith is sin. So for prayer to get the expected results, your words must agree with God's word on the things you pray about. Jesus once said to His disciples,

> "... for I say unto you, if ye have faith as a grain of mustard see,
> ye shall say unto this mountain, Remove hence to yonder place;
> and it shall remove; and nothing shall be impossible unto you"
> (Matthew 17:20).

I also think this passage suggests you do not even have to pray about everything; you have the power and authority to speak things into existence. Doubts and unbelief will always creep in, but because you are fighting a war of words, you need to keep speaking positive words; contend and insist on what you want, through the words you speak.

Many people are in trouble today because of the negative things they confessed yesterday. Prayer success depends ultimately on your confession, not your intercession. So, keep expressing or announcing only what you want. It may start as a seed but words, once sown and maintained, will grow and there will be a time of harvest. You can not run away from this principle because,

> "A man's belly shall be satisfied with the fruit of his mouth; and
> with the increase of his lips shall he be filled. Death and life are
> in the power of the tongue: and they that love it shall eat the
> fruit thereof." (Proverbs 18:20-21).

The negative things you speak will gradually permeate your life – spirit, soul and body, with the result that your faith becomes diluted and you lose the ability to keep trusting God.

Connect the Dots

Your words will announce you. What you say after you have prayed can either connect or disconnect you from your blessings. The children of Israel repeatedly spoke things that were contrary to what God told or promised them. During every major crisis they had a reason to speak against Moses, God and His word. God was very displeased with them.

Confession is the connection between God's word and His promises to you. Plenty of praying cannot override this; that is the way it works-confession keeps you connected.

Confession Precedes Possession

God's Word teaches that your words will either bring you life or death (Proverbs 18:21); the tongue of the wise promotes health (Proverbs 12:18); your words can encourage and lift the spirit of the weary (Isaiah 50:4); your speech should always be gracious and seasoned with salt (Colossians 4:5); your mouth is a well of life (Proverbs 10:11).

Three Types of Confession

There are three common types of confession in the bible:

1. The sinner's confession.
   The bible says with the heart a person believes unto righteousness and with the mouth confession is made unto salvation; this is the sinner's confession of sin.

2. The believer's confession of sin if they step out of God's boundaries.

3. Confession of faith.
   It entails the affirmation of your belief, a testimony of what you know and the declaration of a truth that you have received, accepted and support. Confession of faith revolves around five pillars:

* What God, through redemption and Christ has done for us
* What God has done for us through the new birth, through His word and infilling of the Holy Spirit
* What we are, or represent to God

- What Jesus is doing for us as He is seated at the right hand of the Father in heaven
- What God is capable of doing through us

Keep praying and keep confessing what the Lord says concerning you. These two must agree to release what you have prayed about. Never cancel your prayer or expectation with the words of your mouth. Everything in existence is a product of the words that God spoke at creation. Your words have a creative force in them. It is alright to pray whatever amount of prayer you want; what counts eventually is what you say. If you keep saying something and keep believing what you say long enough, you will soon have the results of your confession. Never forget that confession brings possession. What you say has the ability to neutralise your prayer, it also has the potential to bring your desires to pass.

21

DELIGHT YOURSELF IN THE LORD

Another powerful secret to daily victories in prayer is to delight yourself in God. A lot of people find it easy to get excited about God only when they have things going well for them. Many people delight in God's benefits or blessings rather than God Himself. Some people are even excited about their gifts, talents and what they can, or have accomplished for God. People who derive pleasure in staying close to God are more inclined to enjoy a healthy prayer life.

Taking delight in God means you are satisfied with Him. You make Him the beginning and the end of your life. You will seek to do His will all the time. In word, deed and thoughts He is all that matters to you. You give Him priority over everything else in your life. You lavish your love on Him. He is in charge of your time, resources and relationships. If the quality of your relationship with God is poor so will the quality of your prayer life. The quality of your communication with God is directly related to the quality of your commitment to Him. The two cannot be separated.

Chosen by God

You are God's own special choice. He wants you to always be with Him. He wants you to take as much interest in Him as He has in you.

> "For thou art a holy people unto the Lord, thy God: The LORD thy God has chosen thee to be a special people unto Himself, above all people that are upon the face of the earth." (Deuteronomy 7:6).

God desires your relationship. Your prayer can only be as rich as your personal love for God.

Married To the Lord

One of the greatest mysteries of the Bible is that of the spiritual marriage between Jesus and the Church. God says in His word:

> ".... As the bridegroom rejoiceth over the bride, so shall thy God rejoice over thee" (Isaiah 62:5). "For thy Maker is thine husband; the Lord of hosts is His name; and thy Redeemer the Holy one of Israel; The God of the whole earth shall He be called." (Isaiah 54:5).

Spouses delight in one another; they get to know, understand and enjoy one another's fellowship. It is usually not about asking or receiving. They are excited to be around one another. God wants your relationship before your prayers- He wants you to have a desire for Him all the time; God first, and everything else takes second place.

Many people erroneously think that doing the work of God is the same thing as loving God. False! Many pastors fall into this trap and so immerse themselves in God's work, replacing God with His work. God wants you to be closer to Him than you are to His work. It is possible to be active for God and still be far from Him. Your joy and fulfilment must not come from what you do for God, but from your fellowship with Him. This is central to having an effective prayer life. It is easy to get actively involved in the work of the Kingdom, and still be pathetically distant from God. Work does not equate to God. A sound prayer life is the result of a sound relationship with our Father in heaven.

Obedience to God's Word

There is no greater way of expressing your delight in God than through obedience to His Word. Obedience to God is an indication that you definitely honour Him. 1 John 3:22 tells us what happens when one lives in obedience to God's word.

> *"And what so ever we ask, we receive of Him, because we keep His commandments, and do those things that are pleasing in His sight."*

Many people think they can have a disjointed and an inconsistent relationship with God and continue to enjoy answers to prayers. Miracles may continue to happen. The anointing may keep flowing, but this is no indication that God is pleased with an individual as they could be living in old or faded glory. It is only a matter of time before they realise how far removed they are from God. Let the presence of God remain your delight every day. Get acquainted with Him and let His life naturally enliven and sustain your prayer life.

Delight yourself in the Lord. Make time for Him. Nourish your relationship with God. Closeness to God will completely transform your prayer life. Your power supply for prayer will never be exhausted because you are always close to the inexhaustible God.

22

DETERMINE DIVINE DIRECTION

It is easy to spend tens or even hundreds of hours in a lifetime praying about things God never intended for you to pray about. If you continue to pray in the wrong direction your prayers will be meaningless, because you need to pray in accordance with God's will in order to receive answers to your prayers and minimise the amount of wasted time. No matter how smart a person is, they are still prone to making mistakes, sometimes very expensive mistakes. This is also true when it comes to prayers. Jeremiah recognised this and said:

> *"O LORD, I know that the way of man is not in himself; it is not in man that walketh to direct his steps."* (Jeremiah 10:23).

There are many situations in which your human wisdom, skills and knowledge will fail you. Several times you will think you have got everything right, but then you could still be miles away from God's perfect will.

Life Is a Maze

No amount of experience can teach you how to navigate all the twists and turns of life before you get to your destination. A familiar problem may present in a totally different way next time, leaving you to keep guessing what to do. When you spend time patiently in God's presence,

He will lead you through the peaks and valleys of life- no matter what it is about. Knowing what to do in the first case reduces the amount of prayer you will have to carry out. Sometimes we pray when all that God wanted us to do is simply speak to someone about the situation. Until you seek direction from Him, you may never know precisely what God wants you to do in a situation- whether to pray, wait or take a plunge.

How to Determine Divine Direction

God speaks to His people in numerous ways. Let us examine some of them:

1. **Through His Word**
   God's word is the most authentic and most authoritative way He speaks to His people. His word is forever settled in heaven and on earth. Every prayer must line up with God's word (2Timothy 3:16). When you pray, you must ask according to the written word of God- believing it, and standing on it.

2. **Through Dreams**
   All through the bible God spoke expressly to His people through dreams- telling them what He is about to do, the dangers that lie ahead, instructions they must carry out or things they must avoid. These can subsequently be turned into prayer topics and used as a guide to prayer. In the Old Testament God spoke to Abraham, Jacob, Joseph, Gideon and many more through dreams. In the New Testament He spoke to the wise men, Pilate's wife and Joseph the earthly father of Jesus in dreams.
   Dreams can guide you in prayer, but overreliance on dreams can be harmful to your spiritual life. Every dream must be critically examined under the 'microscope' of God's Word.

3. **Through Visions**
   God may also choose to guide us through visions- these may be flashes of images through the mind or spirit's eyes. God

encouraged Paul through a vision (Acts 18:9-10); through visions Daniel saw and was able to pray about future events (Daniel 8:1-2; 10:4-7); the Angel Gabriel spoke to Zacharias (father of John the Baptist) through a vision (Luke 11:13,22). God warns against false visions (Jeremiah 23:16; Lamentations 2:14). Also, as you would do with dreams turn the visions into prayer topics- everything God reveals is for a purpose, and prayer will expedite the purpose of God for your life.

4. Through Circumstances

God also speaks to His people through unique circumstances by making it obvious that He is in those circumstances. God told David to attack the Philistines when he hears some movements on top of the mulberry trees (2Samuel 5:22-25). Certain circumstances in your life could simply be an indication that God is telling, or about to tell you something.

5. Through the Inner Witness of the Spirit

Every child of God has a regenerated spirit. Through this God can express His will to you. It may come in the form of a desire, a clear or faint conviction, or just an unusual feeling that makes you know that God is speaking to you (Proverbs 16:1; Proverbs 21:1). However, just because you strongly want something does not mean God is in it; also, the fact that you do not want it does not mean God is against it. He may whisper to you to do something that you are unwilling to do. God can settle something peacefully in your heart, indicating His will to you on a specific matter.

6. Through Prophecies

God also uses prophets and prophecies to speak to His people. The bible clearly states the importance of prophecy although God wants His children to depend more on His word. God put His words in the mouth of Jeremiah (Jeremiah 1:9); God spoke to the early Church through prophets (Acts 13:1-2). Every child of God should watch against false prophecies. There are so many false prophets today who speak lies and deceit for their personal gratification and exaltation. God can reveal His will to us through prophecy to aid and guide us on how to pray.

The Supremacy of God's Will

It does not matter how much a person prays, God's will always comes to pass. Daniel recognised that:

> "...the Most High rules in the kingdom of men, Gives it to whomever He will..." (Daniel 4:17). God told Jeremiah, "Therefore do not pray for this people, nor lift up a cry or prayer for them, nor make intercession to me; for I will not hear you" (Jeremiah 67:16). NKJV

If you pray for something or someone when God does not want you to, it is impossible to receive answers to those prayers. Prayer is more effective when you are in agreement with God. Prayer is particularly successful when God guides or directs you on what to pray. When God told Ezekiel to prophesy to the dry bones, the bones received life and began to live again. You should pray as the need arises, however there are times when God gives specific instructions, or you must seek specific instructions from God on a matter. God told Ezekiel, "... Prophesy upon these bones, and say unto them, O ye dry bones, hear the word of the LORD" (Ezekiel 37:4).

During the idolatrous reign of King Ahab, God told Elijah to inform the king there would be no rain, and so it was. Years later God told Elijah to pray for rain, he did, and the land received bountiful rain as a result of Elijah's prayer. God's instruction can make a big difference to your prayers. If He tells you not to pray about a thing, it will be no use praying. If He instructs you to stop praying or change prayer direction, you must not do otherwise.

DEATH TO SELF

To die to self means thinking less of yourself and giving more thought and consideration to others. You can only be a blessing to the world if you make yourself generously available to others. You will not achieve much in prayer if the emphasis is just on yourself and your loved ones. When you give more of yourself to God and people, you will attract more of God's grace to accomplish greater things. Prayer gets better when we remember others, life becomes bigger when we see beyond ourselves.

Prayer Is Made Easy

The easiest way to attract the power of God for fruitful praying is to place greater emphasis on God and others. Your prayer becomes more effective when you learn to pray and give to others, when your prayer focus becomes less of you and more of others.

The richest forms of prayer are those prayed for others. From my personal experience, I have found that my best prayer times are when I pray for other people. I have always felt more of God's grace and anointing when carrying out intercessory prayers. Fast and pray for people even if they do not know you are doing so. Selflessness is the nature of God, and putting on the nature of God will make you enjoy more of His power at the place of prayers.

The Cornerstone of Christianity

Christianity is founded upon, and flourishes on the foundation of selfless giving. Jesus laid down His life, that we may live.

> *"For the love of Christ constraineth us; because we thus judge that if one died for all, then were all dead: And that He died for all, that they which live should not hence forth live unto themselves, but unto Him which died for them, and rose again"*
> (2 Corinthians 5:14-15).

This is the cornerstone of Christianity, and the bedrock of prayer. It is only a life that has died and is resurrected that will manifest the fullness of God's grace. The un-surrendered life may never know the blessings of intimacy with God. When we are completely dead to self, we will be totally reliant upon God's power to pray. Until a Christian is completely dead to self they cannot fully experience a release of the Spirit's anointing for prayer.

Grace and Glory

God's grace represents His favour, generosity and kindness. God's grace enhances your prayer life and ushers you daily into new levels of prayer experience. Jesus taught that anyone who loses their life will save it, those who forsake all and follow Him will receive a hundred-fold and those who serve Him will be honoured by the Father. The bible gives a lot of instances of people who had little regard for themselves so that they can fulfil the will of God:

- When there was contention between the herdsmen of Abraham and his nephew Lot, Abraham gave Lot the right to choose the best part of the land for grazing. God blessed Abraham much more than Lot. (Genesis 13:9). Prayer cannot prosper anything God has not blessed.

- When the poor widow of Zarephath gave Elijah her very last meal at the risk of the death of her family, the left over barrel of meal and her only cruse of oil continued to multiply. She did not need to pray. She simply gave herself freely to the work of God (1 Kings 17:8-16). If we learn to give our all to God, God will be willing to release His all to us, with little or no prayer.

- When a little boy gave what was probably his entire lunch of five loaves and two fish to Jesus, a miracle happened in his life. The five loaves and two fish fed over five thousand people and several baskets of left overs were gathered. Only God can tell how much of personal blessings the lad received through his selfless giving, which prayer alone could never have brought into his life.

The bible is filled with examples of selfless people who lived both for God and others outside their immediate circle. When you sacrifice yourself to God, He rewards you with His grace. With plenty of sacrifice, you will only require a minimum amount of prayer, and sometimes prayer may even become unnecessary. The more you give, the more you receive and the less you will need to pray.

24

DEVELOP YOUR PRAYER LIFE

Continuous personal development (CPD) or Continuous Personal and Professional Development (CPPD) have become two buzzwords in every field or profession. More than ever before, organisations are now taking deliberate steps to ensure their personnel are developing on a continuous basis. The value of your prayer life places a demand on you to grow continuously in your relationship with the Lord. To this end the Bible urges:

> *"But grow in grace, and in the knowledge of our Lord and saviour Jesus Christ. To Him be the glory now and forever. Amen."* (2 Peter3:18).

Not taking measured and consistent steps to grow your prayer life will lead to spiritual dryness over time. It is difficult to imagine a more important area of the Christian life where continuous growth is desperately needed. If your prayer life is weak and erratic, so will your relationship with God and your ability to stand firm in difficult times. Organisations deploy enormous amounts of resources on professional and organisational development. They continuously address issues such as:

- Quality Assurance
- Meeting professional standards
- Gaining a competitive edge

- Meeting legal requirements
- Adapting to an ever changing world, and customers' demands and
- Employee competence

God also expects His people to keep improving. Some Christians continue to remain at the baby stages of prayer which they acquired when they were still new to the faith. Not much has changed even though they may have grown in some other areas of their lives. I suppose things are this way because they have never really seen the need to grow their prayer life. There are phases and sizes in prayer. Deliberate developmental efforts are required to take you to the next prayer level; no matter what stage you have attained in your personal relationship with God, there is always a next level. Start doing something today that will usher you into a new spiritual realm.

From Strength To Strength

In Psalm 84:7, the scriptures tell us that:

> "They go from strength to strength; every one of them in Zion appeareth before God."

God wants you to grow from strength to strength, spiritually. The more you grow your prayer life the better the results you will get from prayers. Try something you have not tried before in prayers. Read books, listen to tapes and participate in some big prayer projects.

Forget The Past

Keep pressing forward. It does not matter how much you have prayed before today. That is already in the past. Keep the light brighter and stop living in past glory. Your prayer life must be better today than yesterday; this week must surpass the last, and this month must outshine the previous one. Cumulatively, the total sum of your prayer (in quality and quantity), must surpass the previous years. Forget the past and reach out for what lies ahead. Something new must happen regularly in your prayer life, then you will continue to see new results as you pray.

Make Big Prayer Plans

Progress from ten to thirty minutes daily. Advance from thirty minutes daily to one hour daily, then to two hours daily. Go for regular personal prayer retreats- alone and away from home, business and loved ones. Practice extended times of prayer. Do what you have never done before in prayer.

> "Enlarge the place of thy tenth, and let them strength forth the curtains of thine habitations: spare not, lengthen thy cords, and strengthen thy stakes" (Isaiah 54:2).

No Pain, No Gain

Prayer is powerful. Powerful praying will drain your energy and sometimes take you through moments of pain. The reason why some people do not embark on aggressive and intensive prayer is because the price is high. The pain is great. Extended prayer hours are neither for the faint-hearted, nor for people whose 'god is their belly'. Preaching may be modernised, but prayer cannot. Christian music may get trendier, funkier and stylish, but prayer must continue to be the old fashioned, heart rending and sometimes exerting exercise. Evangelism can be modernised. Church facilities can be up graded and made contemporary, but prayer cannot be diluted or adjusted to suit modern times. It requires spiritual and physical energy, especially when you have to pray with fasting. As in physical exercise, if you pray consistently and progressively, your physical gains will be a reflection of your efforts.

> "For it became Him, for whom are all things, and by whom are all things, in bringing many sons unto glory, to make the captain of their salvation perfect through suffering" (Hebrews 2:10).

Strong praying can lead to a dimension of physical tiredness, but prayer experience can equally act as a 'pain killer' and energiser. Jesus wept when He prayed. He suffered pains when He fasted for weeks without food. He rose to pray while others slept. He prayed alone when no one agreed to join Him. He prayed until His countenance changed. He purposefully developed His spiritual life. If you are still at the same level of prayer compared to a year ago, then you need to do something to move on from that level.

EVALUATE YOUR PRAYER LIFE

In simple terms, evaluation refers to the orderly determination of the merit, and worth of something or a person. This is usually done by measuring against a set of standards. It is a process of gauging how well you are doing. What has gone well? What could be done better? What corrective measures can be taken? The prophet Jeremiah supported the need for personal evaluation:

> *"Let us search and try our ways, and turn again to the Lord."*
> (Lamentations 3:40).

Evaluation can take the form of very simple methods of rating success. It could also involve very complex systems of appraisal.

The Deming Cycle

W. Edwards Deming (1900-1993) was an American statistician, professor, author and lecturer who was mostly recognised and remembered for his contribution to the Japanese innovation and economic power, especially in manufacturing and business. He was regarded as the father of the Japanese post-war industrial revival. The impact of his contributions on the Japanese people brought about a paradigm shift in the world's perception of Japanese products. One of his tools was the Deming Cycle grounded upon the principles of continual improvement.

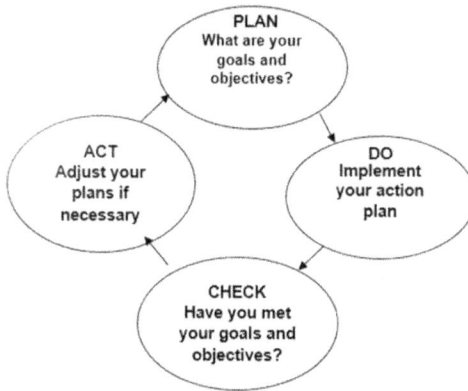

PDCA cycle (Deming, 1900-1993)

Also known as the PDCA cycle the Deming Cycle is a simple four-step problem solving process used in measuring success in the business environment; its four steps can also be applied to any area of life:

Plan

This brings us back to the earlier segment on establishing prayer aims. Every prayer exercise should have its goals or objectives. Every prayer project by groups or individuals should be thoroughly planned. Intentionally plan your prayers – the amount, place, time, duration and resources. Plan in little and big steps.

Do

A plan is useless unless it is carried out. If you ever thought you could pray an hour or two a day, plan it out and begin today. Carry out your plan every single day. Just do it.

Check

After you have planned and prayed, what difference has your prayer made? Have you received your expected results? If not, why not? Do you need to pray more or do you need the help of others? Have you prayed rightly or wrongly? What adjustments do you need to make to have a more productive prayer life? There are so many questions you may choose to ask at this stage. Were you discouraged? If so why or what impact did that have on your prayers? What did God tell you to do and how will you go about doing it?

Act

Make necessary improvements to your prayer plan. Let the process start from stage one all over again, that makes it a cycle. Go back to planning. Then do and check. Keep acting on the results of your evaluation. There will always be something to adjust. In any area of life when you stop evaluating, you stop improving, and start losing value. Spiritual self-assessment should touch on the following:

- Your relationship with God and others and how these affect your prayer life.
- What adjustments need to be made to your prayer plan?
- Your place and time of prayer; what negative or positive impact do they have on you?
- Your commitments. Do they distract from or contribute to your prayer life?
- If regular prayer and fasting will be needed, how would you incorporate this into your lifestyle?
- Whether you need to pray more or less. What should you do next?
- Are there weights and sins that constitute a hindrance to your prayer life? How could you overcome these?

The cycle continues. Plan. Do. Review. Plan again. Most organisations regularly evaluate their programs, policies, procedures, personnel and products. As they keep appraising, they keep appreciating. Regularly evaluate your prayer life. If you do not evaluate you could depreciate. What gets evaluated gets corrected. Continuous improvement enhances continuity, consistency and efficiency. Make it an important aspect of your spiritual life to continue to gauge how you have prayed, and how you can make improvements; do this for every area of your spiritual life.

26

EXCUSES ARE BAD FOR PRAYERS

One of the hall marks of unsuccessful people is excuses. A life full of excuses is often dotted with failures. Successful people take ownership for their mistakes or failures. Unsuccessful people blame everything and everyone else but themselves. It is a lot easier to rise from defeat when you take responsibility. It is possible to find an excuse every day for not praying, if anyone choses to.

When people take responsibility for failure in prayers, they create more possibilities for success. Excuses are usually a smokescreen for something else people are not willing to uncover. It's not me! I have heard children scream or even cry 'it's not me', when in fact they are the culprit. It is time to grow up and take responsibility for our prayer calling. You are responsible for creating the needed time for prayer. Do not blame your job, your family or something else. You own your time and can utilise it for whatever you deem fit. It is a matter of priority. At the Garden of Eden, Adam blamed Eve for his disobedience. Eve blamed the serpent for deceiving her. Neither of them accepted any blame for their action.

"And the man said, the woman whom thou gavest to be with me, she gave me of the tree, and I did eat". And the Lord God said unto the woman, "what is this that though hast done"?

And the women said "The serpent beguiled me, and I did eat."
(Genesis 3:12-13).

So who was to blame for their disobedience? Let us put the blame where it belongs. No more excuses. Start praying today. Start changing lives and situations today through your prayers. Do not wait till tomorrow. It is always easy to find a reason for failing to pay the price for success.

Feeling Inadequate

A possible excuse for not praying is a feeling of inadequacy. Moses felt inadequate when God called him to deliver His people from the Egyptian bondage. He complained about his inability to communicate fluently (Exodus 4:10). When God asked Gideon to go and deliver Israel from Midianite oppression, Gideon complained that his family was poor, and that he was the least esteemed in his family. Once again the excuse was 'I am inadequate'. Gideon eventually went in to deliver the people of Israel from Midianite oppression. God helped him to put aside his excuses, and empowered him to fulfil God's purpose for his life.

This did not stop Jeremiah from complaining about his youthfulness. He told God he was too young for His call. For various reasons, even with God's promises and backing, humans naturally prefer to give an excuse for not obeying God's instructions. You can do all things. You can pray more than you have ever imagined. Just do it and the grace to pray will be upon you. God's power is all that you need, if you are willing and obedient.

An Excuse for Everything

Anybody can give an excuse for anything. The truth is you can do everything you set your heart on. Too often people blame:

- The lecturer for giving short deadlines.
- The computer and printer for packing up.
- The alarm clock for not going off.

- The children for distracting.
- Their spouse for being uncooperative.
- Politicians for not keeping their promises, not giving opportunities.

The list can go on for as long as we want. Yet every reason for failure can be overcome. Do not let anything stop you because the bible tells us that with God all things are possible. Overcome excuses, and you will do wonders through the ministry of prayers.

There Is No Convenient Time

A convenient time will never come. Something will always compete for your precious time. Now is the best time. All worthwhile endeavours contain a certain level of inconvenience. Prayer is one of the easiest things to do because we can get divine enablement to pray. It is also one of the most difficult tasks to see through because many people are waiting for a more convenient time.

It is inconvenient to rise up as early as 5.00 am to pray before distractions set in early in the morning; it is rather more convenient to pull up the cover for another half hour of sleep which is capable of robbing you of valuable prayer time. It is inconvenient to rise from the sofa and dash into your bedroom for the much needed 30 minutes of prayer after a hard day's work; it is far more convenient to sink into the sofa because you have had enough after a difficult day. It is inconvenient to miss your meals (and fast) for twenty-four or forty-eight hours in order to enrich your prayer life. It is convenient to pretend that you do not need fasting. You just want to stay healthy and eat healthy; after all the most important thing is to pray – not fast!

Our ability to accept discomfort and inconvenience is crucial to having a vibrant prayer life. The best time to pray is when you lack the time and the urge to do it. Find the time to pray. Let nothing stand between you and your prayer life. Overcome all the excuses and take advantage of the weapon of prayer on a daily basis.

27

EXTENDED TIMES OF PRAYER

Having extended times of prayer involve setting longer periods of time aside to spend with God in prayers. This should usually go beyond the durations of your regular prayer times. It is like taking a short or long break away to be with God, and the benefits can be astounding. Spending a long time in God's presence can forever change your life. To develop, or grow your prayer life one of the keys you must employ is deliberate extension of your time alone with God every now and then. Just stay there and you will have fresh experiences with the Lord each time you dwell in His presence. You need to practice praying for extended periods of time.

Extend Your Prayer Times

More time in God's presence will bring you into closer intimacy with Him. The more we stay in His presence the more we get to understand Him and the richer our prayer life will be. The Psalmist shares his experience:

"Thou wilt show me the path of life: in thy presence is fullness of joy; at thy right hand there are pleasures for ever more." (Psalm 16:11).

The benefits of sharing prolonged personal fellowship with God are too great to be missed.

Practice makes perfect

When you spend ample time with God, you will become closer to His heart; closeness to His heart will bring you closer to His blessings. Like in sports and other physical exercises the more you train, the more you gain. Physical exercise helps improve flexibility, strengthen your muscles and increase your endurance. Similarly training to stay in His presence will help to develop your spiritual muscles and put you in top spiritual shape to wage war against the enemy.

Stay spiritually FIT

F = Frequency.

To stay spiritually fit you must maintain frequent prayer times with God. Take frequent times away to pray and talk to God. The longer and the more frequent, the richer your experience will be. Frequent and extended times with God will continue to give you the needed edge over the devil.

I = Intensity.

You must intensify your prayer. Increase the level and temple of prayer. The more heat you apply, the more likely the enemy will yield to the pressure. Protracted and intense prayers will pile up unbearable pressure on Satan and cause him to take his hands off whatever you are praying about.

T =Time.

In prayer, time is a valuable asset. Quality is good. Quantity and quality together is even better. Deliberately stay longer than usual when you go before God to pray. More time is better than less time. Every extra minute you spend with God brings an extra blessing to you or someone else. Give prayer more time. More will be said on this later in the book.

Personal renewal

One of the greatest benefits of spending prolonged times with God is personal renewal; a time of letting God cleanse you from every dust or dross. The habit of staying in His presence will make you cleaner and brighter spiritually.

Self-examination

This will be addressed extensively in a later section of this book. Quality time with God affords you the opportunity of self-assessment. The Holy Spirit will beam His light on you, and you will become more aware of what needs to be put right in your life as you bask in His presence.

Planning and preparation

Planning and preparation should naturally precede every major project or event of our lives. No matter how clever or skilled you are, you can still make mistakes due to human limitations. Spending hours, days or even weeks in God's presence will give you the chance to present your plans before God for approval. Make the time for it. Let Him speak His heart to you. Present your plans before Him and let Him guide and speak to you about your life.

Focus

When you spend extended times in God's presence, away from home and daily routine you will find it easier to detach from every day distractions. You will able to focus. The power of focus is the power of success.

Choose a place to stay alone with God. Choose a date in your calendar and stick to it. Take your bible, note book and pen with you. Protect yourself against every possible obstacle or distraction- even legitimate ones. Pray ahead that God prepares and visits you during your time away. Keep a record of whatever God tells you during your time away.

Be sure to act upon whatever he says to you during these special times. Even long after you have returned from your prayer trip, keep going through the notes you made as it is very easy to forget the things he told you.

28

FORGIVENESS

God wants you to pardon rather than hold grudges against people. Forgiveness involves 'letting off', turning a blind eye to an offense and exonerating the offender. The path towards peace and forgiveness can be backbreaking, but bitterness never makes anyone better. Unforgiveness is a decision to cling to past pains, injuries and hurts. Forgiveness is particularly difficult when the other person fails to ask for it. It is extremely difficult when you feel the person does not 'deserve' it. No one can have a fruitful prayer life if they harbour or brood unforgiveness in their hearts.

The Bedrock of Christianity

Christianity is founded upon forgiveness. Any Christian that fails to forgive is denying the faith. It may be hard to do but forgiveness is not optional. No pretending, or living in denial about this, Jesus is very clear on forgiveness in Matthew 6:15:

> *"But if ye forgive not men their trespasses, neither will your father forgive your trespasses."*

Jesus laid down an example of forgiveness during His last moments on the cross when He asked the Father to forgive the same people who nailed Him to the Cross. God wants His people to be: *"... kind one to another, tender- hearted, forgiving one another, even as God for Christ's sake hath forgiven you"* (Ephesians 4:32).

Negative Responses to Offences.

Getting even, and repaying the offender is the cheapest and easiest option when someone grieves you. Strong people do not choose this path. Weak people do, because it is very easy. You want to make them 'pay' but that is not the way God wants His children to treat offenders. Neither does God want you to continue dwelling on the offence. Pre-occupying your mind with the offense, or the offender only exposes you to further problems.

Bitterness and grudging are twin evils. Anger is a God- given emotion which can be used positively to initiate and advance good causes. The bible says to be angry but not to sin. When anger is not well managed it can lead to a catalogue of other problems. The easiest way to overcome hurts and offenses is to pray for those who cause you harm. Bless them. If you leave them to God He will take care of them the way He chooses. If you do not handle it God's way it will become a stumbling block to your prayers.

The offender does not have to be your biological brother, it could be just anyone|. An altar is a place of sacrifice, worship or prayer. Bitterness and failure to forgive are capable of hindering your prayers in ways you may never imagine. Unforgiveness obstructs your access to God – to the flow of the Holy Spirit in your prayer hour.

Give the Grudges to God

Think of the number of times you have tried to pray or do some other important thing but you could not just because someone has hurt or wronged you. Then, imagine leaving yourself in that condition any longer than that particular moment. What a loss that would be to you! Experts agree that forgiving others have a number of advantages including the following:

Increased spiritual and psychological well-being

Healthy relationships

Reduced anxiety, stress and hostility

Lesser symptoms of depression

Lesser likelihood of alcohol and substance abuse

(www.Mayoclinic.org).

Anything that can cause you stress can also harm your prayer life. Things that can affect physical relationships will also impact negatively on spiritual relationships. Anything that can rob you of your peace is also very likely to rob you of the power to pray.

Mercy to the Merciful

Answer to pray is the outcome of God's mercy towards us. He answers our prayers not because we are prayer warriors, great intercessors, eloquent or qualified by any means. It is only because of His mercies; and He wants us to extend this mercy to others so we can continue to have access to His throne:

With the merciful God will be merciful (Psalm 18:25)

Blessed are the merciful for they shall obtain mercy (Matthew 5:7)

If you forgive men their trespasses, your Heavenly father will also forgive you your trespasses (Matthew 6:14)

Condemn not, and you shall not be condemned: forgive, and you shall be forgiven (Luke 6:37).

Forgiveness may not always be easy but it is God's own standard for keeping our relationship with Him; holding things against others will definitely obstruct your communion with God. God may not rebuke you sharply when you come into the prayer closet, but He expects you to meet this condition before He can answer your prayer.

29

FAILURE IS NOT AN OPTION

Everyone experiences failure in life. Failure in prayer could lead to failure in many other aspects of life. It is easy to pray. It is also easy not to pray. Everyone can pray, but everyone will not always have effective prayer times. Failure in prayer could be due to a range of reasons. Whatever the reasons for failing in prayer, God wants you to be able to pray and get results. Delayed answers to prayer do not make you a spiritual failure. Delays are sometimes part of God's answers to your prayer. He will never turn His back on His people:

> *"For the Lord God will help Me, Therefore I will not be disgraced; Therefore I have set My face like a flint, And I know that I will not be ashamed."* (Isaiah 50:7).

Why People Fail In Prayers

Much of the information in this section has been discussed elsewhere in this book, so they will be treated briefly here.

Secret Sins

Sin can pose a major obstacle to your access to God's presence. God wants all His children to gain unlimited access to His presence. Sin includes failure to meet divine standard, flagrantly defying the known will of God or failing to carry out your duties. Doing something that is inherently wrong or forbidden by God's word is also a form of sin. It will be futile to try and make a list of sins here. Quite often people know in their heart when they have committed a sin. Getting sin out of the way will give you express access into God's presence.

Procrastination

There is no better time to talk to God about that problem than now. There is no better day to commence that fasting programme than today. If it means a lot to you, if your life or someone else's life will benefit from it, the ideal time to pray about the matter is today. Every act of procrastination is a step towards failure. Each time you postpone your praying you delay your blessings, and give the enemy further room to carry out his activities.

Lack of Planning

Failure to plan means you are planning to fail. People who pray effectively are those who deliberately and decisively factor prayer into their daily routines. Have a plan. Have an aim. Schedule prayer times like you will do other activities and be committed to it. If you do not want to leave prayer to chance you must be intentional about it.

Over-dependence on Others

Many people fail to develop or grow their prayer lives because they rely excessively on others. You cannot leave your prayer matters to anyone, whoever they are - your pastor, the prayer group, older Christians or some other person. Learn to pray. Get to pray. Pray until you become self-reliant, and until you know God for yourself.

Distractions

Never get too distracted to pray. Prayer brings the influence of God on every area of your life. If you really want God in the matter, then you must pray. You must pray with all your might, all your heart and all the time. You need to develop the power to say no to certain things and people. Prayer must be given priority on your list, and the best place for it is number one.

Discouragement

Stop living in regrets, learn from your disappointments and make adjustments. Do not give up no matter how long the problem has endured. Some prayers take a long time before you see positive signs of change. Do whatever it will take to maintain your passion. Remember that God has promised never to leave nor forsake you. You can keep counting on Him. If possible get a prayer partner or join a prayer group to keep your fire burning. Overcome discouragement like Caleb did:

> "And Caleb stilled the people before Moses, and said, Let us go
> up at once, and possess it; for we are well able to overcome it."
> (Numbers 13:30)

Let God's glory light up your darkest hour, He can use your sufferings and troubles to display His strength. You must continue to hope against hope like Abraham did. Endure every challenge because God hears your sighs and counts your tears. Wait for Him and He will not fail. You must be determined never to fail at praying. There should be no room for prayer failure in the lives of God's children.

30

FASTING AND PRAYER

So much has been written on the subject of fasting, but unfortunately majority of Christians never avail themselves of this powerful and much needed spiritual tool. Not a lot would be covered on fasting in this book as there are many good books on the subject which can be found in literally every Christian bookstore.

Fasting is refraining from food for a period of time for spiritual purposes. People fast for a variety of reasons, some spiritual and others physical. Mere abstinence from food therefore, does not necessarily constitute a Christian fast. A Christian fast is undergirded by a time of prayer, worship, bible study and fellowship with God. To simply forgo food or something else through self-denial or self-restraint does not equate fasting. Christian fasting involves abstinence from food as well as engagement in some form of spiritual exercise. When nothing else works, the unbeatable and powerful combination of fasting and prayer will neutralise both the power of the flesh and the power of Satan.

Spiritual Benefits of Fasting

Fasting brings manifold blessings to the believer. We will discuss just a few of them in this section.

Humble Yourself with Fasting

Fasting is a very powerful instrument for humbling the flesh and bringing oneself into alignment with God and His will. Fasting helps the body to observe an attitude of submission to God. It will break you down, and give you both physical and emotional soundness. It crushes and chastens the body, and brings about spiritual revival. Fasting produces such physical weakness that makes you surrender totally to God, compelling you to cry out, "all to Jesus I surrender; all to Him I freely give". Total surrender is required to get into the heart of God. Fasting takes you quickly to that point.

Power and Anointing

Prior to launching His ministry, Jesus had a lengthy period of fasting; He obtained power and anointing before commencing ministry (Luke 4:14). Christians have been called both to advance the kingdom of God and to enforce the will of God upon those bound by the devil, through the power of the Holy Spirit. Jesus called his disciples together in Matthew 10:1 and gave them power over demonic spirits, yet subsequently they could not cast out an epileptic spirit from a young boy, brought to them by the mother. Jesus rebuked the disciples' faithlessness and added,

> *"Howbeit this kind goeth not out but by prayer and fasting"*
> (Mathew 17:21).

Jesus was very categorical about the role of fasting in the demonstration of God's power, reaffirming the vitality of fasting and prayer. Fasting multiplies your prayer ability several folds, it revives your prayer life; it boosts your ability to carry out ministry more effectively.

Self-discipline

In an undisciplined age, fasting is an indispensable instrument for building self-discipline. Indiscipline is one of the enemy's tactics for weakening people's prayer life. Fasting breaks, moulds and moves the body closer to the realm of God. Unsurprisingly, the body will rebel, sometimes aggressively, when you embark on a fast. It is a sign that you are doing the will of God. A flesh dominated life cannot obtain maximum victory in spiritual warfare.

Victory in Spiritual warfare

The book of 2Chronicles 20:3 records an account of a military alliance against Jehoshaphat, king of Judah. The adversaries were the Ammonites, Moabites and the Midianites. Jehoshaphat proclaimed a fast for the inhabitants of Judah. This invoked the power of God against the evil alliance and the enemies were discomfited. They were in so much disarray that they turned their sword one against another. They literally slaughtered themselves, and Jehoshaphat and Judah triumphed over their adversaries.

Physical Benefits of Fasting

The benefits of fasting are far reaching. Not only is fasting beneficial to your spiritual life, the broader effects of fasting extend to the physical, emotional and mental realms.

Fasting gives the much needed break to the digestive system. Fasting helps to cleanse and detoxify the body, together with managing our eating patterns. It makes the mind clear and sharp; it also increases our level of energy and makes us feel lighter. When you fast you enjoy inner tranquillity and assurance.

When your body takes a break from food, it automatically goes through the process of detoxification, elimination and reparation. Your system will take a break from overload, overwork and over indulgence. This leads to sound physical health, which in turn results in the sound physical and emotional state necessary for a healthy prayer life. Each act of fasting takes you through a journey of physical rejuvenation and spiritual fitness. Fasting gives you the physical, spiritual and emotional health needed for effective praying. Never fail to take advantage of fasting on a regular basis.

Mental and Emotional Strength

Fasting ushers you into a new dimension of clarity, calmness and happiness. Despite the pains and strains that accompany fasting, many believers will find that fasting leaves them in the best spiritual and physical form to achieve greater prayer results. Fasting gives the child of God the wonderful benefits of spiritual, physical and emotional resuscitation and recuperation.

A Christian without an active life of fasting will experience seasons of spiritual draught, physical drag and emotional drain. Give fasting a chance in your life from today and you will continue to experience greater peace, better health and fewer spiritual defeats. Fasting fans the flames of prayer.

31

FAMILY ALTAR

What Is An Altar?

An altar is an elevated place or structure where sacrifices are offered; it is a place of slaughter or death. Important religious activities often revolve around the altar, a place of sacrifice and meeting between God and His people. A regular altar of prayer will repel evil forces and bring God's power into a family, city or nation. The family altar is a time when a family engages in bible study, worship and prayer on a routine basis to develop individual and collective faith. Unbroken fellowship and experiences with God at the altar is the surest way to keep your prayer strength ever renewed.

A Nation of Priests

God called Israel to be a nation of priests unto Him. Every born again Christian is also called to be a priest —we offer sacrifices to, and declare the praises of the one who has called us out of darkness to His marvellous light. As priests, when we stand in God's presence to offer spiritual sacrifices, we:

Promote the presence of the Lord over our land.

Bridge the gap between the people and God, through intercession

Represent God and engineer His move over the land

Generate the power of God over the demonic forces that rule the land

Bring the rule of God to bear upon the land (Mulinde & Daniel 2010).

Just as we can become God's channels of blessings upon the land, we can also position ourselves to convey divine blessings over our family through the family altar because God says:

> "But ye are a chosen generation, a royal priesthood, an holy nation, a peculiar people; that ye should shew forth the praises of him who hath called you out of darkness into his marvellous light;" (1Peter 2:9).

The Altar Is A Place

1. **A Meeting Place with God.** Jacob met with God and built an altar as a memorial at the same place he encountered God.

> "Then Jacob made a vow, saying, 'If God will be with me, and keep me in this way that I am going ... this stone which I have set as a pillar shall be God's house..." (Genesis 28:20-22) NKJV.

It was a day after God met Jacob in his crisis that he built an altar at the same place where he once had a divine encounter. Altars are meeting places. Individually, and as a family Christians should have regular meeting places with God – a place where you deliberately plan to fellowship with your creator on a regular basis.

2. **A Place of Forgiveness.** The brazen (brass) altar in the tabernacle of Moses represented a place of slaughter and substitution. It foreshadowed the once-and-for all sacrifice of Christ on the Cross (Hebrews 13:10-13). The family altar gives you the privilege to seek forgiveness and cleansing

for you and your family. It also presents the family with an opportunity to settle faults with one another.

3. A Place of Intercession. Jesus is continually making intercession for us. At the family altar we mirror the example of Jesus by spending time to pray for a range of issues including the unsaved, our nation and leaders, missionary work, the sick and needy, and whatever God leads you to pray about. Everyone learns to intercede. It is a spiritual factory for breeding spiritual products and building up our prayer lives.

4. A Place of Covenant. Abraham built an altar unto the Lord after having a life changing encounter with Him. *"The LORD appeared to Abram and said, 'To your offspring I will give this land.' So he built an altar there to the LORD, who had appeared to him"* (Genesis 12:7) NIV. At the altar we can both make and renew spiritual covenants. We are covenant partners praying to a covenant keeping God.

5. A Place of Worship. As priests of the Most High God we are to continually offer worship and praise unto the Lord. This is symbolised by the altar of incense in the Old Testament where the priests offered worship to God on behalf of themselves and the people. Worship is an essential part of prayer. Indeed, worship is a powerful type of prayer.

When you build a family or personal altar unto God you are testifying that you have surrendered to Him, to do anything He wishes with you. It is an indication that you value your covenant with Him and that you are totally dependent on Him. At the altar you are announcing to God that you have come to represent your family, your city, your nation and other people He lays in your heart to pray for. Raise an altar unto God; make it a place of unbroken fellowship with your heavenly Father.

Benefits of the Family Altar

Combined Worship

The family altar represents a time of family worship. It is a mini church in the home, where all the elements of a bigger congregation come together in the family context.

Interactive study of God's word.

In the more relaxed and free atmosphere of the home, everyone can study God's word together, adopting the most flexible and most adaptable ways for the family.

Growing In Faith

It is an opportunity to develop the faith of family members. The word of God and worship increases faith. Many times when I finish family devotions with my family the children tend to shower me with plenty of thanks, sometimes with passionate hugs. Why? The reason is that their faith and love for God has been enhanced, and they never failed to express their gratitude. I have also noticed that it helps to re-ignite everyone's prayer life, and revive spiritual commitment.

Raising Godly Children

If God has blessed your family with children, you are simply a custodian of those children. He wants you to train and teach them on His behalf. One powerful tool for this is the family altar, a place for raising godly children.

Affirmation of God's Headship

When a family regularly comes together to worship, study and pray, it is a declaration that God is their head. It is simply not enough to put up a poster on the wall saying "Christ is the head of this family". It must be demonstrated by giving Him regular time within the family. This can be neglected easily when you become distracted. The results of a neglected altar will include an unhealthy spiritual life, a dormant prayer life and a dysfunctional family unit.

Giving God the rightful place in your home, shows that you have given your heart entirely to Him. Not having a regular family altar does not necessarily mean a family does not love God, but it does indicate that they need to give more priority to their time together with God. A family will be more effective physically and spiritually if they can discipline themselves to maintain a regular time together in God's presence. Individual prayer lives will stay strong and everyone will become spiritually refreshed on a daily basis.

32

FACE YOUR FEARS

Fear is 'a feeling of distress, apprehension or alarm caused by impending danger or pain (Collins Dictionary and Thesaurus).

In today's world people suffer from all kinds of fears- fear of divorce, illness, death, accidents, terrorism, loss of job and war are but a few. Fear can be real, imagined or anticipated. It emanates from the unconscious mind. On the positive side, fear is a God given ability to help us in certain ways.

Fear becomes debilitating when it begins to dictate your lifestyle and when it becomes harmful to you or other people. Fear can stop you from praying and trusting God; it can also make you to take irrational steps that will drag you further into problems and cause you to need more prayer than you should.

In a positive way fear:

- Helps you overcome complacency.
- Helps you avoid dangerous and unpleasant situations.
- Fosters change and development.
- Prevents you from doing the wrong things.
- Helps you trust in divinity rather than humanity.
- Makes you fight, instead of fleeing from a situation.

The Fear Factor

Fear can stop you from praying. In the same way prayer can stop you from living in fear. The word of God is a sure medicine for fear. Unfortunately most people forget the word of God when fear creeps into their life. Fear can manifest in the form of doubt, discouragement, negative confession, anxiety or worry- all of which are enemies of prayer, but God says, *"Be not dismayed; for I am thy God: I will strengthen thee: yea, I will uphold thee with the right hand of my righteousness"*

(Isaiah 41:10).

There are numerous reasons why God doesn't want you to fear:

Fear steals your morale.

Fear can even cause illness.

Fear exposes you to demons.

Fear can lead to apathy.

Fear stops you from doing the will of God.

Fear stops you from believing God.

Fear is sin. It means you call God a liar, which He is not.

Fear stops you from doing what you need to do.

Fear can lead to a myriad of problems which can seriously hamper your ability to pray.

Sources of Fear

It is understandable that when people have bad experiences, they tend to live in fear of similar problems or situations. People also fear because they lack the revelation of God's Word and God's ability to meet their needs. Another source of fear could be demons; some people are under the attack of the spirit of fear. In more serious forms this could lead to phobia, anxiety and panic attacks. In some cases, fear may be the result of past negative involvements currently leading to a guilty conscience. Whatever the situation, God's power is available to everyone who is battling with the spirit of fear. Pray seriously about it. Seek help if need be. If you do not 'kill' your fears, they will destroy your ability to pray and obstruct your progress.

Face Your Fears

Without faith it is impossible to please God. Come to God with boldness and not with apprehension.

Confront your fears:

1. Look unto Jesus. Focus on God and His word. Let God be true and the devil (the father of fear) be a liar.

2. Do not let the past pin you down. Break free from the past and let God give you a new start.

3. Meditate upon God's word daily. Find scriptures that address the problem you are grappling with. Meditate on, confess and apply them to your situation.

4. Ask God to heal your emotions. Pray until you receive this healing. Solicit the prayer of others if necessary.

5. Block the enemy out of your life. Refuse to let the enemy into your life anymore.

6. Resist the devil. You must resist him each time you feel like fear is creeping into your life. Shut the devil out of your mind. Confess the word. Pray and fast until you overcome.

Fear can rob you of your power to pray and open the door to the enemy. Until you deal fear a killing blow, it will continue to stand in the way. Fear can slow down your prayer momentum or stop you altogether from praying, because people who have been seriously overcome by the spirit of fear find it difficult to take important steps in their lives. Fear can also plunge you into deeper problems which will create the need for more prayers.

33

GOD'S GOODNESS

Goodness is the state of being kind, compassionate and benevolent. It is also a reflection of pleasantness, excellence and great value. God's nature means that He takes delight in the happiness, pleasure and prosperity of His people. God is only capable of doing good; hence the Psalmist states, *"Thou art good, and doest good"* (Psalm 119:68). God is the sum total of excellence. He is faultless, perfect and pure. His nature and composition cannot be improved. Therefore, His value cannot be measured or mended. When you come to God in prayer you must bear in mind that,

> *"Every good gift and every perfect gift is from above, and cometh down from the Father of lights, with whom is no variableness, neither shadow of turning"* (James 1:17).

God is infinitely and indescribably good. Taking comfort in the fact that God is too good to deny you the best, is the beginning of effective prayer. If you believe that God is good, when you appear before Him in prayer, you will expect Him to do good to you as you bring your requests before Him.

God Is Good To All

God's goodness extends to all creation, irrespective of race, age or geographical location. Nothing or nobody is too bad to experience the goodness of God. Originally God filled everything He created with His goodness, until Satan tempted man and robbed humanity of God's blessings.

Whatever the shortfall in your life, God wants to restore everything to His original plan, so you can bank on Him when you approach His throne in prayer. He is good to both those who have surrendered to Him and those who have not, *"...for He maketh his sun to rise on the evil and on the good, and sendeth rain on the just and the unjust"* (Matthew 5:45). *"No good thing does He withhold from those who walk uprightly"* (Psalm 84:11).

To fully tap into the goodness of God, you must give your life to Jesus and totally surrender to God.

Everything God Does Is Good

The goodness of God is both an aspect, and the totality of who He is. He is the source of everything that is good. If what you are asking for is good and aligns with the will of God, you can be sure He will grant it. Good things emanate from our good God. Take confidence in this, and no matter how long it may seem to get what you want, wait for it. *"... The LORD God is a sun and shield: the LORD will give grace and glory: no good thing will He withhold from them that walk uprightly"* (Psalm 84:11).

The Human Predicament

The trouble with humans is that we think we know what is best for us. Just because it will make you happy, give you status or make you famous does not mean it is God's best for you. God knows everything about you, in His infinite knowledge He also understands what is in your best interest. He knows your future and what is the perfect fit for your situation. The volume or intensity of prayer will not alter this. Jesus understood this, hence He prayed, *"... Father, if thou be willing, remove this cup from me: nevertheless not my will, but thine, be done"* (Luke 22:42).

Jesus never had the cup of suffering removed from Him despite the prayer – actually His prayer expressed a total submission to the Father's will. So He went to the Cross. The Cross was a painful experience, yet it was the best thing that ever happened in God's agenda for humanity. Was the Father good to Jesus? Yes, of course. The Cross was part of God's goodness to restore the human race to Himself. God may allow painful things to happen to you, yet in those things He will reveal His glory in a greater measure in your life. At such times, the devil will make you doubt God's love for you, and you will begin to wonder, 'Is God really good to me?' Truth is, God is good all the time, and you can always rely on Him to do good to you as you pray.

So, why would anyone for once think that God does not, will not, or may not answer their prayers? Every prayer has an answer to it which may take a form different from your expectation. Every answer is an expression of God's goodness and love. You may not like the result of your prayer, nevertheless God is able to turn every evil into good, failure into success and lack into abundance. God is good!

34

GROW IN GRACE

Grace is the undeserved, unearned and unmerited favour of God bestowed upon (sinful) men. God's plan of redemption is founded upon grace. When Adam and Eve (Man) fell at the Garden of Eden, God's grace provided a substitute victim to atone for their sins. God's grace meant that although they did not deserve it, God went out of His way to provide redemption. Grace is the platform for every prayer we pray.

Whatever God does is a personal gift to an undeserving beneficiary. Some people believe that their ability to fast and pray earns them answers to prayers. Nothing can be much further from the truth. It is only by grace. Our salvation is by grace through faith. (Ephesians 1:6-7:2:4). God's grace empowers you for God's service, including prayers. (1Corinthians 3:10, 15:10).Grace completely eliminates human righteousness or ability from the picture. The anointing to pray and the answers to prayer are both products of God's grace.

God's Grace Is Sufficient

Regarding Paul's 'thorn in the flesh' for which he besought God for relief, God's reply to him was, "*...My grace is sufficient for you, for my strength is made perfect in weakness...*" (2Corinthians 12:9).

People often complain that they are not able to pray. Some Christians think the grace of prayer is extended to a 'special' few. Some Christians are regarded as intercessors, or prayer warriors. This may be true in a few cases; however, the grace to pray, the strength to intercede and the privilege of answered prayer are all within the reach of every child of God. The same Holy Spirit works in us all. No exceptions, preferences or favouritism. We can all pray. We can all succeed in prayer. If anybody can, so can you. If someone else can move or shake mountains through prayer, you too can do it.

What Grace Is Not

Grace is not permission to sin. It is not a licence for carelessness and laziness. Although it is all by grace, you can be bypassed by grace if you take God for granted. It is a distortion of grace to neglect prayer, bible study, fasting, holiness, and expect God to still fulfil His obligations to you. Grace cannot make up for abdication of spiritual responsibility. God has provided all the grace that you need for anything, that is why His response to the apostle Paul was, "my grace is sufficient for you". The more you tap into God's grace for prayer or anything else, the more grace He will make available to you. You have the grace to pray, wait, exercise faith and do wonders through prayers.

Keep Growing In Grace

As in everything, we all need to keep growing in grace. God wants you to grow in the grace of prayer. 2Peter 3:18 says: *"But grow in the grace and knowledge of our Lord and saviour Jesus Christ. To Him is glory both now and forever, amen."*

Growth produces character, knowledge and understanding. It generates ability and increases capacity. Grow in the knowledge of God, His word and in the amount of prayer you pray. Grow in character and become more like Jesus. Develop in your ability to stay in God's presence until something happens. If you continue to grow in Grace, your prayer life will become more consistent and productive.

Weak but Strong

Grace overrides your weakness; it exchanges what you do not have for what God has, so you can put on the ability of God at the time of prayer. At the place of prayer God uses weak instrumentalities to wreak havoc in the spiritual realm. We are simply

> "... treasures in jars of clay to show that this all-surpassing power is from God and not from us" (2Corinthians 4:7) NIV.

When the Moabites and Ammonites waged war against King Jehoshaphat and his people, Jehoshaphat knew he could not withstand the alliance, so he prayed: *"O our God, wilt thou not judge them? For we have no might against this great company that cometh against us; neither know we what to do: but now our eyes upon thee."* (2Chronicles 20:12).

As a result of this prayer, God made the enemy alliance turn the sword against themselves, and gave Jehoshaphat and his people victory. Jesus tells us that He is the vine and we are the branches, it is only as we abide in Him that we can bring forth fruits; without Him we can do nothing (John 15:15). Every believer is endowed with a measure of grace; you do not need an additional amount of grace, but you can grow within the existing grace of God upon your life. Without grace we cannot pray effectively; we cannot reach certain dimensions of prayers.

35

GENERATIONAL CLEANSING

Certain problems persist for reasons far beyond the human eye. You do not have to know everything about a problem before you can pray successfully. We pray by faith, but there are many situations where what you know will determine your results. Many 'faith' Christians completely dismiss the idea of generational curses or hereditary problems because, they say, 'with God all things are possible', or because Jesus finished it all on the cross. Whilst this is definitely the case all of the time, there are times when things are not as straight forward as they should. Certain problems need to be resolved layer after layer, and some of these layers are ultimately connected to people's past, such as parents and spiritual environments in which they were raised.

Generational Curse

The word generation in the Bible has multiple meanings – the offspring of an individual or succession of offspring. It also means a period of time or successive divisions of time. Generation also relate to the persons who make up a specific generation; an age or the people living in a particular age. The entire body of people connected together by similarity can also be referred to as a generation (Unger 1988).

A generational curse is an iniquity that increases in strength from one generation to the next, affecting that family and all who have a relationship with it (Hickey 2000). God warns His people of the repercussions of worshipping idols (anything that we esteem above God is an idol) on present and future generations: (Exodus 20:5-5).

Certainly, Jesus finished the work of salvation, healing and deliverance on the Cross. We appropriate these by faith; however, specific incidents of failure, a pattern of premature death of a large number of people, an unusual number of accidents, suicides, mental illness and much more, could be traced to generational roots. These will usually be beyond what is normal, and create cause for concern. Some of these events may have possible connections with what happened in past generations which have not been properly dealt with. A problem rooted in generational background is likely to drain more prayer energy and endure much longer despite prayer efforts. This does not suggest that whenever we face resistance in prayers, we must blame our ancestry, but should there be a link between these incidences and our roots, if they are not specifically and aggressively dealt with, spiritual victory could remain elusive.

Caught In the Middle

We were all born into this world as innocent little babies but, unknown to a lot of people, their destinies have been tampered with by someone else's past involvements:

> *"What mean ye that ye use this proverb concerning the land of Israel, saying, the fathers have eaten sour grapes, and the children's teeth are set on edge?"* (Ezekiel 18:2).

People can either be inhibited or uplifted by their 'inheritance'- that which has been transferred from parents or past generations to them.

The Webster dictionary defines inheritance as:

"The act of inheriting property; the reception of genetic offspring: the acquisition of a possession, condition or trait from past generations". Inheritance can be either bad or good; inheritance could be physical or spiritual in nature. Some generational baggage is offloaded at salvation, but others may require ongoing efforts- a combination of prayer, character change and (in some cases) righting some past wrongs. Knowledge of ancestral demonic past can be frightening to some people, and it is possible to resign to fate and hold other people or your past responsible for current predicaments. There is no place for such attitude in the bible because the just shall live by faith. You must stand your ground and release your destiny from the grips of your past.

If you have struggled with a situation for too long and nothing seems to be changing, it may be that you need to try another way of handling the problem. It could also be that you need to change something in your own life. After you have done all your best, you may need to look into other things. This is where ancestral history might become relevant. Use the information you have gathered as a help for prayer; get prayer support if you need more help.

Two good examples that illustrate the possible impact of generational carry-over is that of two American families. The first Max Jukes, was an atheist and godless man; the other, Jonathan Edwards was not only a Christian, he was godly and paved the way for his future generations to serve God and reap the blessings of godly ancestry.

Max Jukes (Atheist), married to godless women.	Jonathan Edwards (Christian) married to a Christian woman.
7 Murderers	1 US President
60 Thieves	3 U.S Senators
50 Women debauchery	3 Governors
130 More convicts	3 Mayors
310 Paupers	13 College presidents
400 Ruined by indulgent living.	30 Judges
Estimated cost to the United States: $1.250.000	65 Professors
	80 Public office holders
	100 Lawyers
	100 Missionaries
	Estimated cost to the United States: $00.00

A Comparison of Max Jukes' and Jonathan Edwards
Generations: A.E Winship (1900)

The above account is not necessary detailed. Max Jukes' family may have had a number of successful people; nonetheless, this account explains the result of negative inheritance. As a Christian you should not live with the consequences of your past generations, knowing what they are and not deliberately dealing with them on time can slow down the pace of progress, and make prayer more difficult, exhausting and frustrating.

36

HEALTH IS WEALTH

You do not need perfect health to be successful in life – certainly not in prayers. Nevertheless a healthy and fit body is crucial to your success as a Christian. A negative physical, emotional or mental condition can become a distraction to any aspect of life. You need a healthy life to maintain a healthy prayer life. More than anyone else God understands the benefits of good health to His people and He makes this clear in 3rd John 2: *"Beloved, I wish above all things that thou mayest prosper and be in good health, even as thy soul prospereth."*

Benefits of Good Health to Prayer

1. **More Energy and Vitality.**
    With the same amount of time, a healthier and fitter person is likely to be more efficient or productive than a person with poor health. Good health allows for a steady flow of stamina, and can significantly reduce laziness and apathy. A sick person can pray. Some sick people pray more than healthy people. But better health will lead to better praying and better results.

2. **Longevity.**
    Healthier people are more likely to (all things being equal) live longer than people with imperfect health. The longer you live

the longer you can contribute to humanity and God's kingdom. Stay alive by staying healthy.

3. You Are More Able To Stretch Yourself.

You can pray longer and harder if your health is great. Fifteen or twenty years ago I could pray for 7 hours non-stop. Today I could still do several hours of prayer at a time, but not as frequently or as long as I used to; however, I have found creative ways to achieve the same level of success in prayers.

4. Feeling and Thinking Brighter.

A good health and a fitter life will more often keep you over the moon. You will feel happier, and brighter. You can also think well when you are healthier, which will in turn impact on your motivation and momentum in prayers. Your moods can be dictated by your health; your health in turn can determine your capacity for prayers.

5. Prevention of Illness.

Likes attract likes. Rich people often get richer. This can equally apply to health. One or two kinds of illness will most probably generate others. Germs may thrive where other germs already exist. Protecting and preserving your health and wellbeing is paramount to your being able to live a lifetime of good health.

Examine Yourself

The bible says we should examine ourselves to ensure our faith is on track, so also should you constantly monitor your health so you can remain in good shape. Effective prayer and good health go hand in hand.

- **Manage Your Weight.**

  You do not need your clothes to be too tight or loose before you know something is wrong. Use your scale weekly. Avoid over or under weight.

- **Manage Your Diet.**

  You will feel better if you control your diet. Keep a balanced diet. Experts advise us to drink a lot of water, reduce fat intake, eat breakfast, eat lots of fruit, vegetables and fibre, and reduce salt and sugar intake.

- **Keep Fitter.**

  Fitness specialists recommend that you use your stairs, take a walk, jog around, go gardening and of course, (if you can afford it) go to the gym. By all means keep fit. The bible tells us there is profit in bodily exercise. One of those areas of profit will be in your prayer life.

  Doctors, dentists and opticians are there for your benefit. Visit them. Some very 'spiritual' people frown at seeing doctors, or opticians. They advocate non-use of medicines. All knowledge and wisdom is a blessing from God, so take advantage of them. Do not delay. You will be more useful to God if you stay fit and healthy.

- **Take Care of Yourself.**

  The stakes are very high. I guess you want to stay alive, enjoy good health, avoid disability, save money and be more productive. 'Listen' to your body. Pick up warning signals. Take care of your mental health. Create a balance between your work and life. Reduce the amount of stress you go through. Enjoy the health benefits of forgiveness.

Enrich your prayer life by enriching your health. Your health is an invaluable asset to everything you do and everyone around you. The healthier, the wealthier. The healthier you are the richer your prayer life will be also. If you are sick in your body, get to see the doctor; and if they are unable to help you, keep talking to God about it until you receive your healing.

Do everything in your power to protect and preserve your health. You need good health to achieve everything God has for you in life. Never take chances with your health. With good health you can easily excel in your prayer life if you do not allow other distractions to have their way.

HABIT OF PRAYER

A habit is a repetitive, (sometimes) unconscious sequence of behaviour gained overtime. It is an established condition of mind or character. Habits are actions performed so frequently until they become almost involuntary or second nature. Good habits drive people towards personal and professional fulfilment, while negative or bad habits rob people of their God given destiny, because people are effectively what they do repetitively. Initially you make your habits, but eventually you are made by your habits. A good prayer habit can be hugely beneficial to a healthy spiritual life.

Make Room for Prayers

Believe it or not, you are not too busy to pray. We can always have an excuse for anything we do not want to do. Jesus was so busy He hardly had time to eat yet, He made time to pray. He understood the importance of prayer, so He:

- Prayed early in the morning when others were 'tucked in' in their sleep (Mark 1:35).
- Sent crowds away (including friends and family) and then created time to pray (Matthew 14:23).

- Found time to pray during the day (Luke 9:18, 29) at the peak of his busyness.
- Prayed in the middle of the night (Matthew 26:36, 39).

We all do the things that matter the most to us. The place of prayer in your priority list will determine the amount of time you allot to it. Jesus says in Luke 18:1,

> "...that men ought always to pray, and not to faint." Here are a few suggestions that will help you in developing a rewarding prayer habit.

Place and Time

The bible encourages us to pray everywhere. Notwithstanding, certain levels and types of prayers are most ideal for particular places and time. The place should be conducive and appropriate for the kind of prayer. Without a regular place and time, it is unlikely you can smoothly develop an ideal prayer habit. Wherever you chose is up to you.

- You can pray everywhere (1Timothy 2:8).
- Jesus prayed in a desert place (Mark 1:35).
- Jesus prayed alone on the mountain (Matthew 14:23).
- The early church prayed in Christian gatherings like we do today.
- Jesus encouraged private prayers, in the closet (Matthew 6:6).

Daniel prayed three times a day. Setting aside a place and time will help to develop your prayer habit. A fixed time and place for regular prayer can help reinforce your prayer habit. Keeping to it may be difficult at first, sticking to it will cause you to excel.

Accountability Partners

Many people develop successful habits by making themselves accountable to a friend, a group of friends or some other close individuals.

> *"Two are better than one, because they have a good reward for their labour: If either of them falls down, one can help the other up. But pity anyone who falls and has no one to help them up"* (Ecclesiastes 4:9-10).

My closest prayer partner is my wife. When I feel unable to follow through with my prayer times, or when my prayer life becomes inconsistent, I meet with her, talk about it and we both go to God and make pledges to uphold our prayer times and targets. Also I tend to plan regular prayer targets with my wife, and we endeavour to hold one another accountable for seeing through individual and family prayer objectives. Accountability helps us to be on the look-out for one another, and therefore, foster consistency.

Join a Regular Prayer Group

Joining a regular prayer group (it could be your family) helps to strengthen your prayer habit. You become duty bound to meet regularly with that group. A healthy prayer group will help to feed your prayer habit. The bible says, *"Iron sharpeneth iron; so a man sharpeneth the countenance of his friend"* (Proverbs 27:17). Group prayer multiplies prayer anointing, strengthens commitment and fuels motivation.

Self-discipline and focus are crucial to developing a healthy habit. You can develop a successful prayer habit by setting prayer goals and striving to achieve them. Developing the habit of praying at a particular time, place and for a particular duration will not only enhance your spiritual life, but will also enrich you in many other ways.

38

HUMILITY

Humbleness is characterised by meekness, unpretentiousness, modesty, and self-abasement. Humility is one of the most taught and talked about but least practiced subjects in Christianity. It is one of God's requirements for enjoying divine blessings. Humility is not synonymous with inferiority, stupidity, hypocrisy or timidity. It is a genuine and sincere demonstration of absolute submission to, and dependence upon the will of God; it is the most fertile ground for effective prayer.

God says if we humble ourselves in His sight, He will lift us up. If we exalt ourselves, we will be abased. If you look into the lives of many great people- preachers, politicians and 'ordinary' people, you will find that pride has led many to their fall. Pride could be very subtle and can easily creep into a person. (Luke 14:11; James 4:10). Pride and prayer do not go together. Arrogance has no place in the presence of God. God will release more grace for prayer upon people who stay humble in His sight.

The Humility of Jesus

Jesus is the perfect example of humility. He ate with, mingled with and dressed like the disciples and ordinary people. He washed the feet of His disciples and served them, leaving us an example to follow: *"Whosoever will be chief among you, let him be your servant: Even as the son of man came not to be ministered unto, but to minister."* (Matthew 20:27-28).

To able to touch God's heart in our prayer times we must follow in the foot-steps of Jesus. From birth to death, Jesus was an embodiment of authentic humility. We can see why He demonstrated the highest level of God's power in everything He did.

The Benefits of Humility

Divine Approval

Humble people are highly esteemed by God. God resists the proud. He has respect for those who recognise Him as the source of all things. He does not want you to devalue yourself, neither does He want you to over value yourself. Humility is not wearing a cloak of inferiority, it is a recognition that whatever you are, can do or have, originates from only one source- God.

Answer To Prayer

God never forgets the cry of the humble (Psalm 9:12). God closes His ears to the prayer of the proud.

God's Presence

God promises to dwell with people who have a 'contrite and humble spirit'. He has promised to 'revive the spirit of the humble, and to revive the heart of the contrite ones'. (Isaiah 57:15).

Prayer and Humility

Two people - a Pharisee and a publican, appeared before God to pray. The Pharisee prayed, *"Oh God, I thank you that I am not like other men are; robbers, extortioners, unjust evil-doers ..."* His opposite, the tax collector also prayed but, *"... the tax collector stood at a distance. He would not even lift up his eyes to look toward heaven, but he beat upon his breast and said, 'God, be merciful to me, a sinner!'* (Luke 18:11-13).

Jesus said to those who were present that the tax collector, rather than the Pharisee, went home justified by God. Simply put, God answered the prayer of the tax collector, not that of the Pharisee. Such is God's respect for humility of heart. You will achieve more in prayer when your life is characterised by humility, and submission to God. A humble person will enjoy more prayer grace, the Spirit's help and continuous favour with God.

Humble people know how to be gracious in defeat, are assertive but not aggressive, and are easily approachable. They never talk too highly of themselves because they recognise that the source of every blessing is God. To tap into God's endless grace of prayer, you need to constantly 'scan' your life for any form of arrogance or anything that does not represent humility in your life- this may be difficult because pride is very subtle, but humility is the only way to please God and get Him to pour His grace upon you.

39

INCREMENTAL STEPS

'Big' prayers are made up of seconds and minutes. Many people see prayer as a difficult, time consuming exercise because they have not quite realised that great prayers do not always mean finding plenty of time to pray. The day is made of seconds, minutes and hours, every one of which matters so much to our success. So also, just a few minutes of prayer here and there can lead to massive prayer achievements over time. It is not always the 'big' prayers that win; it is the tiny, consistent amounts of prayer carried out on a daily basis that accumulate into success stories.

Little Things Matter

The most effective way to pray is to carry out bite-size prayer sessions. This is a much easier and steady way to achieve prayer success. Praying five minutes a day over a one year period on any subject will yield better results than praying an hour on the same subject on a one-off, irregular basis. Little things can sometimes result in enormous breakthrough. That extra amount of salt on your plate, compounded over many years might be the killer habit for many people. Little acts of kindness carried out every day can transform your relationships with your spouse or other people. In just the same way little displays of negative attitudes can badly damage your relationships if you engage in them long enough.

God will often test people with little things before entrusting them with greater ones because, *"He that is faithful in that which is least, is faithful also in much: and he that is unjust in the least is unjust also in much."* (Luke 16:10). God believes in taking little steps. He demonstrated this in Deuteronomy 7:22 when speaking to the children of Israel about delivering them from the enemy:

> *"The LORD your God will drive out those nations before you, little by little. You will not be allowed to eliminate them all at once, or the wild animals will multiply around you."*

If you want to accomplish great things in prayer, do a bit of it every day, on that matter at the centre of your heart. Do not leave things till the last minute- till when you are completely or almost out of time. Try and project how much time you will need to put into praying about a subject to get things accomplished; I know this cannot always be predicted, but in most cases there are many issues on which you can control the amount of time you need to pray. Starting early, and putting in a few minutes a day will make the prayer job easy for you.

Compound Your Prayer

When you take baby steps in whatever you do the result may not show up immediately but every step takes you nearer the end of your journey. Stop complaining of time to pray because everyone has more than enough time to pray. Jesus said,

> *"The kingdom of heaven is like to a grain of mustard seed, which a man took and sowed in his field: which indeed is the least of all seeds: but when it is grown, it is the greatest among herbs, and becometh a tree, so that the birds of the air come and lodge in the branches thereof"* (Matthew 13:31-32).

Keep sowing your mustard seeds of prayer and give them time to grow. People who have the most success in prayer are not always those who put in the longest hours once in a while, but those who prayed a few minutes each time for a long period. As a younger Christian I preferred praying long hours. I enjoyed praying for hours- sometimes up to 7 hours at one given time, but then in many cases I stop praying about that problem for several weeks or months. This was not a very effective way of praying – although the training was good for my spiritual development. Today I pray differently; I have a few daily prayer items, each of which I pray over for 10 to 30 minutes daily. I have found this to be a very effective way of praying. I am having better and more consistent results.

Five Minutes a Day

Just five minutes of prayer a day can forever transform your life. I would like to give a few examples of how you can take advantage of breaking your prayer requests into a few minutes daily, and how much this could mean to you in twelve months.

Prayer Item	Daily Minutes	Weekly Total	Monthly Total	Twelve Months (approximated)
Spiritual Growth	5 Minutes	35 Minutes	2.5 hours	28 hours
Financial Prosperity	5 Minutes	35 Minutes	2.5 hours	28 hours
Church and Leaders	5 Minutes	35 Minutes	2.5 hours	28 hours
Job or Ministry	5 Minutes	35 Minutes	2.5 hours	28 hours
Country and the World	5 Minutes	35 Minutes	2.5 hours	28 hours
Totals	25 MINUTES	3 HOURS	12.5 HOURS	140 hours

The above table illustrates the power of the minute. A few minutes spent praying daily will amount to several numbers of hours weekly, monthly and annually. Our table tells us that:

1. If you pray 5 minutes daily on one item, that makes 35 minutes at the end of the week- I think that should be easy for anyone who depends on God's grace. Many people will do a lot more.

2. If you pray 35 minutes weekly about an issue, at the end of four weeks that makes a total of two and a half hours. A lot of people will do this with relative ease.

3. Then, comes the big issue! Keep praying like that month after month and see what you get- an astonishing 28 hours at the end of twelve months. That amount of praying will literally change anything you pray about.

All you need to do is just find those 5 minutes from your daily schedule to pray over that thing that means a lot to you- it could be one, two or three main subjects a day. It is up to you, what matters is that you develop the habit of transforming tiny minutes into mighty victories. Never complain again that you have no time to pray. Find a few minutes daily from your twenty four hours, and you will be only five minutes away every day from a major victory.

40

JOY AND GLADNESS

When your heart is full of joy, prayer will naturally and freely flow from within you. Your faith in God will be activated and you will make yourself a living source of blessings to others also. The Webster's dictionary defines joy or rejoice as:

1. to experience great pleasure or delight
2. the emotion evoked by well-being, success, or good fortune or by the prospect of possessing what one desires.

The Hebrew words for Joy or Rejoice (Simchah and Sim-kha), were used in relation to the joy and celebration experienced during festivals and other ceremonies- and mean to be glad, pleased, rejoice. The Greek word for Joy or Rejoice Chara means cheerfulness- calm delight, gladness and exceeding joy.

The Joy of the Lord Is Your Strength

Joy is very critical to a continuously thriving prayer life. Nehemiah once told repentant Israelites: *"...Go your way, eat the fat, and drink the sweet, and send portions unto them for whom nothing is prepared: for this day is holy unto our Lord: neither be ye sorry; for the joy of the LORD is your strength"* (Nehemiah 8:10).

The devil will do everything to steal your joy by orchestrating negative events that will overwhelm you and undermine the joy of God in your life. The Spirit of God within you is your fountain of joy- whatever the 'weather'. You will lack the ability and tenacity to pray if you allow Satan to rob you of your joy. Even when the believers were beaten and humiliated in the Acts of the Apostles, the bible records that they rejoiced that they were counted worthy to suffer such things for Christ.

There will always come moments of doubts when you will experience bouts of sadness. Rather than whining and wallowing in self-pity and discouragement you must grab and cling onto the joy which lies within us. The joy of the Lord is your lifeline, energy and propeller to get out of difficult situations. If you let Satan steal your joy, you will become too feeble to prayer. An individual filled with joy will be better motivated to pray, and is more likely to find the strength to persist in spiritual warfare.

Joy Is Different From Happiness

Joy is not the same thing as happiness. A lot of people really want to be happy in life, but what they actually need is joy- which is more authentic and long lasting. It is happiness when it is induced by external events. If you just bought a new car, it makes you happy for some days, weeks or even months. If your family recently had a new baby, this could make you very delighted for some time to come. However, if something happened to your car- may be an accident, and you still have some peace within you because of your faith in God, this is joy.

God forbid, something unpleasant happened to your new born child, and yet you retain your integrity and confidence in God, refusing to be sad, but glad that your heavenly Father is still in charge- this is joy. Happiness is transitory and fleeting; it does not last forever. Happiness is based on materialism and influences, but joy rests absolutely on God and what He is capable of doing in your life. Hence, a Christian can be in a state of grief, and still enjoy an overflow of joy from within- independent of external occurrences. In the event of a tragedy or crisis, if you lack joy you may also lack the ability and will power to pray.

Rejoice In the Lord Always

Joy is so important to the Christian that the bible admonishes us to rejoice in the Lord always. Joy is a fruit of the Holy Spirit (Galatians 5:22). For you to stay joyful, you must:

1. Constantly worship the Lord- make it a habit (1chronicles 15:16)
2. Let the Holy spirit mature the gift of joy (fruit of the Spirit) in you (Galatians 5:22)
3. Keep doing the will of God. The more you do for God, the happier you will become
4. Never let anything rob you of your joy. The joy of the Lord is your strength. If you lose your joy, you could lose the power to pray, and the will to do many other things
5. Avoid sin all the time. Sin is the greatest thief of joy. If you sin, the Holy Spirit in you gets upset, as a result your joy will be affected, until you confess and repent.
6. Stop counting your failures, keep counting your blessings (1Timothy 6:6)
7. Immerse yourself in God's Word (Psalm 19:8; Psalm 104:34; Jeremiah 15:16)

A long time ago, San Francisco, California was badly damaged by an earthquake which led to the destruction of many buildings. Fire triggered by the tremors also gutted several more buildings. In the middle of it all, an elderly grandmother was seen sitting and singing in her rocking chair on her front lawn. Someone passing by stopped and asked how she could be so calm and happy in the midst of the crisis. She replied that she was simply waiting to see how her God would turn things around.

The joy of the Lord is what keeps you going- whether you are praying or doing some other thing, you need the joy of the Lord to see you through. Therein lies your strength to pray, win souls and carry out every day activity successfully. You must never seek joy from outside your being- it lives within you. Joy is the result of salvation and abiding in Christ. People who continue to look for it elsewhere will always meet with disappointment. It is not available in the world, and that is why Jesus says, *"Peace I leave with you; my peace I give you. I do not give to you as the world gives. Do not let your hearts be troubled and do not be afraid"* (John 14:27) NIV

Your joy should be flowing constantly because its source is not natural; it is a product of the eternal Spirit living within you. This is why you can be joyful every day of your life, all you need is to tap into the well of joy within you.

41

JOURNALS

A journal is a daily record of events on experiences, occurrences and observations. A prayer journal can be a very rewarding aspect of a person's prayer activities. Keeping a prayer journal is an exercise worth every second spent on it. It will enable you to keep a record of your prayer experiences from worship, meditation and the actual act of prayer. Your journal will serve as a reference point for making prayer decisions, including adjusting and making improvements to your prayer life. There are many types of journal, and they all serve different purposes:

Reflective Journal - Feelings, insights, and perceptions are expressed through reflective journals. They are very useful for trainees, and practitioners in various professions. They can also be used to record your feelings and experiences during and outside the prayer closet.

Travel Journal - Travelling is a great thing on its own. Travel memories are worth preserving, so people keep travel journals to protect their travel experiences and information. In the same way, prayer is a journey. No day of prayer is ever the same. Record keeping means you are able to safeguard your experiences and information.

Weight Journal – Weight journals serve the purpose of recording weight loss for those who work towards losing weight (weight gain for those who need to). A child of God could find themselves carrying unwanted spiritual weights. In your journal you can record the things you want to give up as a Christian, including how you have managed to deal with them. Anything that is capable of weighing you down spiritually and emotionally is most likely to impact negatively on your prayer life. Do something about this daily and keep your record.

Idea Journal - Ideas come and go very quickly. The best way to keep them is by trapping them in a journal. During prayer, meditation and worship times, the Holy Spirit can give you all sorts of ideas. Each of them must be handled with great care- your destiny may well depend on them. Let them go into your journal.

Professional Journals - Different Professions and academic institutions publish their own journals or periodicals. These are more academic in nature and very different from the personal or prayer journal, which are the main focal of this section. Periodicals, such as medical journals write articles on particular subjects. Accountants keep a daily record of financial entries, also referred to as journals.

Why Keep a Prayer Journal?

A prayer journal can serve multiple purposes to the believer. It is a beautiful thing to always be able to look back to God's dealings with you written in black and white. Each time I read things I recorded a long time ago about my encounters with God, I get very refreshed; I also feel pleased that I had them written down. Your prayer journal can become a point of reference for God's current dealings with you.

1. Tracking of Prayer Requests

Keeping a log of prayer points both for yourself and others is one of the signs of an organised prayer life. It can also help you develop a sense of discipline and consistency. You are able to then tick off each prayer item once you have received the answer.

2. Prayer Goals

Prayer goals can be written into your journals. How many hours do you wish to pray ultimately on a particular matter? How many minutes do you intend to pray daily or weekly on a subject? Write your objectives in the journal. Keep a daily record of the time you spent daily on prayer, review this weekly and monthly.

3. Instructions, Reflections and Revelations

How else can you capture and retain what the Lord whispered to you the other day during prayer? What about the visions, impressions and inspirations from the Lord. They will fly away unless they are written in your prayer journal. Those powerful night time dreams will be forgotten after a few days unless you have written them down. Record and peep regularly into them for they shall come to pass. Act on, and pray about them; God gave them to you for a reason.

4. Progress Evaluation

Record the amount of prayer you carry out daily. Regularly evaluate your prayer life for consistency, quality and quantity. Study the trends, and events recorded in your record book. Sometimes you may feel you are doing well in prayer. Other times you may feel you are falling behind. The only way you can judge this is through your records.

5. Telling Your Story

Your walk with God is made up of a stack of stories. Every child of God has a story- special to him, and originating from God. Sooner or later answered prayers, divine instructions and other things recorded in your notebook, will become a source of encouragement to others. That is only if you can remember, or retrieve them. With record keeping, you will be able to one day tell a story that will inspire others. Some of the information may find their way into your book, preaching and conversations with other people.

How to Keep a Prayer Journal

There is no one - size - fits all way to keeping your journal. Whatever suits you is best because it is personal to you.

- Choose a format that you find easier to adapt. It is yours - yours alone.
- Purchase a book that is good enough - durable and useable.
- Always start with date (day, month, year and may be, time); this is crucial.
- Keep your journal on a daily basis. There is always something to write about.
- Whether it is a line or five hundred lines, it is up to you. Size is irrelevant. The record is more important.

Keeping a prayer journal requires discipline. Initially you may not enjoy it, but with time you will fall in love with it and it will become a part of your life. It will usher you into a special dimension in your relationship with God. It will enhance, enrich and make your prayer life more interesting. Give it a try. It will add tremendous value to your spiritual life.

42

Kingdom mindedness

Christianity goes far beyond praying and getting your prayer answered. Neither is it merely about what God can do for us. It centres on worshipping God and doing His work on earth. Christianity will be incomplete and unfulfilling until we have committed ourselves to doing God's will on earth. If you take interest in the things of God, you will draw His attention to the things that matter to you.

We have been called to be a blessing to the world. It is about the bigger picture- representing God on earth. When we do this we show that we are kingdom minded. Jesus says to seek first the kingdom and everything else will become an addition. Prayer is less exciting and least rewarding when you make yourself the main focus. A kingdom mind-set will get you faster to your prayer destination than a selfish mind-set that cares less about the things of God and other people's problems.

Ambassadors of Christ

We are God's ambassadors on earth. Ambassadors represent their own country's interest. Ambassadors protect their country's stake wherever they are. They are appointed to stand in for their country in another country. An ambassador is an embodiment of the state they represent. They speak and do things on behalf of their country. You are not a citizen of your current country of residence- your true nationality is in heaven. So your prayers should very much reflect a zeal for, and commitment to the things of God. When an ambassador carries out their ambassadorial responsibilities, their country of origin becomes duty bound to take absolute responsibility for their provision, protection and prosperity. This is where too many Christians miss it- they abandon God's work and concerns, and expect God to honour their prayers.

Your position as an ambassador of Christ gives you unlimited access to the blessings of God's kingdom:

1. An ambassador must be a citizen of the country they represent. God, *"… hath delivered us from the power of darkness, and hath translated us into the kingdom of His dear Son"* (Colossians 1:13).

2. An ambassador is appointed by a home country or state to represent them in a foreign country. No ambassador appoints themselves into the office. *"Then said Jesus to them again, peace be unto you: as my Father hath sent me, even so send I you"* (John 20:21).

3. Ambassadors do not represent their personal interest. They represent their home country. As Christians we live on earth, but our citizenship is in heaven. *"For our citizenship is in heaven, from which also we eagerly wait for the Saviour, the Lord Jesus"* (Philippians' 3:20).

4. The position of an ambassador is a high calling. Their performance must be worthy of their calling. *"I press toward the mark for the prize of the high calling of God in Christ Jesus"* (Philipians3:14).

5. Ambassadors are protected and provided for, by their state. They are immune from the law of the country where they serve. They cannot afford to be lawless however, as they are bound by the laws of their country of origin.

6. Their personal opinion or ambition is never projected. They speak only on behalf of the country they represent.

7. An ambassador has a written instruction from their country of origin- this is the equivalent of God's word to the believer.

8. Christ's ambassadors carry God's kingdom wherever they go. *"Neither shall they say, Lo here! Or, lo there! For, behold, the kingdom of God is within you"* (Luke 17:21).

9. Ambassadors do not just represent, they also reconcile and restore. Two friendly nations have reciprocal posts, each in the other's country. If things go wrong with two countries, ambassadors tend to carry out reconciliatory work. If relations break down and, two countries later agree to normalise things, ambassadors go between to restore normal relationships. *"And they that shall be of thee shall build the old waste places: thou shalt raise up the foundations of many generations; and thou shalt be called, the repairer of the breach, the restorer of paths to dwell in"* (Isaiah 58:12).

All prayer efforts must essentially reflect our roles and responsibilities as Christ's ambassadors. When you get immersed in the things of God - pray about and defend Kingdom interests, God will continue to make His resources available to you in abundant proportions. When you commit yourself to doing kingdom work, God will unleash His anointing and resources upon your life. This will reduce the amount of prayer you will need to pray on a daily basis. It is time we stopped wasting energy 'begging' for things that rightly belong to us. Fully represent the Kingdom and watch kingdom blessings flow freely to you.

You are God's ambassador. He wants to live in and work through you. He wants people to experience His kingdom as a result of your prayer. He wants the emphasis to shift from you to the kingdom, so assume the role of an intercessor today. As you shift the focus of prayer from you to God's kingdom, you will see what a big change it will make to your life. Ambassadors get their protection and provision from their own state. When they continue to represent their state, in return they have the full support of their country behind them at all times. Continue to make God's kingdom your prayer emphasis and He will see to it that your needs are met.

43

KNOW WHO YOU ARE

Knowing who you are is a major to key to success. A free-flowing prayer life will be helped by understanding who you are in Christ. Your relationship to God, position in Christ and your impression of how God sees you will impact on your prayer effectiveness. Knowing who, and whose you are will determine your level of confidence before the throne of grace.

Doctors have distinguishing characteristics that define who they are. So do lawyers, teachers or pastors. A child of God has certain attributes that make up their identity. Your identity can influence your destiny and the quality of whatever you do. Knowing who you are and who is behind you is the major platform for success in prayer.

Your Identity: Adam or Jesus.

Everyone on earth falls into one or two families – the family of Adam or the family of Jesus. When Adam sinned, he 'died' and all of human race went down with him. Then Jesus came with life and all those who receive Him receive the life of God and are born into God's family. Where you belong in this equation determines your identity, it will also affect your revelation of God and how you understand the things of the kingdom.

"For as in Adam all die, even so in Christ shall all be made alive. (1corinthians 15:22).

When an individual receives Christ, he is transferred from the family of Adam – sin, death, failure, and separation from God, into a new family- the family of God. Here old things (consequences of the fall) are passed away and all things are become new. This brings about a change of identity. You can now boldly go to God as a member of His family, having all the rights and privileges of a child of God. You must keep operating from this position to fully tap into the blessings God has made available to His children.

Your Primary Identity

Many people are not necessarily who they think they are. Just because you have failed several times does not make you a failure. Failure is not your identity. Do not let a problem define your identity no matter how long you have grappled with that situation. You may think you are good-for-nothing, but that does not make it true. It is just your thinking, which can and must be changed. If you believe nothing ever works well for you, even when you go to God in prayer you will have no confidence that He will answer your prayers.

If you fail to understand, or doubt your true identity as a Christian, you will have great difficulties trusting God, because you have no conviction that you are one of His. If you do not identify yourself accurately, you are bound to experience painful (sometimes perpetual) defeats in your prayer life. Many people continue to define their lives by the things that happened in the past- some of these, even in their childhood past. What a sad thing, because, *"…if any man be in Christ, he is a new creature: old things are passed away; behold, all things are become new"* (2Corinthians 5:17).

Your real identity is in Christ. Your identity in Christ is your primary identity. God does not reckon with your past, including the negative things that happened an hour ago, so do not let them hold you back.

God's Word Is Forever Settled

1. Do not let your shortcomings cast a shadow over your fellowship with God. He has a lot more for you than your bitter past. Go before God with boldness and excitement. God loves you just the way you are: *"…God commendeth His love toward us, in that while we were yet sinners, Christ died for us"* (Romans 5:8). He loves you just the way you are, so approach Him just the way you are.

2. You are worth more than you can ever imagine. *"And they sung a new song, saying, thou art worthy to take the book, and to open the seals thereof: for thou was slain, and hast redeemed us to God by thy blood out of every kindred, and tongue, and people, and nation"* (Revelation 5:9).

3. Before God, you are justified and guiltless. Put your past behind you. Go before God with a clean slate *"Knowing that a man is not justified by the works of the law, but by the faith of Jesus Christ, even we have believed in Christ, that we might be justified by the faith of Christ, and not by the works of the law: for by the works of the law shall no flesh be justified"* (Galatians 2:16).

4. In Christ you are a totally new person, so *"… put on the new man, which after God is created in righteousness and true holiness"* (Ephesians 4:24).

5. You have a new inheritance in God. God has made you a joint heir with Christ (Galatians 4:7); partaker of His divine nature (2Peter 1:4) and you have inherited every spiritual blessing (Ephesians 1:3).

6. Never be enslaved by your negative past *because "… it is God which worketh in you both to will and to do of His good pleasure."* (Philippians' 2:13). Trust God to pray through you, and to answer your prayers.

Every day pray with the conviction that you are who God says you are – you can do all things through Christ that strengthens you. God's grace is sufficient for you. You have been set apart for great things by God and He has a glorious future for you. Believe and expect nothing less than God's view of you. God's concept of you overrides every other conclusion you or others may have drawn about you. A good perception of yourself is a principal ingredient for success in prayers. Some people feel so worthless, incapable and irrelevant before others; painfully many of these people still feel the same way when they are in God's presence. This feeling has huge implications for their spiritual victory in prayer

44

LISTEN TO GOD

Prayer is the highest form of communication. Effective communication involves passing across your message in the best possible way, as well as listening to all that your recipient has to say. Too often God's children do all the talking. They never give God their ears because they want God to keep doing the listening. Some people are even too frightened to listen to God speak because they think that God's instructions might be too difficult to obey.

Some people have heard God say the same thing too many times on the same subject without obeying, that God has given up speaking about the matter. Others are incapable of hearing God speak personally to them because they are not born again, or they are too distracted by the many other voices they listen to. You cannot pray effectively unless you are able to listen to and obey what God has to say. Many times you do not need to pray, the key to solving a good number of problems is to listen to God and do whatever He asks you to do. Hearing more from God will make you pray less because simply following His instructions eliminates the need to pray about certain things.

The Command to Listen

"But whoever listens to me will dwell safely, and will be secure, without fear or evil" (Proverbs 1:33).

So many years ago I lost a bunch of keys that was so important to me. After searching unsuccessfully for a while, I concluded that the best way to go about it was to take the matter to God and ask Him to show me where to locate the keys. One of the nights after I had prayed, God showed me in a dream where the keys were misplaced. I went straight to the spot and the keys were there, exactly at the location God had revealed to me. Never be afraid to ask God questions, and never be afraid to do what He instructs you to do. Listening to God will cut down on the amount of 'blind' praying you do.

The bible distinguishes between three categories of hearers- the "dull of hearing", those with "itching ears" and those with a "noble and good heart".

The Dull of Hearing

Dullness speaks of lifelessness, deadness and heaviness. It also means indifference, apathy and insensitivity. Dull hearers are unresponsive to God's voice. No matter what you preach or how you preach it, their hearing remain impaired. They are spiritually lifeless, and trying to make them understand a spiritual message is often useless. (Hebrews 5:11). A lot of people continue to pray for things God has been speaking to them about, which no longer require prayer. All that is needed is either obedience or spiritual healing for their ears (if they are suffering from spiritual deafness). If anyone fails to listen to and obey God's voice they will continue in an endless and fruitless prayer journey.

The Itching Ears

The medical term for itching ears is Pruritus. In his epistle to Timothy, Paul warned that there will come a time when certain people will not endure sound teaching, but because of their selfish desires and interests, they will have *"Itching ears and look out for teachers well suited to them, turning away from the truth"* (2Timothy 4:3 – 4).

Christians with itching ears listen only to what they want to hear, they also surround themselves with teachers and preachers whose sermons support their beliefs and lifestyles. Even when God convicts them or speaks to them personally or through other means, they wave it off and live in denial. God will only hear the prayers of people who listen to Him.

Physically, itching ears have underlying root cause. Similarly, Christians with itching ears definitely have some deep seated inner spiritual problems that make them uncomfortable with the truth of God's word. People with itching ears will not listen to God; they will also not listen to any preacher who tells the truth. How can anyone expect God to listen to them when they are not willing to listen to Him?

The Noble and Good Heart

This is the kind of listener God wants His children to be- willing to hear what God or His messengers have to say. They sincerely receive the Word of God without being selective. This class of Christians is willing to do everything to obey God's instructions.

Obedience is better than prayer. Listening to God is better than talking to Him. God has a reason for whatever He says to us. His commandments are not a burden. Everything He says is for your good. You know what God has been speaking about. Listen to Him today. A word from God is worth more than a million words of prayer.

45

LIFESTYLE OF PRAYER

A lifestyle is a way of living which mirrors a person's values and attitudes. A lifestyle projects an individual's fashion, manner, mode or style of living. People's lifestyle represents their set of attitudes or habits. To every child of God prayer should become a lifestyle, not a past time. Prayer was never intended by God to be ceremonious, cumbersome or burdensome.

Prayer is a connection and communication between God and His people. This may take different forms or shapes as we have observed all through this book. You can pray silently. You can also pray aloud. You can pray as an individual. You can equally pray in a group. Prayer can be carried out at anytime, anywhere and on just about anything. God wants you to make prayer a lifestyle- a way of living, something you cannot do without, something you do with ease, and for which you are known.

Your Lifestyle Reveals Your Heart Cry

Every individual, household or society has certain things they hold very dearly. Some are prepared to do everything to maintain their lifestyle. Some people's lifestyle reflects their identity. Your lifestyle dictates what you do on a daily basis. Wherever you are- at home, work or leisure; it displays what you value the most in your life. People's tastes, interests and opinions are generally expressed by their lifestyles. You can deliberately chose to make prayer a daily priority- put it at the top of your list, create time for it and refuse to be distracted from it.

1. Jesus regularly woke up very early in the morning to pray. It was his lifestyle
2. Daniel had the habit of praying three times a day and would not let the threat of being thrown into the lion's den deter him from his consuming lifestyle.
3. The early church prayed and broke bread daily in the temple and from house to house. It was something they valued and paid great attention to.
4. Job regularly consecrated his children to God. He did it very religiously. He valued it. It was part of his family's life.

A strong and consistent prayer life can be developed and sustained by anyone – just one step at a time. To take your relationship with your heavenly father to a powerful phase, prayer needs to become your way of life. That does not mean abandoning everything else. When l drive, l hardly listen to tapes – it is one of my greatest moments of prayers. I pray for hours sometimes whilst driving. The Bible says we should pray without ceasing, and that we should lift up holy hands everywhere in prayers. I do not lift up hands when I am driving – that would be stupid. In fact when I drive and pray I do it with very little emotion, I am mindful of the possible risks involved. I would not recommend for anyone to do very intensive praying when driving.

Pray before and after meals, before going to bed and when you wake up. Pray in understanding and in the spirit. Pray before you go to work and when you return from work. Saturate every appointment or interview with prayers. Pray while you walk and (whenever possible) while you work. Take advantage of short breaks to cover a prayer item, even if it is for a minute- it all adds up. Women, while you do dishes or cook the meals, pray in the spirit or in understanding. It will amaze you how much time you put into prayer if you are praying and walking or praying and working. Make prayer a lifestyle.

People complain of lack of time for prayer. There is plenty of time to reach your prayer goals – if you have any. Prayer can be done aggressively. You can also pray silently, just moving your lips like Hannah did. That makes the job easy and uncomplicated. Pray in waiting rooms and lobbies. I pray at the airport, in the aeroplane – just about everywhere, so long as I am not disturbing or distracting any one. If you arrive early at the airport or your flight is delayed or cancelled, it is another opportunity to pray. Always find a reason and a place to pray. Some airports even have prayer rooms- arrive early and use them.

Pray when you are sad and when you are happy- the more reasons why you should pray. Your prayer times must exceed the amount of time you spend eating, watching the TV, and hanging out with friends. Every prayer time carries a reward – whether praying for yourself, someone else or something else.

God desires your fellowship. You deserve God's blessings. You can pray about everything. You can pray everywhere. And of course, you can pray anyhow, so long as your praying does not constitute a nuisance to other people. You have a call to prayer. Make prayer your lifestyle today and you will never regret it. If you need a lifestyle change so that you can create more time for prayer, do so quickly.

46

LABOUR IN PRAYERS

Labour represents effort, pain, sweat and travail. It reflects hard work, rigours, toil or struggle. A woman in the process of delivering a baby is said to be in labour as she goes through the pangs, contractions and pains of delivery. Prayer is akin to the process of pregnancy, labour and delivery. In prayer you carry a burden, a weight that you must carry to the very end. It involves your entire being and at some point you must deliver, but before then you must go through the pangs of labour.

It is true that success in prayer is the work of the Holy Spirit; however, most result oriented prayers have the element of hard work attached to it. These efforts include emotional, spiritual and physical dimensions. The casual, effortless types of prayer may be alright for ordinary situations, but most dire situations require desperate approaches to prayer.

Labour Fervently In Prayers

Paul wrote to the Colossian Christians informing them that:

> *"Epaphras, who is one of you, a bondservant of Christ, greet you; always labouring fervently for you in prayers that you may stand perfect and complete in all the will of God"* (Colossians 4:12).

Prayer is not a casual activity. It sometimes requires plenty of energy (spiritual and physical) to push your prayers through satanic opposition- one of the reasons Christians are said to be engaged in spiritual warfare. Of course God does answer quiet or silently uttered prayer from the depth of our heart when done in faith, but for the most part, effective prayer requires toil and travail. Some people might be critical of this but those who have experienced or understood prayer at this level will completely agree with me.

Prayer can sometimes be an act of labour and the bible states that in every labour there is reward. If you have been toiling in prayer never give up because God has promised that he would never forget your labour of love. Keep praying until your light shines out of the thickest darkness.

As Soon As Zion Travailed

"Who hath heard such a thing? who hath seen such things? Shall the earth be made to bring forth in one day? or shall a nation be born at once? for as soon as Zion travailed, she brought forth her children" (Isaiah 66:8).

Zion has several biblical meanings which cannot all be explored here. It was the place from which king David governed the nation of Israel. It was also the religious capital of the nation of Israel. Zion symbolises God's throne in heaven, and spiritually, it signifies God's presence and God's people on earth.

Travail and delivery by Zion is a reference to how God moves to help his people who are in any form of 'labour'. God's miraculous power delivers His blessings to people who diligently seek His face. Labouring in prayer is only possible as an act of the Holy Spirit who energizes God's people to deliver every burden they carry at the place of prayer. It is a crucial experience that God's people must have frequently, when they come before His throne to seek His face. In Galatians 4:19 Paul writes to the Galatian converts, *"My little children for whom I Labour in birth again until Christ is formed in you."*

Effective prayer requires the input of all your faculties, everything within you must go into the prayer for it to be fruitful, especially when it comes to difficult cases. Of course, a one- word prayer can work wonders if prayed in faith, however, it does not always work that way. Jesus prayed a few words on several occasions. He also prayed long and repeated prayers at other times.

Whenever I observe people pray passively I really query whether they are expecting any answer to their prayer. Most powerful prayers are a combination of your physical, mental, and emotional energy. It takes everything you have to pray to get the results you desire. Physical strength does not make you prevail, the power of the Spirit does, but as in everything else, you need to focus all your energies if you want results in prayer.

Prayer is similar to seed sowing. Sowing time can be a difficult, painful and tearful period. The good news is that after sowing then comes reaping.

The Spirit Helps Our Weakness

When the Holy Spirit is involved the job is easier no matter the situation. This is made clear in (Romans 8:26):

> *"Likewise the Spirit also helpeth our infirmities: for we know not what we should pray for as we ought: but the Spirit itself maketh intercession for us with groanings which cannot be uttered."*

The Bible indicates that success in Christian life is neither by might nor by power. It is the spirit of God that enables the labouring and birthing process of prayer.

When Jacob laboured in prayer all night, he was physically impacted. Abraham wrestled with God not to destroy Sodom, and Jesus wrestled with the Father at the Garden of Gethsemane. Not all prayers get to these levels, but these are a few examples of what it is like to labour in prayer. When we mean business with God, God will do business with us. Labouring in prayer is one of the ways we can demonstrate that we mean business with God. Prayer is both a painful and painstaking affair.

47

LOVE AND PRAY

Love and prayer are inseparable. Prayer cannot be effective without love. If you love someone you would like to be around them. Your love for God should draw you constantly into His presence. You just want to be where He is. When you have great love for people, you are interested in their well-being and being around them; you will wish them success and progress in all of their endeavours. Love can be expressed through tenderness, passionate affection and a strong personal liking. One of the pillars of a solid prayer life is authentic love. There are two sides to this love – love for God, and love for others.

Unconditional Love

God's kind of love is unconditional, unselfish and without blemish. This kind of love is hardly understood by many people, and therefore they claim to love when in actual sense they are either doing the opposite or something that is an imitation of the authentic. Some people's exhibition of love is possessive, controlling, and in many cases, for personal aggrandisement or personal advantage.

For your prayer to be acceptable to God your love for Him and people need to be unequivocal and absolute. It is easy to love someone when they are nice and kind to you. If you love when people turn out negative and become antagonistic to you, this is called unconditional love.

When it is more about you, your feelings or your needs, then it is not true love. Unconditional love is not tied to physical things and family relationships- your love is unconditional when it is extended to people whom you have no reason to love; their beliefs and values are in clear contrast to yours, they have hurt you without cause, and are never able to see or accept your point of view on matters- *"For scarcely for a righteous man will one die: yet peradventure for a good man some would even dare to die. But God commendeth his love toward us, in that, while we were yet sinners, Christ died for us"* (Romans 5:7-8).

Jesus exemplified unqualified love when He died on the Cross for us while we were yet sinners. He forgave on the Cross even when no one had asked forgiveness from Him.

When we were no good, Christ died for us. When we were incapable of doing anything good, God sent His son to die for us. We were ungodly and undeserving when Christ took our place. Unless you are motivated by this kind of love, you will never see the need to pay the price to pray for others. You will also never enjoy the full benefits of prayer. Unqualified love will drive you to pray for others when you will get nothing in return. This is the foundation of intercessory prayers, and it lies at the root of every sound Christian life.

The Greatest Commandment

Jesus taught the pre-eminence of love when He was asked by a lawyer, 'which is the greatest commandment?' Jesus' response was:

> *"Thou shalt love the Lord thy God with all thy heart, and with all thy soul, and with all thy mind. This is the first and great commandment. And the second is like unto it, Thou shalt love thy neighbour as thyself. On these two commandments hang all the law and the prophets"* (Mathew 22:37-40).

You will enjoy more victories in prayers if you let God live a life of love through you. Many Christians love ministry, money and miracles more than God and people. When you love your neighbour, it is an indication that you definitely love God. Your prayer motivation and momentum must originate from your love for God and people, your capacity to pray is largely dependent upon your capacity to love.

Faith Works by Love

No matter your level of faith and how fervently you pray, it is unlikely you will get results in the absence of genuine love. Faith is principally an instrument for tapping into God and unlocking His blessings, but faith that is not mingled will love will not be recognised by God. Just like faith without works is dead, so also, faith without love is dead (Galatians 5:6).

Perfect Love Casts Away Fear

Love for God and people will boost your confidence to come into God's presence. Loving God keeps us away from offending Him, hurting or neglecting others; it also qualifies us to come before Him in prayers.

Pray For Those Who Hate You

This might be a difficult one. Jesus commands us to love our enemies, do good to those who hate us, bless those who curse us, and pray for those who spitefully use and abuse us. (Luke 6:27-28). It takes rock solid love to do this. Some enemies need vengeance and judgement, but God says He will take care of that on your behalf (Romans 12:17-19). Prayer that is void of unrestricted love for others can only be described as mechanical, worst still, hypocritical. The most authentic drive for prayer should be the love of God and people. Nothing else can replace this, and nothing less will please God.

Everything Jesus did was motivated by love. Every prayer He prayed, every miracle He worked, every act of kindness He showed and every act of firmness He exhibited were all on the platform of love. Your prayer will be weak, and probably worthless if the inspiration and motivation behind it is anything but love. You must therefore, love and pray!

48

MATURITY

It is God's desire for His children to increase in size, number, value and strength. Growth is the emergence of a new you on a continuous basis. There are certain depths of prayer that only growing and mature Christians can experience. The interesting thing is that Christian maturity is not determined by how long you have been born again or being in Church, but by how well you have submitted to, and known God.

Born into God's Family

Similar to human growth and development, Christian growth is not automatic. When you became born again you received the spirit of adoption. Adoption is the act of God whereby a born again person is placed as son and bestowed with the full privileges of sonship. Your adoption into the family of God, effected through the new birth, is the equivalence of the birth of a new baby into a natural family. From that point onwards, the born again child must continue to grow. As a child of God you must keep growing, meeting every developmental milestone in order to get the most out of your relationship with your Father. Growth in prayer is directly related to growth in other areas of your spiritual life.

Stages of Christian Growth

Just like a new-born baby undergoes several stages to attain maturity, so must a child of God go through the necessary process of attaining to full maturity. Until this happens you are likely to be limited in the amount of results you get in prayer.

> *"Now I say, That the heir, as long as he is a child, differeth nothing from a servant, though he be lord of all; But is under tutors and governors until the time appointed of the father. Even so we, when we were children, were in bondage under the elements of the world"* (Galatians 4:1-3).

Your prayer life will only be as progressive as your spiritual development. If you are growing spiritually, your prayer life will continue to grow. If your spiritual growth is stunted, your prayer life will be affected. Spiritual growth is comparable to the human developmental stages.

The Baby or Infant Stage (0-2 years)

This is a range between 0 -2 years of age. In the natural it represents new born infant- innocent, unable to speak, untaught and without skill. Christians at this phase still depend on milk, not the meat of God's word as they cannot stand strong teachings (1corinthians 3:1, Hebrews 5:13). The stage is characterised by limited knowledge and experience of God and dependence on others to do much of your praying. The earlier a Christian moves on from this phase, the better he can achieve in prayer. Quick transition from this level can be achieved through a personal hunger for God and support from more experienced Christians.

The Little Child Phase (2-10 years)

Paul lamented over these category of Christians:

"My little children, of whom I travail in birth again until Christ be formed in you... for I stand in doubt of you ..." (Galatians 4:19, 20). Little children are impressionable. They easily blend with the environment

and people around them at the expense of their own identity. Too many Christians want God to treat them like adults when they still exhibit all the traits of a child- they ask God to give them things that they cannot manage when they have not proved themselves in smaller blessings. A loving father will not put his children at risk, we never give our children more than they can handle. A quick transition from this phase will open up great possibilities in a person's life.

The Teenage Phase

This growth phase is characterised by better physical and psychological development. The child becomes an adolescent, a youth or a minor. A boy may now be referred to as a young man, with more freedom and privileges. The child can be trusted to a considerable degree. In most societies there is multiple expectation from the young person - in education, employment, community service, independence and home-leaving.

Some people in this phase still manifest the features of a child – they cannot be trusted to drive certain types of cars in some countries, and in many cases, are below the legal age to be able to purchase certain items. Christians that remain in this phase cannot be fully trusted by God with greater responsibilities- this will limit the level of God's power they can enjoy in prayer and how much God can entrust them with. If you pray for what you cannot handle God is not likely to grant your request, grown-ups can have unrestricted access to many things that are not within the reach of children.

The bible also refers to people in this stage as "young men", (1 John 2:13-14; proverbs 20:29). It is an ongoing stage of growth, not a full-grown one. Many people at this level can demonstrate strong prayer lives and make better use of spiritual resources; hence they can be trusted with more grace. They still have plenty of room to grow into spiritual adulthood.

The Mature Phase

In this phase you have truly (not fully) known God and can do exploits through prayers. The journey to this place can be long and arduous, but that's where God wants you to be – totally relying upon and being led by the Holy Spirit, able to forgive easily, able to respond to difficult instructions from God. You have severed ties with the world, and are fully yielded to God. Mature Christians possess the required stamina to tackle tougher spiritual problems through prayers.

Some people never go beyond the stage of infants or little children. This makes it difficult for them to enjoy a fruitful relationship with God. Prayer becomes a burden to them and their limited spiritual experience and understanding gives them less motivation to pray. Mature Christians are more mature in prayers. So, it is time to grow up.

49

MOTIVES

We all have motivations for everything we do. Some of these motives are right while others may be wrong. Wrong motives can be very subtle and may not be easily identified. Your motive is the reason, inspiration or inducement behind your actions. If the motive behind your prayer is wrong, every likelihood is that you will not go far, let alone expect answers.

Mixed and Wrong Motives

Paul wrote to Titus regarding the early church of Crete, a church where people had questionable reputation, and false teachings were rife:

> *"Young men likewise exhort to be sober minded. In all things shewing thyself a pattern of good works: in doctrine shewing uncorruptness, gravity, sincerity, Sound speech, that cannot be condemned; that he that is of the contrary part may be ashamed, having no evil thing to say of you"* (Titus 2: 6-8).

Some of the key parts of this scripture are integrity, reverence and incorruptibility. It is easy for prayers no matter how serious they may be to be mixed with insincerity, irreverence, and wrong motives. A wrong motive will constitute an impediment to your prayer. Wrong motives may take any of the following forms:

Personal Pleasures

Most prayers are so self- centred that heaven does not appreciate them. The Apostle James recognised and addressed this: *"You ask and do not receive because you ask amiss, that you may spend it on your pleasures."* (James 4:3).

The Lord cannot be pleased with self-seeking prayers which have little or no focus on His kingdom and other people. Any prayer which centres on the needs of others and the work of God, will draw quick attention from God. People who make personal pleasure their prayer focus will get very little from God.

Questionable Sincerity

Let us examine the case of King Saul in the bible. God raised him out of obscurity to be a king over His people. He came from a little known tribe and was the least in his family when God commissioned him to go and utterly destroy the Amalekites, sworn enemies of Israel. The Amalekites attacked Israel during their exodus from Egypt. Israel was forbidden from plundering the Amalekites- they were forbidden from taking any booty of war after they have defeated the Amalekites. King Saul won the war, nevertheless, he did contrary to God's instructions, by keeping *"The best of the sheep, the oxen, the fatlings, the lambs and all that was good"* (1 Samuel 15:8).

When confronted by God through Prophet Samuel, Saul blamed his subjects for his dishonesty and insincerity and pleaded innocence. He pretended to be in repentance:

> *"And Saul said unto Samuel, I have sinned: for I have transgressed the commandment of the LORD, and thy words: because I feared the people, and obeyed their voice. Now therefore, I pray thee, pardon my sin, and turn again with me, that I may worship the LORD"* (I Samuel 8:24-25).

His prayer was not sincere. His heart was not right. His claim of innocence and repentance were doubtful. God refused to answer His prayer and instead, stripped him of his kingship and the throne.

How many people pretend to be repenting in prayers when they are not? How many times people make promises to God in prayers and God sees insincerity and dishonesty within their heart? God cannot be manipulated; no one can get God to do things through deceit; He sees deep within every heart.

Keeping Up With the Joneses

Many people ask God for things they do not really need, and sometimes out of envy and competitive jealousy. They go ahead to fast and pray about such things. Of course, God wants us to live a good life. He wants you to prosper and have the best. Nevertheless, you do not have to obtain certain things just because other people have acquired them, or simply because you want to enhance your status and boost your personal ego. It is important to draw a line between legitimate aspiration and sinful covetousness. God knows better than dishing out blessings just to boost a person's sense of value.

Personal Glory

All prayers must meet the 'glory of God' criteria. This does not mean praying about the kingdom and soul winning alone. It has more to do with whether your request will serve God's purpose in anyway. Where is God in your prayer? *"Therefore, whether you eat or drink, or whatever you do, do all to the glory of God."* (1Corinthians 10:31).

Make sure your prayer meets the standard of God's word and will give praise to God in every way.

Loving the Gift More Than the Giver

Do not take your personal need more seriously than your need for for God. God cannot be used that way. You cannot have anything from

God unless you first have God. The Jesus you do not have cannot meet your needs. Exceptionally, God may answer your prayer or someone else's prayer on your behalf to draw your attention. This must not be misunderstood to mean that you can receive from God without first entering into a relationship with Him.

Incorrect prayer motives, will lead to prayer failure. Defective and dishonest state of heart will deny you access to God's treasure house and render your prayers ineffective. The right attitude and motives are essential keys to very effective praying.

50

MORNING BY MORNING

There is no best time or place to pray, I believe it depends on the need, circumstances and urgency required by the situation. Prayer can be done any day, anytime and anywhere. However, the discipline of rising early in the morning to pray has un-surpassing rewards. For the majority of people, the ideal time to meet face to face with God is early in the morning. Quiet periods with the heavenly Father can hold any time and at any place. Although Jesus prayed in a variety of places, He distinctively modelled the early morning prayers whilst He was on earth.

Why Rise Early To Pray

Strength for the Day

It is impossible to predict the surprises that will spring up as you face each day. No two days are ever the same, and you need God's help and guidance to tackle whatever the day throws at you. You need physical strength to go through the day. You also need emotional and spiritual stamina to keep you throughout the day. Early in the morning, at the place of prayers God will release His power to energise you to be able to wrestle with the 'forces' that you may encounter the rest of the day. No matter how strong and smart you are, you need divine intervention to get the utmost out of each day. When you spend time praying early in the morning and commit your day to God, you will give Him a chance to breathe His life and power into your day.

Divine Direction

I have learned from personal experience that during prayer times my spirit, mind and body receive divine illumination and invigoration. It never ceases to amaze me how many things I needed to remember and plan for, which were completely out of my mind prior to praying. Without exception I have found that each time I meet with God in prayers He brings to my remembrance all the key, urgent and important things that require my attention for the day- sometimes for the week and even a month. My early morning prayers are food for my brain, inspiration to my spirit, and strength to my physical body. My best days of the week are those initiated with prayer and personal fellowship with God. Make time for the Lord every morning before the start of your day. There is no better way to commence your daily journey.

Early Risers in the Bible

The bible contains several examples of people who rose early to either pray or worship God:

1) Abraham rose early in the Morning (Genesis 19:27; Genesis 22:3).
2) Moses rose early in the morning to appear before the Lord (Exodus 24:4).
3) Samuel's parents (Hannah and Elkannah) rose up early in the morning to worship the Lord (1 Samuel 1:19).
4) King Hezekiah rose up early in the morning to rally the rulers of Israel to go up to the House of God (2Chronicles 29:20).
5) Job rose early in the morning to offer sacrifices on behalf of his children to God for purification and cleansing (Job 1:5).
6) David rose early in the morning to worship God (Psalm 57:8).

7) Jesus rose up a great while before day to a solitary place to pray (Mark1:35).
8) Isaiah promised to seek God with his sprit early (Isaiah 26:9).

So much can be learned from these great people of God. It may be difficult initially but once the habit is formed the benefits of rising early in the morning to pray far outweigh those of wrapping up inside your blanket for an extra hour of sleep.

How to Rise Early

The importance of rising early to pray means the devil will do everything within his reach to sabotage it. You must do everything you can to protect your precious prayer times. Anything that succeeds is the product of determination and hard work.

Determination

Determination is at the heart of everything we do. If you are not determined to wake up early, a lot of things will distract you from doing so. The value you place on your time alone with God will determine how much efforts you put into making it happen.

Early to Bed

'Early to bed, early to rise' is a common saying, but the advice is not taken seriously by many people. Unless you give priority to going to bed early, you might keep struggling with giving God the best time of the day. God should always be first in our life- and that includes giving Him first place in the morning.

Multiple Alarm Clocks

A lot of people have no difficulty waking up early but if you are one of those who do, one alarm clock may be insufficient to get you out of bed. If you are having problems rising early, try using more than one alarm, set at a few minutes interval. This has helped some people overcome the challenges of getting out of bed at the quietest time of the day.

Get a Buddy

You may need to agree with a friend or someone who is used to rising early, to give you an early morning wake up call. Most people are better at carrying out difficult tasks when they work with a close person.

Do It for a Month

If you are just learning to rise early you may need to work hard to do it consistently every day for the first 21 to 30 days. That is about what (they say) it takes to make a new habit stick. Hopefully you will be a winner after that period. Mind you, you will still need some efforts to keep the habit going.

No Pain, No Gain

Remember the popular saying, 'no pain, and no gain'. There is so much to gain from rising early to pray. What can be more valuable than starting the day with your heavenly Father? It would make a world of difference to your life. Give it a go. Go through the pain and the reward will be great.

51

MEASURE YOUR SUCCESS

Whatever you do, it is important to measure how much progress is being made. Everyone has plans, written and unwritten, in the head and on paper; we must find ways to ensure that everything is going according to plan. Prayer is a major event in our lives, needless to say. It is more important than most things that compete for your time. If planning is crucial in other areas, it is no less important in prayer.

Anyone who wants to get the most out of prayer needs a workable plan, which must be carefully followed and monitored on a regular basis. A basic or very simple plan is all you need. Not only will this help to map out your prayer journey, it will also enable you to assess when you are on track and when you are falling behind.

What Gets Measured Gets Done

There is a popular saying that whatever gets measured gets done. Generally, people monitor their bank accounts, sometimes several times a day on line. A lot of people monitor what they eat, their blood pressure, cholesterol levels and the fuel level in their car, but not their spiritual lives. A lot of God's children tend to wait until something seriously goes wrong and then begin to fire fight. Fire fighting problems is a gamble especially when things get out of hand. Monitoring your prayer accomplishments ensures you remain on track with your prayer goals, and that things are not in disarray.

Clear and Realistic Objectives

Nothing can be effectively achieved or monitored unless the objectives were initially defined. We all have a set of objectives at places of work, we either set them or someone else does. What are your prayer intentions? How much time (in minutes or hours) do you plan to put into each prayer item daily, weekly, monthly, quarterly or yearly? Making it clearly defined will determine how well you can appraise your effectiveness. If you fail to picture your end product, prayer will simply be a game of convenience and hit-and-miss. More will be discussed on prayer objectives in subsequent sections.

How to Monitor Your Prayer Progress

Here are some of the questions which have helped me in monitoring and ensuring my prayer life remains on course.

1) Have my prayers been successful- partially, completely or not all?
2) What about the quality of my prayer- have l been praying through and experiencing the help of the Holy Spirit?
3) What about the quantity of prayer- have l been praying too little and falling short of my daily targets?
4) Have I been getting prayer results; do I have testimonies to share with others?
5) How can l deal with distractions or create more time for prayer? Is there anything else l can do at all? If so what are they?
6) What is the next step l must take to re-align my prayer life? How can l regain lost prayer time? How can l rekindle or re-energise myself for prayers?

7) Are there any besetting sins or 'weights' that stand in my way and hinder my relationship with God?

8) What is stopping me, if any?

You can certainly ask yourself many more questions. Meditate on your answers and use the information to make necessary improvement to your prayer activities. Check on your prayer life regularly to make sure everything is fine.

A Lapse Is Not a Collapse

Some people give up on themselves and their plans too quickly when they discover how 'woefully' (they think) they have failed. It is alright to fail in prayers, but not alright to lose hope and abandon your goals. Pick up from where you stopped, and if necessary, start all over again. Prayer is not everything, and prayer does not do everything. That said, I still firmly believe that effective praying will lead to effective homes, more effective churches and ministries- in fact there will be a sharper edge to whatever you do. Make prayer the platform and pillar of all that you do, and never stop measuring your success.

Always have a plan in place. This will help define, direct and keep your prayer life steady. It will also help you to compare your results with your goals, and to identify where improvement is needed. This way, you will be able to remedy any gap between your plan and actual achievements. If you fail to plan your prayer life, you are prone to fail in prayer. Planning will direct and keep you on course to achieve your prayer goals. If you do not plan your prayer life, things that appear more urgent (but are not) will take the place of prayer, and the devil will be very happy about that.

52

MORE PRAYERS

We can never do enough of praying- it is like the air we breathe; we constantly need air to survive- good quality air, flowing constantly in abundance. More prayers will lead to more miracles and more of God's intervention over His creation. Less prayer will result in little divine influence over human affairs. I believe we need to do our physical best to make things work, I also believe we need to pray our best to get more help from God.

You Need to Pray More

You need:

More prayers when you are just learning to pray

More prayers when you continue to grow in prayers

More prayers after you have grown in praying confidently

More prayers when you are struggling to maintain your prayer life

More prayers when you are already experiencing great success in prayers

More prayers when you suffer lack and poverty

More prayers when you enjoy plenty and abundance

More prayers when you are afraid or confused and unsure of what to do

More prayers when you feel bold, strong and courageous

More prayers if you are battling to live above sin

More prayers if you are living absolutely above sin

More prayers if you feel rejected and isolated

More prayers when you feel surrounded with love, and accepted by all

The bible says, *"Be careful for nothing; but in everything by prayer and supplication with thanksgiving let your requests be made known unto God"* (Philippians 4:6).

Prayer sharpens your mind

Prayer shapes your destiny

Prayer is the 'water' in your 'garden'

Prayer initiates your blessings

Prayer secures your blessings

Prayer prospers the works of your hands

Prayer preserves the works of your hands

Prayer keeps you out of trouble

Prayer keeps you close and connected to God

Prayer is God's vehicle for your supplies

Prayer helps when you are happy

Prayer heals when you are unhappy

Prayer will take care of many things

Prayer will multiply God's presence in your life

When Hudson Taylor was Eighteen years old, he stumbled into a gospel track in his father's library. He read the tract, but the message in it stuck to his head until he eventually fell on his knees, receiving Christ as his saviour. His mother had been away from home, and on her return, Hudson told her of his encounter with Jesus. The mother replied that she knew of Hudson's encounter with God ten days earlier, as God had given her the assurance as she prayed an entire afternoon for Hudson's salvation.

The story could have been different if Hudson's mother prayed simply on a few occasions and then gave up. She most probably had been praying for weeks, months or even years, until that day when he felt she needed to pray more- not less, as her child remained "wayward". Rather than giving up on him, scolding, shouting, crying and blaming God for her deviant child, she saw the need to pray more. More prayer will pile up the heat on your problem until the situation 'bows' to the power of the Holy Spirit.

53

NOURISH YOUR SPIRITUAL LIFE

Feed and nourish your spiritual life consistently. A healthy spiritual life is the bedrock of quality prayer life. A flourishing prayer life cannot be achieved in isolation from spiritual fitness. Fruitfulness in prayer can only result from a viable spiritual life.

When you ingest food or other nourishing materials, the expectation is that it will result in wholesomeness and give the benefits of promoting and supporting your physical, mental or emotional wellbeing. I have seen people who give little or no seriousness to their Christianity wonder why they cannot pray successfully or why their prayer life is so shallow. I have also seen many so called 'great' Christians whose prayer lives are anything but desirable. The root cause of ineffective prayer times can be traced to poor spiritual health.

3rd John 2 highlights God's desire for the health of His Children:

"Beloved, I wish above all things that thou mayest prosper and be in health, even as thy soul prospereth." Everything about your Christian life works in concert to produce a sound spiritual being. A smooth prayer life is a product of a robust spiritual state, and an undesirable spiritual condition will breed unsatisfactory and unproductive prayer closet.

7 Ways to Nourish Your Spiritual Life

In 2 Peter 1:5-7, the bible highlights certain things we must do to lead a stable and reliable Christian life.

1. **Add Virtue to your faith**
   Other words for virtue are goodness, integrity, morality, uprightness, dignity and propriety. With these elements in the correct proportions you should have fewer struggles with your praying.

2. **Add Knowledge to Virtue** (2 Peter 1:5)
   This is the ability to discern the truth from falsehood, and right from wrong. God wants you to keep feeding yourself with knowledge- knowledge of Him, His Word and everything else that can contribute to a steady flow of His grace when you pray.

3. **Add Temperance to Knowledge** (Galatians 5:22).
   Self-control or discipline enables you to persevere in the midst of difficulties. Are you growing or diminishing in quality? Self-control gives you control over every aspect of your life. It helps you to put a handle on everything including your prayer life.

4. **Add to temperance patience**
   The bible says that patience leads to perfection. Everyone can learn to be patient- wait patiently for God, patiently make decisions, be patient when dealing with others especially those with whom you do not agree. Essentially, your patience will be tested nearly every time you pray. Losing your patience could mean losing your blessings.

5. **Add to patience godliness** (1Timothy 3:16)
   Godliness means to be god-like in word and action. Demonstrate godliness in loving others, being merciful and in exercising

justice. A godly person is separated unto, and has a right standing with God.

6. **Add to godliness brotherly kindness**
   The Church of Christ is one body. Living in unity with, and loving God's children ensures you continue to stay nourished by the head of the body- Jesus Christ. Brotherly kindness includes forgiving, supporting and accommodating God's children everywhere no matter their denomination.

7. **Add to brotherly kindness love (1 Corinthians 13:40)**
   Love is characterised by forgiveness, patience, kindness and humility. We can only enjoy God's blessings on the platform of love. No matter how we pray, give or try to serve God, without love God will not be pleased.

Feed on God's Word

God's Word is the source of faith. (Romans 10: 17). In the absence of faith your prayers will be essentially wasted as faith is very crucial to receiving from God. God says you must feed on His word like a new born babe feeds on milk (1Peter 2:2).This is also reiterated in Matthew 4:4 by our Lord Jesus Christ: *"...Man shall not live by bread alone, but by every word that proceeds from the mouth of God."*

When you read or study your bible daily, your mind will be renewed, your faith will be built and strengthened and your spirit will be fully fed. Failing to study the bible will inevitably result in a weak prayer life. Prayer and the Word are the pair of wings with which every Christian may soar to greater spiritual heights. You need both to make great prayer strides.

Tapes and CDs

Christian teachings on tapes come in various forms and on just about any subject. Buy them; listen to them over and again until you are truly fed with God's message through them. Christian and other targeted audio messages have the ability to positively affect your spirit and mind. Be careful though to make a good selection of appropriate materials that will adequately feed your spirit and soul.

Read, Read and Read

A lot of people never completely read a single book in an entire year. A good book can forever transform your life. Find time to read- read on the train; on the plane and at the lobby. You can read during your break and waiting times. Turn your TV times into reading times. Unproductive times spent with certain people can be utilised for reading. Fifteen minutes a day will enable you to read several medium sized books in a year. That you are baptised in the Holy Ghost, work miracles, signs and wonders or attend church regularly does not guarantee powerful prayer encounters. Feed your spirit and it will reflect in your prayer. If you take proper care of your spirit, you will enjoy powerful prayer times.

54

NEGATIVE MINDSETS PRODUCE NEGATIVE OUTCOMES

A negative mind-set will undermine your ability to pray. The bible says that two people cannot work together unless they are in agreement. You are a partner with God in Kingdom business as well as your personal and professional life. A positive mind-set is cardinal to success in everything we do. Anyone who comes before God feeling hopeless is already on the path of failure; your state of mind will shape your life.

The Battle Begins In the Mind

Your mind is conditioned by many things including what you learned from school, family, friends and the media. The things you listen to and observe can have a lasting impact on your state of mind, and will combine to shape your personal philosophy. If your memory of past experiences is inaccurate, it could define your present state. If your perception of present challenges is off the mark, you will react accordingly. Genesis 11:6 reveals the possibilities of the human mind:

"And the Lord said, Behold the people is one, and they have all one language, and this they begin to do and now noting will be restrained from them, which they have imagined to do." This passage suggests that whatever people imagine in their heart, they will achieve if they embark on it.

Romans 12:12 equally adds: *"And do not be conformed to this world, but be transformed by the renewing of your mind, that you may prove what is that good and acceptable, and perfect will of God"*.

At salvation our spirit is renewed but the mind is not. The mind remains a battle field long after you give your life to Christ. If you lose the fight in the region of the mind you will almost certainly be a casualty of spiritual warfare. Whatever your mind attracts or accepts is what you get in life. Your state of mind will determine your prayer outcome.

What the Bible Says About the Mind

In several instances reference to the mind in the bible denotes the seat of reflection- the place of perception, understanding, feeling, judgement and decision. The mind is the faculty of knowing, and the cradle of understanding. If an individual is defeated in their mind regarding a problem, prayer may not be able to redeem the situation. If your mind convinces you that God will not hear you or that you do not deserve answers from God, this will stand in your way as you pray. Your mind must not only agree with God's word when you pray, it must also believe that God loves and cares enough about you to grant your request. God wants you to have:

- A spiritual mind (Romans 8:6)
- A renewed mind (Ephesians 4:23)
- A right mind (Mark5:15)
- A fervent mind (2Corrinthians7:7)
- A pure mind (2peter 3:1)
- A mind that is stayed on God (Isaiah 26:3)
- A sound mind (2 Timothy 1:7)
- A sober mind (Titus 2:6)
- A mind that continually thinks God's thoughts (Isaiah 55:8-9)
- The mind of Christ (1 Corinthians 2:16, Philippians 2:5).

A wholesome Christian life is a product of a sound, stable and sober mind. A mind that continually thinks God's thoughts, stays pure, and is progressively renewed by God's word is perfectly positioned to receive from God. It will also be able to pray and believe God for the impossible. A healthy mind will persist longer in prayer and be able to resist the devil tenaciously. You can receive healing for your mind through God's word and by the power of the Holy Spirit. The greatest challenge a lot of people have is not the actual conflict they face, it is the battle that rages in their mind (2 Corinthians 10:5).

Some people are just too anxious, worried and wearied by life's problems that the centre of their mind cannot hold things together; this hampers their ability to pray or trust God. You need a sound state of mind to initiate and maintain a great prayer life.

What Is On Your Mind?

Your mind can either be filled with the thoughts of God, victory, success and God's promises, or with fear, anxiety, sorrow and vanity. Are you harbouring defeat, rejection, poor self-image, guilt and condemnation in your mind? Is your mind burdened with insecurity, lack, self-pity and impossibility? Whatever is on your mind can dictate the direction and success of your prayer.

Resist the Devil

God cannot resist the devil on your behalf. Everyone must take responsibility for confronting and putting the devil to flight from their life. You need to confess with your mouth what God says concerning you. Tell Satan to get out of your mind and get behind you. Satan needs to hear that prosperity and not poverty is your portion and that you are worthy to receive all that God has for you, even today in prayer.

Do not let Satan's weeds overgrow in your mind. Root them out when they are still tender, better still, keep them out whilst they are still knocking at the door of your mind. Keeping your mind healthy will make your prayer life fruitful.

55

OVERCOME OVERCONFIDENCE

Do you remember sitting for an exam, very certain you will achieve high grades, only to experience disappointment and failure? It could happen with exams, keeping appointments, catching a flight, meeting office deadlines and in virtually everything we do. Some people get so confident to the point that the high level of confidence becomes their undoing.

Overconfidence is excessive confidence. It is good to be confident, but dangerous to be overconfident. Overconfidence sometimes indicate high self-esteem, and could be a catalyst for success. However, too much confidence becomes a disadvantage when it makes you procrastinate, under-estimate consequences, or altogether make you underperform because you are certain nothing can go wrong.

Dangers of Overconfidence

Self-confidence is great. Faith in God is much better. Overconfidence, if not well managed can have negative consequences. The bible warns: *"Therefore let him who thinks he stands take heed lest he fall."* (1 Corinthians 10:12).

Exaggerated belief in yourself can lead to self-delusion, an unteachable spirit and taking God for granted. Overconfidence can also result in underestimation of risks and refusal to accept criticism. It can endanger you and other people whose lives may be impacted by steps you take or failed to take. Overconfident people are often at risk of overestimating their knowledge, underestimating risks and exaggerating their own ability to manage events.

Overestimate knowledge And Underestimate Risk

The bible says, *"…the world through wisdom did not know God."* (1 Corithians1:21).

In other words, the people of the world have rejected Christ because they failed to understand God through their natural understanding. They believe they know it all. Paul prayed that the eyes of people's understanding may be enlightened. This was a prayer for Christians who thought they knew enough about God and were therefore complacent about spiritual things. The people who undertook to build the Tower of Babel were overconfident. They were very convinced they could build a tower tall enough to reach heaven, but alas! God proved them wrong and demonstrated the limitations of human ingenuity (Genesis11:4). Being overconfident can make you depend less on God. Rather than praying and putting things in God's hands, you will rely more on your own ability.

The Titanic: "Practically Unsinkable"

Several lessons in overconfidence can be learned from the titanic, a ship that was widely believed to be unsinkable but actually sank on its maiden voyage. It was April 15, 1912. An iceberg punctured and caused the RMS Titanic to sink into the bottom of the Atlantic Ocean, to the amazement of millions of people all over the world. Apart from the loss of over 1,500 lives the most shocking and unbelievable of it all was the sinking of a ship that was firmly believed to be so watertight that various people commented:

It is "practically unsinkable",

"Not even God could sink this ship"

"The Captain may, by simply moving an electric switch, instantly close the doors throughout, and make the vessel practically unsinkable"

"We place absolute confidence in the Titanic. We believe that the boat is unsinkable"

Such was the level of confidence the ship builders, the media and the Captain of the ship had in the vessel that many things were taken for granted. It was said for example that:

- Although the ship was capable of carrying 3,000 people, it had life boats for only 1,178
- Men in the Crow's Nest (look-out tower) had no looking glasses. The looking glasses in the ship had been misplaced
- During the voyage, crew received several messages from other ships warning them of existing icebergs on the path of the titanic, but the warnings were somehow ignored
- Many passengers believed (until it became too late), that the ship would not sink, so they could not be saved

Life is neither smooth nor safe if God is taken out of the equation. God is all-powerful and all-knowing. We need to place implicit trust in Him rather than human creativity and ability. Never put your trust in yourself, anyone or anything else. Secure your destiny by placing implicit trust in god alone. Of course you should not live in fear and unbelief, neither should you trust in your own ability.

Exaggerated Ability (to control events)

Overconfidence can deceive people into overestimating their ability to control things. An overinflated mind-set can be a recipe for failure in prayer and other things. An overblown picture of oneself make a lot of people less reliant on God and the power of prayer. They forget that:

1. Winners are not always the fastest or strongest (Ecclesiastes 9:11)
2. The spirit is willing but the flesh is weak (Mark 14:38)
3. He who thinks he stands should take heed lest he falls (1Corinthians 10:12)
4. You cannot tell what will happen tomorrow (4:13-14; Luke 12:16-21)
5. One needs to pay earnest heed to the Word of God (Hebrews 2:1-3)

By all means have faith in God, believe Him for great things, go for the very best you can get from God and add as much value as you can to your life; but by no means trust too much in your natural instincts, ability and wisdom. Commit your life and work into God's hands. Trust in God's ability to see you through every challenge you face. Work like everything depends on work and; pray like everything depends on prayer and the power of God.

56

OFFENSIVE PRAYER

Offensive praying is the act of taking prayer initiative and imposing your will upon the enemy. Offensive warfare sets the pace and determines the direction of conflicts. The offensive is a disposition of forward, aggressive and continuous deployment of resources in order to gain an objective or achieve warfare goal without waiting to be attacked first by the enemy.

Attack, Your Best Form of Defence

It is more beneficial to persistently take the battle to the enemy's territory than to wait for him to harass you before making frantic moves to defend yourself. A premeditated and planned push into the opponents' territory puts them on their back heels, and helps you to quickly gain grounds. In spiritual warfare it is more economical and rewarding to continuously attack the devil on every front on a steady basis. This leaves him with less room to effectively deploy his forces. This method of praying will require you (as earlier discussed) to always have a simple but carefully crafted prayer plan which you must stick to.

Pray persistently and aggressively over every aspect of your life, ministry and business. Regularly destroy all the plans and works of the enemy over your family, finances, projects, businesses and job. Do this on a daily basis, because when you are not, the enemy will gain the upper hand. If you allow the devil to strike you first, it will take you time to undo your losses; it is a lot cheaper and easier to remain on the offensive than to wait and allow the devil to gain advantage over you.

Always Seize the Initiative

Keep maintaining a combative stance, never allow evil to advance towards you; never allow an inch of the enemy's incursions into your space. Why wait for something to go wrong before you pray when it will cost a lot more to do so? Assume your prayer responsibilities, devise a prayer plan to cover everything in the short, medium, and long-term. Rather than blame circumstances, shape circumstances by taking the initiative. Let people see you pray and be moved to pray. Pray for today, tomorrow, next month and next year. Cover the next one, two, three or more years in prayer. At first you may not see the fruits, but you must never relent in your efforts. You avert future crisis by praying in the offensive, and before problems show up.

Offensive and Aggressive

Be single-minded and tireless in praying about issues that you want resolved, be dogged and unyielding in attacking the enemy before he shows up in any aspect of your life. Last minute prayers very rarely win spiritual battles. In most cases very little can be achieved in prayers if we allow things to run amok before we pray. The bible calls Satan the thief; if you fail to stop a thief before they gain access to your priced possession they would have caused irreversible damage before you realise it.

> "Fight the good fight of faith; take hold of the eternal life to which you were called, and you made your good confession in the presence of many witnesses" (1Timothy 6:12). NIV

Defensive praying will only help you to manage your losses. Some damages are irreparable, but being on the offensive enables you to dictate the tempo of the battle and take the momentum off the hands of your opponent. Seizing the initiative puts you in charge of the situation, ahead of the adversary. In essence you will be dictating the direction of events and the enemy will only fight to fend off your attacks. The easiest way to achieve victory is to act before the other side commences hostilities.

Offensive and Progressive

Whatever your goals in life or ministry, playing the defensive is not going to get you far enough. Look ahead, see things coming and halt the advancement of evil before your enemy takes off. Take no prayer breaks and holidays because if you sleep the enemy will sneak through your defences. Proactively and rapidly chase the enemy beyond your borders- to their own gates, and then lay a permanent siege against them until you wreak total havoc on their territory. Offensive prayer is the only means by which you can execute God's pre-designed plans for your life and ministry.

Offensive and Relentless

> *"...Ye shall chase your enemies; and they shall fall before you by the sword. And five of you shall chase an hundred, and an hundred of you shall put ten thousand to flight: and your enemies shall fall before you by the sword"* (Leviticus 26:7-8).

The only way to constantly keep the devil on the run is to vigorously pursue him out of your vicinity, flustering and unnerving him in every possible way. When you are not pursuing the devil, he will be after you. A little payer every day is better than many hours of prayer, once in a while. In Luke 22:40 Jesus exhorted His disciples to seize the future through prayer, warning them: *"...pray that you enter not enter into temptation."*

Never wait for the need for prayers before you pray. Every time there is an urgent need to pray, it means there is a problem, many of which could have been avoided in the first case. There will always be emergencies, however, many spiritual emergencies are borne out of negligence and failure to take pre-emptive steps in prayers.

"Onward, Christian soldiers, marching as to war,
With the cross of Jesus going on before.
Christ, the royal Master, leads against the foe;
Forward into battle see His banners go!"
- Sabine Baring-Gould (1865).

57

PROTECTION PRAYERS

In life one problem can easily escalate into another, one crisis can quickly give rise to several others. Jesus encouraged us to pray that the Father delivers us from evil. Problems are a fact of life, but unnecessary problems can easily sap your energy and resources, as well as keep you extra busy and stressed. One way to pre-empt this is to plan your prayer life such that you can screen yourself and loved ones from preventable troubles. You must aim to protect yourself before the enemy strikes; also launch pre-emptive strikes against the enemies before they make the first move.

I believe in praying regularly for protection, whilst taking every precaution to keep myself and loved ones safe and secure. The prayer of protection also enables you to preserve the victory already gained in a variety of ways. The devil is ever looking for inroads to your life. He is ever on the lookout for weak or non-existing lines of defence. A football side need defence players as good as, or even better than strikers. Whatever you achieve in life can be easily wiped out if you are not well insulated against the enemy's onslaughts.

The prayer of protection can be likened to defensive warfare. It is true that the best form of defence is attack, it is equally true that when you attack you do not have to leave yourself exposed to the enemy's activities. You must protect yourself and supplies from the enemy. In warfare even when you are continually advancing you will have to constantly protect yourself in all directions. In protective praying, you simply cover your life, achievements and belongings from the hands of the evil one. God Has Promised that:

> *"He shall cover thee with his feathers, and under his wings shall thou trust: His truth shall be thy shield and buckler. For He shall give his angels charge over thee, to keep thee in all thy ways."* (Psal91:4, 11).

It can be said that if God has promised to protect us what is the point of praying? Well, the same God has said we must ask, seek and knock to tap into His blessings.

God Protects His People

During their wilderness journey God protected the children of Israel with the pillars of cloud and fire day and night (Numbers 10:35).

- God protected Shadrach, Meshach and Abednego from the fiery furnace (Daniel 3: 22-27).
- God protected Daniel in the Lion's den (Daniel 6: 13-24).
- God has designated His angels as ministering spirits to believers, also giving them the responsibility of safe-guarding us (Hebrew 1:14).
- During their wilderness journeys God put his terror upon the cities round about His people (Genesis 35:5).
- God protected and delivered Ezra and his colleagues from marauders when they travelled to rebuild the walls of Jerusalem, carrying large sums of money (Ezra 8:31).

Pray deliberately for protection over your family, finances, job and other aspects. One major crisis is enough to completely upset and dis-stabilise your life, plunge you into untold hardship, and cost you unwarranted prayer hours. The best way to prevent this is to pre-empt the enemy.

Pray daily for protection for yourself, loved ones and your society from evil activities.

A Story of Divine Protection

Several years ago whilst pastoring a church in Ibadan, Nigeria, a team of our senior church leaders travelled to represent our church at a funeral ceremony. The team was made up of nearly all the senior leaders of the church. On their way back late in the night, for some mysterious reason the driver of the minibus in which they travelled veered completely off the road and drove into the woods, narrowly missing ramming into a tree. Thanks to God, everyone came out of the vehicle unhurt in what could have ended up as major disaster. None of the passengers could explain why there was such a great escape.

A day or two prior to that trip, I had reported in my church office in the morning with some prayer burden and restlessness in my spirit. The urge to pray was so strong I knew something serious was about to happen. I told my secretary I would not be seeing anyone for a while, and shut myself in to pray. I found myself engaged in a fierce and unusual spiritual warfare that persisted. I prayed for an hour, but the burden would not lift from my heart. I continued for about another hour until I felt relieved and God assured me the battle was over. When the team returned from that trip and narrated their experience, I immediately remembered my spiritual experience, and quickly connected the accident with my earlier spiritual battle, which was won at the place of prayer. Prayer can protect God's people from a lot of trouble.

God will always defend his people. He never wants us to be taken by surprise. Commit yourself to Him on a continuous basis. Respond promptly to his leadings, pray when He spurs you to. I cannot imagine what would have happened if I had not prayed when he laid the burden in my heart that blessed morning. Pray for God's protection over every aspect of your life. God wants to protect you and your loved ones. He wants to shield your business, job and all your undertakings. Your ministry, dream and vision need protecting. Pray continually for God to insulate you against satanic activities. God is *"...a strength to the poor. Strength to the needy in his distress, A refuge from the storm, A shade from the heat, from the blast of the terrible ones as a storm against the wall"* (Isaiah 25:4).

Praying for protection shields you from fighting unwarranted battles. In physical warfare, unnecessary battles lead to unplanned and wasteful use of manpower, money and time. It can lead to costly detractions from original aims and objections. Praying for divine covering has the benefit of safeguarding you and your belongings from everything that would potentially distract you from your main focus in life. Make the prayer of protection a normal part of your daily prayer.

58

POSITIONS OF PRAYER

Effective prayer has little to do with position or physical postures adopted at the time of praying. Some people believe one must kneel every prayer time. This is an awesome position to assume in prayer. Nonetheless, the heart posture is more important to God than physical comportment. Whatever is convenient for you is fine with God. Only be honest with yourself- on a cold winter morning it may not be wise to cover yourself with a blanket whilst lying in bed to pray when you are only half awake. I guess you know what is likely to happen.

The bible teaches us to do all things decently and in order as God is not the author of confusion. This is the most important thing about the position you adopt when you pray. If it is decent, orderly, convenient and sustainable, and your heart is right before God, I believe it is acceptable to Him.

The Kneeling Position

Kneeling to pray makes some people feel like they are really honouring God in prayer. I personally love and enjoy it, but these days I cannot kneel for as long as I used to do about 20 years ago. This is a great way to pray so long as it is convenient for you. Some people might find this posture difficult due to health or age issues, but for those who can, it is a reverential position to adopt in prayer. It is entirely up to you; if it is your preferred method, and your health permits, by all means enjoy kneeling before God to pray.

- Jesus knelt to pray (Luke 22:41)
- Solomon knelt to pray (1Kings 8:54)
- Paul knelt in prayer (Ephesians 3:14)
- Peter knelt before God in prayer (Acts 9:40)

Kneeling to pray can enhance concentration. It may also signify self-discipline, especially if done for long hours. It could sometimes be an endurance test as it may be a less comfortable position than others. Kneeling to pray may portray surrender to, and reverence for our heavenly father.

Standing / Walking to Pray

You are perfectly at liberty to stand and talk to your father in heaven. Standing to pray could involve walking and praying. Often when l stand or walk whilst praying, l tend to be more effective except when I am too tired. During warfare or more aggressive prayers- (binding and loosing), l find this a very dynamic and effective position to adopt.

Apart from the spiritual benefits l always end up feeling like l have worked out in the gym especially when prayer-walking on the street for anything between 30 minutes and one hour. I end up feeling very refreshed and physically fit. Walking and praying daily for 30 minutes or more could save you the cost of a fitness club membership. Jesus made reference to standing to pray, in the bible (Mark11:25). When you stand to pray, it signals that you are set for battle. Standing to pray is a fighting position which may indicate battle-readiness. I have also found this posture very stimulating- when I am having difficulty initiating prayer momentum, standing or walking to pray has frequently given me the boost needed for effective take off.

Prostrating and Praying

Lying prostrate before God is a reflection of humility, surrender and resignation to God. Nothing can portray humility and total submission to God than lying prostrate before Him. Some people fall flat on their face when they pray. A lot of us Christians do this occasionally especially when we are gripped by the awesomeness of God. What an awesome way to pray! Some people do it when they feel overcome by God's glory. Before His crucifixion, Jesus fell on His face and prayed: *"O My Father, if it is possible, let this cup pass from me; nevertheless, not as I will"* (Mathew 26:39).

Laying Down to Pray

Some people may query lying down to pray. So long as this does not become a habit, I see nothing wrong with it, if done particularly in private prayers. It could encourage you to drift into sleep instead of praying, and may not be best suited for aggressive praying when needed. For some people it could even be a sign of laziness in rising from bed. What is important is your ability to pray effectively. It is better to lay and pray than not to pray at all. A sick person may find this the only way they can pray. In the winter months when it is usually very cold in the morning you will need a lot of discipline to pray in this position.

Some nights I pray in bed before I sleep, sometimes for a reasonable amount of time. On a number of occasions I have had flashes of vision whilst in bed; I immediately commit the matter to God before I finally drift off. God does not care so long as you can pray effectively (Psalm 63:6).

Sitting to Pray

This could be very helpful when you are tired and you must pray. When I am very tired I find it useful to sit on the floor and pray. It is not always comfortable, but who wants to be too comfortable at prayer times, anyway?

There are other prayer positions not addressed in this section. Varying your prayer postures might be helpful in achieving your daily prayer goals. Some people sleep off on their knees because they are adamant about kneeling to pray. Many people find themselves wandering off in their thoughts and getting visually distracted when they stand and pray. Some people end up never praying just because they choose to lay and pray. It is possible to sit comfortably on your sofa to pray and end up sleeping because you feel too comfortable.

Any position most suitable to you is acceptable to God in as much as you can achieve your prayer objectives. In some group prayers, the prayer leader may specifically tell people what posture to take depending on the prevailing situation. I do not believe there is a superior prayer posture unless God specifically instructs otherwise. Sometimes you may be so awed by God's presence that you cannot stand or sit before Him. You may sometimes find that in a prayer session, you will adopt a combination of all or some of the postures discussed above. Any position that helps you to best accomplish your prayer goals should be adopted whenever you go before the Lord in prayer.

59

PRAY UNTIL SOMETHING HAPPENS (P.U.S.H)

If God did not want you to get results in prayer, He would not ask you to pray. Why give up on your prayer goals shortly or long before you receive the answers? A few Christians have yet to learn how to hold unto God in prayer until they have a breakthrough. You must pray until something happens. A lot of people pray, but have little or no patience to continue until something happens. Keep 'pushing' your prayer, like a woman in labour until you get your expected results.

Great problems require substantial prayers, and most extensive prayers demand enormous amount of time to carry through. For instance praying for a revival or national transformation are not projects that are likely to be achieved in a few weeks or months; of course God does not need long prayers over a long period before He shows up in a situation. The Bible records several instances when people prayed and did not immediately get the answers. They went on to pray until something happened; never give up knocking before the door is answered.

How Long Do I have To Pray about One Thing?

The question of how long an individual should pray about an item has no single answer. It all depends on what you are praying about- its seriousness, urgency and how much longer you can wait before you get the answer. As you will find elsewhere in this book, just because there is delay does not mean God has not heard your prayers. However, you may have to keep praying until you receive a physical manifestation, or to the point when you receive the Holy Spirit's conviction in your heart that your prayer has been answered.

There could be a wide range of reasons why certain prayers take longer than others before the answers manifest. Whatever the case, it is nothing to do with God's ability or willingness to help us. Like in the case of Daniel for example (Daniel 10:2), it could be that there is some demonic opposition to your victory which God will expect you to overcome through spiritual warfare. Other reasons may be that God wants you to learn some lessons or has even answered the prayer in a different way. Some of the reasons why answer to prayers could delay have been treated in another section of this book.

How Many Times Do I Have To Pray For One Thing?

Jesus taught in Luke 18:1 that we ought to always pray and not to faint. A lot of people believe that once you pray about anything in a session of prayer, you do not need to continue praying. Some believe it is a demonstration of lack of faith to keep praying about one item over and again- after all God is not deaf. Let us examine the following passages of scriptures and what they say about praying until something happens.

1. The Wall of Jericho did not fall in one day, although God could have done it in one minute. God asked His people to march round the city, once every day for six days. And on the seventh day they were instructed to march round the city seven times with the priests blowing the trumpet- and then the miracle happened! The Wall and the city fell to the hands of the Israelites. God could have asked them to march around the city once and for all, instead He choose to do it a different way (Joshua 6: 3-4).

2. Through prayers Elijah shut up the heavens from giving rain in the days of evil King Ahab. When Elijah wanted rain again, he prayed- once, twice and thrice, but it failed to rain. Then he continued to have sessions of prayers for up to seven times before it rained. God could have sent down rain the first, second or third time. But He chose otherwise. Some problems require a series of prayer retreats or fasting and prayer sessions before something eventually happens. Never give up until you see the manifestation of the answer to your prayers. (1kings 18: 42-44; James 5: 17-18). Elijah was human like you and I. He had the same weaknesses, challenges, fears, doubts and obstacles. He was probably more discouraged than you and I at a point in his life, but he persisted in prayer until he prayed through.

3. Daniel was a great man of God- a prophet, a scholar and a man of unusual faith who received and interpreted dreams and visions. Even with all these qualifications, Daniel needed to pray on a particular occasion for 21 days before he received answers to his prayers. God could have removed every obstacle from the way much earlier. From the very first day he prayed God heard him, but the answer did not arrive until 21 days later (Daniel 10: 2).

4. Elisha was a mighty prophet who performed at least twice the recorded miracles of Elijah. He was a man well acquainted with, and anointed by God. He too had to pray and lay himself upon a dead child several times before the child came back to life. This was the same Elisha whose skeletons later brought a dead man back to life – by mere contact. I cannot understand why God did not answer his prayer the first time when he wanted to raise a dead child to life. The key issue is that Elisha kept praying until his prayers were answered, God choses to do it that way sometimes (1kings 4: 34-35).

5. Jesus had to go through two sessions of prayer to open the eyes of a particular blind man in Bethsaida (Mark 8: 22-25). The first

time Jesus prayed for the man he saw only faintly, even seeing humans as trees. Jesus did not need a long or repeated process of prayer to heal the blind. Only one word from Him could have settled the matter. God alone understands why it took two prayer sessions for the blind to regain full sight. Yours is to learn lessons from it. Trust the Father like He did and keep praying until your heart desires come to pass.

Continue in prayer until something happens. Never give up too quickly. God has your interest at heart. He is touched by every pain you experience and moved by every tear you shed. Establish clear deadlines on when you must complete a prayer project and press towards your target until your prayers are answered. Never give up praying until you see the treasures of heaven released to you.

60

PRAYER PARTNERSHIP

Partnership is a very popular phenomenon in today's world. Partnership relationships have grown increasingly popular over the years, and in business circles many organisations can trace their survival and competitiveness to it. Partnership involves co-operation, association or alliance between one or more groups or individuals working towards a common goal.

Jesus underscored the importance of partnership in Matthew 18:19:

> *"...again I say unto you, that if two of you shall agree on earth as touching anything that they shall ask, it shall be done for them of my father which is in heaven."* Furthermore, Ecclesiastes 4:11-12, states: *"Again, if two lie together, then they have heat: but how can one be warm alone? And if one prevails against him, two shall withstand him; and a threefold cord is not quickly broken."*

These passages emphasise the importance of partnerships in whatever we do. Prayer partnership is a very powerful tool for accomplishing more for God in intercession and spiritual warfare. When Christians come together in prayers, God multiplies their prayer power much more than individual prayers would attract.

Partners in Progress

> *"Iron sharpeneth iron; so a man sharpeneth the countenance of his friend"* (Proverbs 27:17).

Uniting and praying with others have something in common with business partnerships, where two parties band together towards a common goal. They may have dissimilar ideas, competences and cultures to some extent, but in most cases, they will have something in common. The difference between them and kingdom partnerships is that the Holy Spirit is a unifying force between God's people, whereas countless numbers of business partnerships somehow collapse along the line.

> *"If two of you shall agree on earth as touching anything that you shall ask, it shall be done for you of my Father which is in heaven."* (Matthew 18:19).

Jesus meant for two or more people to mingle together for prayer and other spiritual activities, and He would show up amongst them. God's blessings flow more freely when His children unite to pursue common objectives.

What the Bible Says About Partnership

1. Two are better than one (Ecclesiastes 4:9-10)
2. Christians are living stones built upon one another into a spiritual house (1Peter 2:5)
3. If we walk in the light like Jesus, we have fellowship with one another (1John 1:7)
4. Where two or three are gathered together in His name Jesus promises to be in their midst (Matthew 18:20)
5. God wants us to bear one another's burden (Galatians 6:2)
6. The bible says we should pray for one another (Galatians 5:16)

The bible is filled with examples of all sorts of partnerships. God believes in people working together; He perfected the idea through marriage relationship

How to Go About It

Prayer partnership may be more effective if it is between individuals with similar interests, vision, mission or profession. Common interests will allow for easy bonding and smoother prayer efforts.

It is not advisable to be a prayer partner with the opposite sex where there are just two of you in the group. Same sex prayer partnership is safer as it gives people the liberty to open up to one another; it can also help to prevent awkward and ungodly ties. A male and female in a prayer relationship could fall into the traps of the devil. This should be avoided at all costs as prevention is better than cure.

Cooperation in prayer should not be limited to spouses, family or people of the same spiritual group alone. The body of Christ is one and it would benefit God's Kingdom for us to join hands in prayer with other Christians at intergroup, regional, national and global levels. Geographical location should not present a barrier; with modern technology it is possible these days to hold video and audio conferences without having to be in the same room or location. The key issue is to have a kindred and united spirit. You can even agree in prayer with other believers around the world on the same subject, at the same hour without being physically present.

God wants us to both love and work with one another. He wants us to maximise the benefits that come with depending on one another. Every believer must extend a hand of fellowship and relationship to other believers. Praying together is one of the best ways to make this happen. As good as individual praying may be, the force that prayer partnership generates is far greater than what any individual can trigger in their private closet.

61

QUENCH NOT THE SPIRIT

The Holy Spirit is behind every prayer success. His absence will eliminate the cutting edge from prayer. Prayer is both communion and communication, and the Spirit is the oil that keeps the process running smoothly. Without the presence and influence of the Holy Spirit prayer will lack potency and dynamism. To grieve means to 'to afflict with deep sorrow', while to quench means to put out, like we pour out water to quench fire.

How the Spirit May Be Quenched

Everyone can tell when a physical fire has been extinguished. There may still be some form of heat but it will no longer be fit for purpose. Some people have spiritual heat but no fire. The fire of the Spirit is the agent that powers your prayer life. When you begin to sense that your spiritual temperature is falling below comfort, it is time to search your heart and discover the reason why you are running low on the presence of the Holy Spirit. Unhealthy association with non-believers, especially the opposite sex, is a fast lane to zero temperature. Seeing, saying, or tasting things forbidden by God can very quickly squeeze the presence of the anointing out of a person's life. Lying, bitterness, un-forgiveness and the absence of regular fellowship with God and His word are a recipe for spiritual disaster. These actions can hinder the move of the Holy Spirit in your life.

The Dangers of Quenching the Spirit

To quench the Spirit simply means doing things that limit the flow of, and extinguish the fire of the Spirit in your life. Any form of sin or disobedience to God can suffocate the Holy Spirit out of a Christian's life. When a child of God grieves the Spirit, it obstructs the flow of His power in their life. Their peace, fellowship with the Father, assurance of salvation and divine influence will be affected. Anyone that continues in disobedience and sin, the Holy Spirit will gradually withdraw from their life, sometimes unnoticed for a long time. Very rarely will the Holy Spirit dramatically exit the life of God's children; this makes it difficult for many people to realise that something has gone wrong.

Quenching or grieving the Spirit will make prayer frustrating, unexciting and passionless. Limited influence of the Spirit in the life of a child of God will lead to boring prayer times, decline in faith, and lack of confidence in fellowship with God. It will usually take some time for many Christians to recover from this state. It is therefore safer in the first instance not to let it happen, because if you slumber, Satan will plunder your estate. Diminished influence of the Holy Spirit in the life of a Child of God can lead to lifelessness. This in turn will lower their spiritual energy levels and render them powerless to tackle evil forces.

Avoid Grieving or Quenching the Holy Spirit

Of course, when a person offends the Spirit, He will be grieved, and the person will definitely know from within that the Holy Spirit is unhappy. If offensive acts against the Holy Spirit continue, it is only a matter of time before a Christian becomes empty of God's presence.

You need the power of the Holy Spirit to sustain you as a Christian and to keep your prayer life in top-flight. The first thing to do is to avoid grieving or quenching the Spirit and if it ever happens, quickly go to God for restoration. Do this swiftly to get yourself back in good form as quickly as possible. The faster you can settle your short comings with

God the better it is for your fellowship with Him. The bible says we cannot continue in sin and expect grace to abound.

Grieve not the Spirit because it will weaken your prayer life. Quench not the Spirit because doing so will extinguish your prayer fire. Listen to and obey God's Spirit all the time. No Christian will survive or thrive without the Spirit's influence, and no prayer life will flourish in the absence of the Holy Spirit. Listen to your inner promptings and cautions on a daily basis, and never take God for granted. In the book of Proverbs God reprimands people who refuse to listen to His reproof:

> *"How long, ye simple ones, will ye love simplicity? And the scorners delight in their scorning, and fools hate knowledge? Turn you at my reproof: behold, I will pour out my Spirit unto you, I will make known my words unto you. Because I have called, and ye refused; I have stretched out my hand, and no man regarded; But ye have set at nought all my counsel, and would non of my reproof: ... Then shall they call upon me, but I will not answer; they shall seek me early, but they shall not find me"* (Proverbs 1:22-25, 28).

God turned His back on Israel whenever they deliberately resisted the Holy Spirit. Grieving the Holy Spirit makes you vulnerable in spiritual warfare. When you stay under the influence of the Spirit, your protection is guaranteed, and you will continue to enjoy divine flow of every blessing that God channels through the Holy Spirit. We see this in the life of Samson. Before he sold out to the philistines, he enjoyed an unusual measure of the power of the Holy Spirit, but when he compromised his call and relationship with God, the Holy Spirit lifted off him. This was a disaster for him as he became hopeless, powerless and defenceless; he became an easy prey to the Philistines. The withdrawal of the Holy Spirit from Samson placed his life in jeopardy. He became a slave to the philistines and eventually died what appeared to be an untimely death. You can only pray as successfully as you yield control of your life to God. The extent to which you allow the work of the Holy Spirit in you will always dictate the flow of the Spirit in your life.

62

QUIETNESS BEFORE GOD

"The LORD shall fight for you, and ye shall hold your peace"
(Exodus 14:14).

Your heavenly father wants to listen to you pray. He also expects you to stay quiet and let Him speak. A quiet spirit calmly looks unto God for salvation and deliverance, is not hasty, does not give up too soon, but waits for God for as long as it takes. It blocks out the noises of the world and calmly listens for what God has to say. A quiet spirit refuses to be restless and rash, rather it hopefully looks unto God for instruction and direction.

Quiet and Confident

"For thus saith the Lord God, the Holy One of Israel; In returning and rest shall ye be saved; in quietness and confidence shall be your strength" (Isaiah 30:15).

It is not easy to connect with an unsettled heart; when your heart is in a peaceful mode it signals a readiness to receive from, and be inspired by God. It also indicates that you are certain that God will listen to and answer your prayers. People who allow themselves to become ruffled by difficult situations will have trouble getting the most from their prayer times. Have you ever tried to communicate important things to someone who was restless and agitated? You may have discovered during or after the conversation that the person was not listening to you with good attention. The same happens when we go before God allowing too many things to overcrowd our minds. God will find it difficult to get our attention, and when He speaks we might not be able to hear Him.

God miraculously delivered His people from Egypt and took them on a journey to the Promised Land. They witnessed unprecedented signs and wonders, yet they failed to rest themselves in the Lord whenever they encountered dangers and powerful enemies. They even clamoured that they wanted to return to Egypt rather than continue to face challenges in the wilderness. They actually began to make plans to return to Egypt- the place of bondage, from which God had previously delivered them. That is what happens when people lose their cool. They become disoriented and irrational. God was very disheartened because He had proved Himself through mighty signs and wonders to these people. Staying calm in God's presence is something every believer must learn just like we develop other habits. Train your spirit to stay still before God. Philippians 4:6-7 says:

> *"Be careful for nothing; but in everything by prayer and supplication with thanksgiving let your requests be made known unto God. And the peace of God, which passeth all understanding shall keep your heart and minds through Christ Jesus." "It is vain for you to rise up early, sit up late, to eat the bread of sorrows: for so He giveth His beloved sleep"* (Psalm 127:2).

What is the point of getting flustered every time the enemy frightens you? If you have prayed, leave it in the hands of God. If you have not prayed, put things in the hands of God. Keep your peace and go to sleep. Jesus once asked His disciples, *"And which of you with taking thought can add to his stature one cubit? If ye then be not able to do that thing which is least why take ye thought for the rest?"* (Luke 12:25-26).

After you have prayed do not be hasty to take decisions without first staying silent in God's presence. It is in those quiet moments that you can receive directions from your heavenly Father. Moving too quickly to act after you have prayed can cause further harm. Remember, prayer is not all about talking to God, listening to God is more helpful that talking to Him. Observing regular quiet periods in God's presence, means your ears and heart are open to receive from Him.

Quietude Leads to Clarity

It is difficult to hear someone speak clearly in a market place. We live in a very noisy world- all kinds of noises. These make it hard to hear when God is ministering to our spirit. A person who cannot hear God speak, or would not listen when God speaks will continue to find prayer a tricky task. In Numbers 9:8, Moses emphasised the importance of quietness in hearing God: *"...Moses said unto them, stand still, and I will hear what the Lord will command me concerning you"* When the psalmist had difficulties quieting his spirit, he prayed, *"Why art thou cast down, O my soul? And why art thou disquieted in me? Hope thou in God: for I shall yet praise Him for the help of His countenance"* (Psalm 42:5).

You must deliberately resist every act of the enemy to unsettle and cripple you from praying triumphantly. Satan will do everything to create crisis within your inner man and your mind to strip you of the power needed to pray. God always has something to say, and unless you stay still you may never hear His voice. Fears, doubts, busyness, daily negative news and personal crisis are some of the things that can hinder us from being still before God. Constantly clear your mind of every unhelpful material and patiently learn to stay calm in God's presence. You cannot receive from God when you are hearing too many voices. You can also not claim to have faith in God if you cannot relax in His presence.

REFRESH AND REFILL

In physical warfare, an army can only be victorious to the degree that they are supplied and replenished with resources. The bible says we are God's soldiers, and are constantly battling spiritual foes. To be successful in this warfare every Christian needs to constantly go before God for a time of refreshing, replenishing and refiling. It is crucial to go before God to cool off and be re-energised because war is characterised by emotional, physical and material 'tear and wear'.

God is the only one that can fortify and breathe new life into you when you become exhausted and burnt-out spiritually. Genuine prayers involves you emptying yourself out completely; although a spiritual exercise, active and continuous praying can sometimes drain you of both physical and emotional energy. You need to constantly go before God for refuelling to avoid becoming a casualty of war.

When to refresh and Refill

A stitch in time saves nine. No one can really prescribe when and how to set time aside to re-enliven your spiritual state. You will need to look out for some of the common characteristics of spiritual burn out. When lack of spiritual desire or motivation begin to set in, it is an indication that you are running out of spiritual steam. If you find yourself compromising your faith in little or major ways then it is time to 'top up'. Lack of motivation for studying the bible and lack of appetite for prayer are red flags that something is amiss. If a Christian begins to find himself unusually and frequently irritant and impatient with people, it means it is time to re-charge their spiritual batteries. God has promised to breathe fresh life into His children:

> "And I will make them and the places round about my hill a blessing, and I will cause the shower to come down in his season; there shall be showers of blessing" (Ezekiel 34:26).

Healing For Spiritual Wounds

Quality prayer life is moderated by a constantly renewed spirit. As a Christian it is not unusual to experience occasional spiritual and emotional drain. Paul recognised this and reflected, *"For which cause we faint not; but though our outward man perish, yet the inward man is renewed day by day"* (2 Corinthians 4:16).

If you get to the point when you feel like your mind, spirit or even your physical body has been squashed, take time out alone with God. Better still, do not wait for this to happen; make every effort to schedule regular times of at least two days or more alone with God so He can 'jump start' your spiritual life again. This is the path to a consistent and sound relationship with God.

Break Up the Fallow Ground

Fallow ground is an agricultural or horticultural terminology. It is land that has been left unused, uncultivated or unplanted for some time. Fallow ground represents inactivity, dormancy and idleness. It is easy to relapse into what I will refer to as 'spiritual sabbaticals'- a long period of silence, quietness and spiritual inactivity. Once, when the people of Israel found themselves in this state, God sent the prophet Hosea to tell them:

"...Sow to yourselves in righteousness, reap in mercy; break up your fallow ground: for it is time to seek the LORD, till He come and rain righteousness upon you" (Hosea 10:12).

Seek the Lord's face, present your fallow ground (heart) to Him and expect His spiritual rain upon you. Do not stay in a dry condition for too long. Every additional day may compound your situation. The longer a child of God stays in a dormant spiritual state, the more complicated things will become. To stay in top prayer form, you need regular times away from family, job and business to spend purely alone with God.

Spiritual Restoration

God is in the business of continually fixing things when they go wrong in the lives of His people. He never leaves His people in a state of disrepair if given the right of way. If you fall out of grace He is available and ever ready to reinstate you. If any part of you is broken, God is waiting to mend it. He is the master restorer, if you spot or feel any spiritual inadequacy, all you need to do is go to Him for a complete overhaul of your state. You must reclaim everything you have ever lost to the enemy. Given the chance to move freely in your life, God will:

- Restore to you what the enemy has stolen (Genesis 20:14).
- Reinstate you to your original glory (Genesis 40:13).
- Restore healing and health to you. (Matthew 12:13).
- Restore double of whatever you have lost (Job 42:10).
- Rebuild the ruins of your life and ministry (Isaiah 58:12).

God never neglects His soldiers if they are wounded in the battle. Some spiritual casualties are due to personal carelessness, not withstanding, God cares so much about us that whenever we run out of morale and strength He is ever ready to lift and reinstate us. Your prayer life will be a shining example if you put in every effort to regularly go before God for a time of spiritual restoration and revival.

64

RESPONSIBILITY

Responsibility, according to BusinessDictionary.com means: "duty or obligation to satisfactorily perform a task (assigned by someone, or created by one's own promise) that one must fulfil, and which has a consequent penalty for failure"

Jesus finished the work of redemption on the cross of Calvary; God has fulfilled His part of the plan of redemption and our total wellbeing. As custodians of God's grace, we can carry out our duties and responsibilities by praying for God's work and our society. Our people and systems will never fall in line on their own, we must shape history through the power of prayer. It is the responsibility of every Christian to do this. Many situations can only be changed by the power of prayer and someone has to do the praying and provoke divine intervention. Prayer can prevent human errors, resolve political and religious crisis and avert economic disasters. Through prayers we can both determine who should and should not lead out societies, the events that happen in our own lives and the degree to which the devil can operate; again someone has to gain this insight, take responsibility and make it happen.

We are individually answerable for prayer success because we have access to everything needed to control events by prayers. God banks on us to shape the events of the world through prayers, but a very small percentage of us care little about anything from which we will have no immediate personal benefit. The fact that we have been redeemed by the Lord automatically places this onus on us, and it is not a matter of choice.

Take Responsibility

Very few people like taking responsibility or being told to do so. No one wants to take the blame when things go wrong.

People who fail to own their situation are more likely to give up in difficult circumstances. They are least inclined to fight their way through by prayer when the going gets tough. They are very quick to blame others when they experience failure. Every child of God will give account for not living a holy life, paying their tithes and not carrying out other Christian duties. Similarly if we fail to pray for perishing souls, or stand in the gap to help others escape evil or disaster, then, we will be accountable to God. We share in the blame because we have access to God's power and are His representatives on earth; in particular, anything God will do on earth, He relies on us to accomplish through prayers. You must maximise the possibilities of prayer and bring God's blessings upon as many people as possible. We will blame other people less frequently if we take our prayer obligation more seriously.

When People Fail To Take Responsibility

When people fail to take responsibility they will find a way to console themselves by doing a number of things:

1. **Accusing**
    Rather than paying the price of prayer, most Christians go about pointing the finger at others. Unfortunately, this does not do anything to change their situation. Even if somebody else is actually the cause of your problem, you can always turn things around through prayers.

2. Whining

When things go wrong, when answers to prayers delay, many people become upset and drift into the habit of moaning, murmuring and complaining. Whimpers are never winners. Grumbling and fault finding will only make things worse. When you accept to take full charge of your situation, you will have the power to pray or deal with it- not before then.

3. Excusing

Failing to sort things out can lead to self-defence or self-justification – both of which are recipes for further failure. People who do not pray often come with excuses such as lack of time and being too busy or tired. Some even suggest they are not great at praying (any one can learn to pray effectively). Excuses are the hallmarks of people who fail to be in charge, while taking responsibility is the greatest strength of successful people.

4. Victim Mentality

People with a victim mentality believe nothing can be done to improve their situation; that no amount of prayer will solve their problem. They feel helpless and hopeless, become disempowered and feel rejected. They give up ownership of their lives, and wallow in self-pity. This crippling attitude does not allow for progress in life. People with a victim mentality may not even want to pray at all, and when they do pray, they find it hard to trust God. It is all part of Satan's attacks on their mind, and God asks us to resist Satan *"… steadfast in the faith, knowing that the same afflictions are accomplished in your brethren that are in the world"* (1 Peter 5:8-9).

You are the architect of your life, the driver of your destiny. Go the extra mile to make things happen. Pray harder until you keep Satan on the run. Satan may withstand for a while, but if you keep up the prayer fight, he is bound to flee ultimately. When Germany invaded

Poland in 1939, and turned its aggression on Britain's neighbours, France, wartime British Prime Minister, Winston Churchill, promised his country that he would offer blood, toil, tears and sweat to deliver victory over Germany. With that unwavering commitment he fought until Germany was defeated by the allies.

Germany was a dreadful enemy at the time, but Churchill and his allies eventually defeated the Germans. It was not easy, but it happened. You can also win through prayers, despite the odds so long as you do not leave control of things to someone else, or hope that things would change on their own. If we all continue to take responsibility for praying Satan will be very limited in his operations and the kingdom of God will have a greater influence on the world.

65

SUBMISSION TO AUTHORITY

Submission to authority is a key teaching of the bible which is vital to successful praying. Authorities represent plural powers such as the government, state officials, organisation, family and other figures (including spiritual leaders) who hold the right, influence and power to determine or direct what we do. God respects every one of these, whether they are Christians or not.

Submission to authority is not about handing your life over to someone else. Neither is it about making yourself a doormat and relinquishing your God given ability and freedom. It is not a licence for anyone to manipulate you, notwithstanding, God's word is very clear on the need for His people to cooperate with, and yield to those who are in positions of authority. *"Obey your leaders and submit to them, for they are keeping watch over your souls, as those who will have to give an account. Let them do this with joy and not groaning, for that would be of no advantage to you"* (Hebrews 13:17).

There is widespread mistrust and suspicion towards people in authority because nobody wants to let someone else take charge of their lives. One of the reasons is that a number of authority figures attempt to intimidate and dominate people who are under their leadership and many others fail to live up to expectation. The bible projects submission as something very positive and pleasing to God. Jesus submitted to the father despite the pain and shame of having to go to the cross (Acts2:27, Colossians

3:5, 12-14), and this brought salvation to the entire world. We must not feel coerced or threatened to submit but must do it as unto the Lord. It is God's own way of making His blessings flow from top to bottom.

Submission and Prayers

All authority is ordained or at least, permitted by God. For this reason God says,

> "Let every soul be subject unto the higher powers. For there is no power but of God: the powers that be are ordained of God. Whosoever therefore resists the powers, resists the ordinance of God: and they that resist shall receive to themselves damnation." (Romans 13:1-2).

The bottom line is that every authority, secular and spiritual are ordained by God. Failing to submit to them is flagrant disobedience to God's Word. One can argue that God expects us to submit only to those rulers who are good and just. The bible does not say so, instead it says, *"Wherefore, ye must needs be subject, not only for wrath, but also for conscience sake"* (Romans 13:5).

When People submit to their leaders, they are invariably submitting to God, and this perfectly positions them for spiritual victory: *"Submit yourselves therefore to God. Resist the devil, and he will flee from you"* (James 4:7). There is a strong connection between victory in spiritual warfare and submission to God and His delegated authority. Rebellion is the opposite of submission and the bible makes it clear that, *"God setteth the solitary in families: He bringeth out those who are bound with chains: but the rebellious dwell in a dry land"* (Psalm 68:6).

People get put off by God's command to submit because they have had nasty experiences with leadership or have found many leaders to be abusive, exploitative and deceptive. Independence from authority has been present in man since the fall. Everyone wants to be completely free to do whatever they like; abusive leaders and father figures have made the situation more complicated.

You can firmly and respectfully confront a leader who is not working according to the will of God without taking matters into your hands. Taking matters into your hands would put you in direct collision with God, who in the first place, permitted a person to be a leader. A rebellious heart towards authority exposes you to demonic attacks. This will make you fight more spiritual battles than you should.

God took part of Moses' anointing and put it into the leaders and elders of Israel, and whenever they rebelled against Moses, God always said they rebelled not against Moses, but against Him. That clarifies how much value God places on spiritual leadership. Leadership structure is God's way of bringing order into His family. Rebellion is a direct affront on God's institution, which is why when Saul disobeyed the command of Samuel to utterly destroy the Amalekites, God rejected Saul and His future generations from ruling over Israel. Saul did pray and ask for forgiveness somehow, but his prayers were never answered because God says,

> "...rebellion is as the sin of witchcraft, and stubbornness is as iniquity and idolatry" (1Samuel 15:23).

Submission and obedience play an important role in effective prayer because if you cannot submit to spiritual and secular authorities that you see every day, you cannot claim that you have yielded control of your life to God. If you have not given full control of your life to God, He will not empower you to put the devil to flight.

66

SECRET SINS CORRUPT PRAYER ANOINTING

Nothing in the world stifles prayer more that sin. A secret sin is the ugly and dark side that you do not wish anyone ever knew something about. A lot of Christians started out brilliantly in their Christian journey but along the line they allowed demonic infiltration and caved in to the pressures of the flesh. They fall into all kinds of sins which no one would dare associate with them. Sin corrupts and erodes your ability to pray productively. Sin dilutes spiritual energy and eliminates the cutting edge from your prayer. God cannot stand sin, and a sinful person cannot stand in God's presence.

Cleanse Me from Secret Faults

A secret fault is so called, because it is exhibited where and when no one can notice. Some would not even let their spouses or loved ones, much less other people know about it. Why? The embarrassment, shame and disgrace will be unthinkable. There are no secrets before God and it is for your own good that you lay bare every secret before God as they cannot be hidden from His watchful eyes. Secret sins are spiritually crippling and can gradually eat away the fabric of your spiritual life. The psalmist prayed: *"Cleanse thou me from secret sins" (Psalm 19: 12).*

Conversely he says: "my body wasted away, but I acknowledged my sin to thee, and my iniquity I did not hide" (Psalm 32:3, 5).

One of the fearful consequences of living in secret sins is highlighted in Matthew 10:26-27: *"...for there is nothing covered that shall not be revealed; and hid that shall not be known."* If you are indulged in secrets sins, it will not take long before the impact begins to show in the open, even if they have been cleverly concealed. Prayer and sin are great enemies; if you are sinning you cannot pray effectively, if you are praying it can keep you from sinning. Desperately ask for God's help to free you from every known secret sin.

Consequences of Sin

God in His mercy disciplines His children when they fail to repent from sin. He is very patient and allows time for repentance and change. If a child of God refuses to heed His warnings, God uses any means to discipline them and this may take any form including humiliation and embarrassment. This is always His last option, He does that because He loves His children and would not want them to face destruction.

David

He started out as a great warrior and anointed King, excellent musician and a great leader. He feared God and was a "man after God's heart". His secret sins included lust which lead to adultery and murder. Every effort to cover the sins failed. Consequently he invited judgement on his whole family and even the nation of Israel. It is never easy to hide it from God, neither is it easy to hide it for long. God never allows us to get away with un-repented sins.

Solomon

Solomon was one of the wisest and richest men that ever lived. He was a great prayer warrior whom God spoke to frequently. He was the richest in his days, and wrote 3000 proverbs and 10,005 songs.

Solomon was the wisest of the wisest. He was plagued by greed, pride and womanising, which blighted his enviable life. He was stripped of his kingdom, became void of God's anointing and ended up in idolatry. Sins which are not forsaken can strip people spiritually naked.

Achan

Joshua chapter seven details the account of Achan's secret sins. He deliberately disobeyed God's command by keeping for himself the things God forbade the children of Israel during their war against the city of Ai. The results were disastrous for him, his family and the entire nation. A secret or double life can be obscured from people but not from God. Secret sins lead to spiritual defeat. It robs people of God's power and anointing. If anyone lives secretly in sin, they might still be able to 'perform' in many areas without others noticing any difference, but their relationship with God will be inhibited. They could still work miracles, signs and wonders, but cannot have a viable relationship with God. Sin builds a wall between you and God which hinders real intimacy, turning prayer time into a casual and lifeless routine.

Dealing with Private Sins

God expects His children to be open and honest before Him about spiritual challenges. Ask for His help and mercy, confess and repent of every hidden sin. Talk to trusted Christian leaders and friends, and where necessary, a Christian counsellor. Humility and sincerity are the keys to obtaining freedom from sinful bondages. If you are desperate and honest enough God will be there to help. You cannot pray with impact if you continue to condone sin. Sin will sap a person of spiritual energy, create a big gulf between them and God, and overweigh them with guilt and other psychological baggage.

All through the bible hidden sins led to defeat, disgrace and degradation. People who live double lives do so, not only at the expense of their soul, but at the price of their communion with God. Hidden sins result in guilt; guilt robs you of the confidence to approach God in prayer. Sin is the greatest obstacle to prayer. Covert sins may be unnoticed for a while, but it will usually come to a point that the impact begin to manifest.

67

SOWING AND REAPING

The law of sowing and reaping is also applicable to praying. Praying is actually seed sowing, and until you understand things from this angle you will not have a good grasp of how prayer works. When writing to the Galatians Paul cautioned:

"Be not deceived; God is not mocked: for whatsoever a man soweth, that shall he also reap" (Galatians 6:7).

The law of sowing and reaping, seed time and harvest practically come into play in our everyday lives, although many are not aware of this. Each time you pray you are sowing a seed; the very first time you prayed about an issue, you sowed the initial seed. A seed that is planted must be tended and protected until it reaches maturity, and then the harvest. Praying also follows this pattern; of a truth, praying is a process that must be nurtured and monitored before you reap the benefits; a one-of prayer does not follow this principle.

No Seed, No Harvest

People will always reap what they sow- sometimes you reap exactly what you have sown, other times you may reap something else; the season of reaping is never the same as that of sowing, and that is where patience is needed. Harvest will always come in greater measure than the seed sown, but the quality of seed sown determines the quality of yield that follows.

If you do not plant you will not harvest, so also if you do not pray you will not receive answers. When you stop sowing you stop reaping; when you stop praying you also stop receiving answers. The bible states that King Uzziah *"... sought God in the days of Zechariah, who had understanding in the visions of God: and as long as he sought the LORD, God made him to prosper."* (2Chronicles 26:5). Some people progressively enjoy great blessings in their personal, family, ministry and business activities when they pray, but when they begin to slack in prayers they will find that things start to go in the reverse. If you continue to sow seeds of prayer you will continue to reap its blessings, but if you cool off, things will begin to slow down.

Nurture Your Seed

It is not enough to present a request before God only once or occasionally; you must keep up your prayer. Keep the momentum up until the deed is done. When a farmer sows seed, they do not just cover it with soil and go to sleep. They will continue to observe and nurture the seed. First, the farmer check to see that the seed has germinated. Farmers do not immediately worry about their harvest; rather they focus their minds on the survival and development of the seed. They will continue to fertilize and weed around the tender plant, doing their best to protect it from everything that is unfriendly and undesirable, such as rodents and insects. A seed or seedling that is not tended and protected will not survive till harvest.

Sow, nurture and protect your prayer seed by continuing to pray, refusing to doubt, and never giving up or abandoning your prayer project, *"For the earth bringeth forth fruit of herself; first the blade, then the ear, after that the full corn in the ear"* (Mark 4:28). Keep watering, weeding, pruning and observing your prayer seed. Remain positive in your mind and confession; take steps of faith that align with your expectation and never stop praying until your prayer is answered. Unattended seedlings left on their own stand very slim chances of making it to harvest.

The Chinese Bamboo Tree

The growth life of the Chinese bamboo tree very well illustrates the prayer life of Christians. The Chinese bamboo seed is an amazing one, which when planted, you fertilize it for one entire year without noticeable results. Second year, you continue to water and fertilize without any visible sign of life. You will continue that discouraging process of hard work for a few more years, and the seed shows no response to your efforts. Then comes the 5th year of watering and fertilizing- and you will begin to notice some encouraging signs. Sometimes within this 5th year you will witness some sprouting, and then astonishingly, the bamboo shoots to 90 FEET IN 6 WEEKS. Unbelievable!

This is exactly how many of our prayer efforts work. Sometimes you pray and there is no indication that anything is happening at all. Just stay with it. Keep praying and expecting, because a lot is happening without your knowledge. No prayer effort is ever wasted. Each time you pray, something keeps happening. As long as you do not give up along the line your prayer seed will definitely end up with a great harvest. So plant your prayer seeds, nurture them until you reap your harvest. Do not lose your prayer vision, do not let go off your prayer goal. Cherish and nourish your request, carry it on your chest every time without having to worry about it. It may take much longer than you expect, but stay with it, if it is important to you.

If the farmer stopped fertilizing the bamboo seed, just for a while it would take a much longer time for the process to be completed. One of the great lessons to learn from the story of the Chinese bamboo tree is continuity. Prayer should not be a sporadic affair. You must stick to your prayer point to the very end- and the very end is that point when you eventually get what you are praying about. For some people this could be one week, for others it could be one month. And, yet for others this could take a whole year or more. If you ever had a reason to pray about anything, let that same reason remain your strong motivation to sustain the momentum. The day you stop watering your seed, things will begin to regress and your seed may experience an untimely death.

68

STRESS IS BAD FOR PRAYERS

Carrying unnecessary weights is detrimental to effective praying. Many cases of stress are the results of taking on too much burden on yourself. Take for example, if you carry beyond your baggage allowance with an airline for whatever reason, there are a few things you will have to do with the excess: ask someone to help you take it back home, leave it at the airport or pay a fee. Paying a fee is usually relatively expensive. I hate it, and I guess many people do. If you do not want the inconvenience or annoyance that goes with overweight baggage, it is better to avoid it all together. If you discover this too late at the airport- just before your flight, it can be extremely stressful and disruptive; in extreme cases you can miss your flight trying to find a solution to the problem. This is exactly what happens if you allow too much stress into your life- it can easily drain you of the strength and motivation to pray. This is in addition to the health problems that you may encounter in the process.

We can all manage minimal stress, but too much of it can create a lot of crisis for us. You may be so weighed down that you will be unable to pray effectively- in worst cases you will not be able to pray at all. Certain types of stress can be a motivating force in prayer, but too much and prolonged stress can drain you of all the desire and stimulation you need to pray. The good news is that you can simply offload your overload into the waiting hands of Jesus- He says:

"Come to me, all you who are weary and burdened, and I will give you rest. Take my yoke upon you and learn from me, for I am gentle and humble in heart, and you will find rest for your souls. For my yoke is easy and my burden is light" (Matthew 11:28-30). NIV

Do Not Be Overpowered By Stress

Signs of stress can manifest in so many ways- some people will begin to shirk responsibilities, loose energy and let go of their sense of purpose. Stress can lead to lack of energy, direction and discretion. Many people need (or wait for) a certain dimension of stress to be able to function successfully, it makes them more productive and enthusiastic. However, a lot of people will naturally react negatively to stress and experience physical symptoms such as too much or little sleep, stomach ulcers and headaches, loss of concentration, inability to make decisions and muscle problems.

Negative Impact of Stress on Spiritual Life

When people experience continuous stress, they may feel overwhelmed by responsibility. They will find many things too much to handle. They could end up losing desire for prayer and other spiritual activities. Stress can make an individual not want to be around anyone, including going to church or relating with other Christians. If a person becomes too stressed they can easily become detached from spiritual things. God wants His people to reorder their lives and put every situation in His hands. *"Except the LORD build the house, they labour in vain that build it: except the LORD keep the city, the watchman waketh but in vain"* (Psalm 127:1-2).

Hand yourself and your burdens over to the Lord and keep resting in His arms. If you want your prayer life to stay powerful, you must learn to let Christ live His life through you. Commit your pressures, the present and the future into God's hands and you will be able to say like the Psalmist: *"Truly my soul finds rest in God; my salvation comes from Him"* (Psalm 62:1). NIV

Stress can keep you off praying; however, it is important to note that the principal way to overcome stress is by praying, in addition to identifying the causes and severing your self from them. You must retrace your steps out of stress. Identifying how you got there means you are half way out of the situation. You can totally de-stress yourself by talking: talk to God, to people who can help out; say 'no' to people and situations that lead you into stress. Continue to speak God's word into your situation until you experience a turn around.

Managing Stress

> *"There hath no temptation taken you but such as is common to man: but God is faithful, who will not suffer you to be tempted above that ye are able; but will with the temptation also make a way to escape, that ye may be able to bear it"* (1 Corinthians 10:13).

Anyone who does not learn to manage stress can be completely overwhelmed by its power. This has little to do with how anointed you are. Prayer is not even a cure-all for stress. There are a number of things you can do to assist you in overcoming stress; we will discuss just a few of them:

Be Realistic

Stop biting more than you can chew. Setting out to do too much can end you up in stress. Also, you will fail to appreciate the little things you accomplish along the way. Taking on too much at a time can make some people feel inadequate; especially if they fail to meet their own expectations.

Take time to be Away

This can be a very powerful tool for de-stressing yourself. Take time off. Take breaks away from work and home on a regular basis. It gives you the sanity and serenity you need to recuperate, and realign your life.

Stay Fit

Exercise has a way of making you feel good; this can in turn place you in a better position to combat stress. Exercise strengthens your mind, emotions and muscles. It gives you what you need to fight back.

Stay Closer To God

Spend more time in worship, praying, studying the bible and in having fellowship with other Christians. Staying closer to God keeps you connected to your maker, the source of life. A constant flow of the life of God into you will replace the exhaustion and loss you may have experienced through stress. Unfortunately, too many people cut off from God and spiritual activities when they are overcome by stress.

Speak To Someone

We do not have to empty our anxieties on people around us, but talking to someone who might be able to advice and guide may well be what you need. It could make a world of difference. You may also want to speak to an expert such as a counsellor or therapist who has the professional knowledge and skills to help you through your difficult times.

Generally stress can act as booster to achievement in some people; in others stress can cause a lot of damage. Stress can be used to an advantage if you learn to manage it well. You must watch out for and respond fast to negative signs of stress in your life. Stress can bring your life to a standstill. It can make you lose the desire for prayer, and completely disrupt your spiritual life. It may altogether stop you from making progress in every area of life when you are at the height of it. Prayer can help you reduce stress, but ironically, a lot of people who are going through stress actually withdraw from God's presence. This should not be the case.

69

SELF-DELIVERANCE

Not every Christian agrees with the fact of God's children ever needing deliverance, let alone accepting the connection between prayer and deliverance. This topic is not popular among many Christians, yet I believe it is a subject deserving mention when addressing the matter of prayer in a broader dimension. Deliverance is one of the most controversial of all Christian subjects, yet it is one of the most crucial and obvious teachings of the bible and should be viewed with an open mind. If a Christian battles with demonic residues, they may also struggle with praying.

The controversy surrounding deliverance appears to focus mainly on who needs deliverance, and whether deliverance is biblical. Deliverance is God's will for His people. It was for this reason that, "...*God anointed Jesus of Nazareth with the Holy Ghost and power: who went about doing good, and healing all that were oppressed of the devil; for God was with Him*" (Acts 10:38).

If you are not totally free, you will not be able to pray freely. Every believer should enjoy the deliverance power of God. It is hard for me to agree that it is only the unsaved that needs deliverance. The weakness I see in this argument is that, if it is at all possible for an unbeliever to get delivered from demons, it is quite likely the demons will be back, because Christ may not yet be in full control of that life. For many Christians, deliverance will be unnecessary, but for some, deliverance will be relevant- either because of their involvements before salvation, or carelessness on their part after they gave their lives to Christ. If a person has had past demonic involvements, it may well be that they will need some help (deliverance prayers) to completely break free from demonic residues. If this does not happen, they could experience struggles in certain aspects of their spiritual lives.

It is important to bear in mind that when you become born again, you can be healed of every sickness and disease immediately, but in many cases a good number of God's children still carry sicknesses in their bodies for a while before they eventually get healed. Deliverance prayers should be considered something similar to healing and prosperity prayers.

Can a Christian Have Demons?

A Christian does not have to have demons, but many do, and they know it! Satan filled the hearts of Ananias and his wife, Saphira (Acts 5:3) Jesus said to Peter, *"Get thee behind me Satan"* (Matthew16:23), A particular daughter of Abraham was in bondage to Satan for many years (Luke 13:16). These were all God's children. I am not arguing that demons have free access to God's children. Nonetheless, many of God's children recklessly expose themselves to demonic activities.

Earlier in the book I discussed the tripartite nature of man- spirit, soul and body (1Thessalonians 5:23) and their relationship with our spiritual lives and prayer. The human spirit relates to God, and is fused to the Holy Spirit at salvation. The Soul (mind) and body can still be under the influence of sickness and demons, although this should not be the case. This is more likely to happen if a believer becomes careless spiritually.

Demons can gain access into anyone (saved or unsaved) if their actions permit. A Christian can be exposed to satanic influence if they make themselves vulnerable to demons by what they think, say or do. God will not give his children immunity if they wilfully permit their humanity to negate the protection of God upon their lives. Writing in Ephesians 4:26-27, Paul warns: *"Be angry, and do not sin: do not let the sun go down on your wrath, nor give place to the devil."*

Christians can give room to the devil, and he will be swift to occupy the space. Demonic interferences can oppose your prayer life. They can hinder the smooth flow of the Spirit in your life, and therefore reduce your prayer effectiveness.

Deliverance is more effective when administered to a believer because when a demon is expelled from an unbeliever who has no relationship with God, the demon goes only for a while, but will later return with many more demons to inhabit the individual. The last state of that person will become worse than the first. (Matthew 12:43-45).

Steps to Self-Deliverance

It is not my intention to make a prescription but the following steps can help you in evicting demons from your life or helping someone to be relieved from demonic influence:

1. Repent totally of every known sin.
2. Spend some minutes in praise and worship
3. Declare your surrender to God, reject and renounce every demonic connection.
4. Stand upon God's word as your grounds for deliverance.
5. Vigorously plead the blood of Christ upon your spirit, soul and body for cleansing, and for victory over demons.
6. Pray in faith. Without faith, you will not get far.
7. Begin to cast out the demons by praying something like this: "Father in heaven, every demon, and everything else in my life which does not belong to you, I destroy, bind and cast them out of my life now in Jesus name". Keep praying this until you experience personal deliverance. Demons leave through many ways. They could simply leave quietly without putting up a

fight and without letting you know they are leaving. At other times when they are leaving, it could take the form of yawning, sneezing, foul odours, vomiting, coughing, spitting, stretching, and a feeling of relief. It can also happen in many other ways.

8. Then ask God to fill you afresh with his Holy Spirit.
9. Give thanks to God and ask him to help you stay off anything that will expose you to further demonic attack.

My conclusion is that a Christian can have demons. It could have happened before they gave their lives to Christ; further demonic inroad is possible after salvation due to sin and other behaviours that give Satan a legal ground to come in. Unresolved demonic influences can be problematic to an individual's prayer life.

70

STRETCH YOURSELF

Continue to break new prayer grounds and take on more prayer responsibility; never stop raising your prayer bar because every time you do, you will take your relationship with God a little further; you would also have reclaimed new space from the devil.

Strangely, only a few Christians find a significant stretch in prayer something attractive. Many people want more miracles, visions, prophesies- anything sensational. Fact is, prayer is the key to entering into these realms and staying there. Prayer can do much more exploits than all forms of spiritual manifestations. When you keep stretching yourself in prayers, you will continue to enter into new territories, and reap more blessings. Each time you raise your prayer bar, you will push the enemy further back, you will earn yourself peculiar victories and enter into the next level.

Stretch Your Strength

> *"But the path of the just is as the shining light, that shineth more and more unto the perfect day"* (Proverbs 4:18)

Life's problems never seem to shrink or get smaller whatever your level of success, instead they tend to grow gradually, and sometimes, aggressively. As you deliberately strive to take on more prayer challenges, you will make yourself ever ready for the next batch of battles that may confront you. Deliberately stretching, growing and toughening yourself in 'peace' times will continue to equip you for unforeseen spiritual contentions. Athletes do not get ready for events on the day of the actual competition, they strain and train well ahead of the real action. You cannot be a prayer success story unless you consciously and consistently develop your prayer stamina.

If you have always prayed 5 minutes why not begin to stretch yourself to pray 10 or 15 minutes. If your regular prayer time averages 30 minutes, extend yourself to go regularly up to 45 minutes or even an hour. Move from one hour to one and a half, then regularly to two hours. If you do not continue to stretch yourself, you will not easily win new battles and will find it difficult to cope when you are confronted by unexpected major crisis.

When I first started out, praying half an hour was a nightmare. But soon I began to hear stories of people who pray for several hours at a time. I took on the challenge and gradually developed myself until I could pray up to seven hours at a go – non-stop. It can be great fun as well as fulfilling. You do not get there in one day. Ever wondered what on earth you will be praying about in seven or more hours? Just look around you - from your home to church, community and country; you will find more than enough to pray about on a daily basis. No one expects you to do this daily in practice. Why not try praying at least double your usual time, every now and then. The experience will take you to another level in your understanding of God.

Why You Should Push Your Prayer Boundaries

No strain, no gain. Paul said I forget those things which are behind me, I press towards the mark of His high calling, straining towards what is ahead. I press on toward the goal to win the prize for which God has called me (Philippians 13:13-14). Whatever the stage you are in presently in your spiritual journey, it is already in the past. Break new grounds. Do something new. Enter into a new realm. There is something you have yet to experience about prayer. Expanding our prayer horizon has numerous blessings for the believer:

Growth

Every form of growth requires a stretch. Whenever you try something new in prayer you have taken off the limit to your spiritual development. When you stop making demands on yourself you will stop growing. When you enlarge your capacity, God has more than enough to fill up your space, so *"enlarge the place of thy tent, and let them stretch forth the curtains of thine habitations: spare not, lengthen thy cords, and strengthen thy stakes, for thou shalt break forth on the right hand and on the left..."* (Isaiah 54:2-3). If you do not push the boundaries, God will not move the boundaries; push beyond your comfort zone and God will go all the way with you.

Fulfilment

Trying something unusual gives a sense of satisfaction. You feel like, 'yes, I have done it'; you will be filled with pride. Take your prayer to a new level frequently and enjoy this feeling.

Fresh Testimonies

There is always something new in God's presence. We will never be able to fully explore who God is even if we lived a million years. You will always discover a little more about God, whenever you go a little further with Him. Open new grounds in prayers, go beyond your current maximum, and see how many people will be blessed by your prayer testimonies.

Prepared For the Future

When big problems arise (and they will), you would have readied yourself big time without having to start building your prayer muscles anew. Get prepared to win future conflicts before they emerge from nowhere.

Never give in to the fear of trying something new. Turn your comfort zone into danger zone; go for the kill. Deep calls unto deep, dig deeper in your communion with the Lord, so you do not miss out on God's greater blessings. Beginning from taking small steps, intentionally lengthen and widen your prayer scope, make demands on yourself and draw out the hidden treasures lying within you. Increase your prayer time by 2, 3, 4, 5, 6 and even ten times. Gold is not found in the surface of the soil. In fact, no natural mineral can be picked up easily from shallow surfaces; miners must dig deep into the earth to discover those expensive gems. If you want new revelations or prayer revolution, you must habitually take a plunge into deeper prayer waters- that is where the riches of the Holy Spirit are hidden.

71

SPIRITUAL MAPPING

Effective spiritual warfare requires sufficient knowledge about the enemy we are up against. Limited knowledge will lead to partial or no victory because poor information about your adversaries will give them an edge over you.

The motivation for spiritual mapping should be evangelism and intercession, and must be aimed at unveiling the obstacles the enemy has erected against the preaching of the gospel in a particular environment. Discovering, dismantling and destroying these barriers (through prayers) is the object of spiritual mapping.

The Purpose of Spiritual Mapping

Several authorities in spiritual mapping have suggested a number of benefits that come with spiritual mapping, including the following:

1. The number one objective of spiritual mapping is to unveil demonic secrets from behind the scene so as to engage in effective spiritual warfare and evangelism.
2. To bring the rule (kingdom) of God to bear upon the earth.
3. Spiritual mapping helps to reveal the specific demonic strongholds that hold a community in bondage.

4. It enables us to view the world from God's own perspective. We are able to see things in their true nature, not through the falsehood, deceptions and camouflages presented by evil forces.

5. Detecting the demonic origin of certain ungodly activities manifesting in the physical.

Spiritual mapping is an investment into finding out more about the enemy. It involves going the extra mile to survey the land, select and sift information with which you later carry out informed spiritual action. Knowing your enemy in as much detail as possible will tip the battle scale in your favour, because you will be engaging the enemy from a platform of superior knowledge.

How to Carry Out Spiritual Mapping

I would like to note that spiritual mapping is a means to an end, - not an end in itself. Indeed, spiritual mapping is not a new phenomenon; it dates back to bible times and can be traced to people like:

Joshua- He sent out spies to spy out the Promised Land (Deuteronomy 1:22-23). Joshua sent out men, instructing them to go and spy out the land of Jericho (Joshua2:1).

Nehemiah- He sought information secretly viewing the land by night in spite of the presence of the enemy (Neh. 2:12-18).

Harold Caballeros (2001) suggests the following keys for embarking on a spiritual mapping project:

Historical Factors – These include the names, nature and history of the territory. What do the names mean or imply? Is the name associated with a blessing or a curse? What does the name say about the original inhabitants of the land, and the characteristics of current inhabitants? Is there any link between the names and demons/religion, cult or beliefs?

What about the territory? What characteristics distinguish it from others, and what is the general response of the people to the gospel? What are the social economic challenges of the territory? The original founders, original purpose and past events may all be central to understanding how to pray for that land.

Physical Factors

The devil nearly always leaves his footprint behind. We can find evidence of his activities on material objects. Does anything ring a bell or echo what you have known or observed previously, and which might have some implications for spiritual warfare? Study and analyse the territorial maps, for adjustments which may give some information away. What do these communicate to you? Look out for and record the monuments, sites, statues and instructions that are present; research the nature and number of the places of worship both of God and the devil. What about pubs and 'red light' (prostitution) structures; how entrenched are they; what are these telling or not telling you? Use the information as an aid to prayer.

Spiritual Factors

Some questions to be asked include, whether the heavens are open, how easy it is to pray in that environment; whether there are variations in the spiritual atmosphere within the territory. God may reveal a name, the "Strong Man" or other form of demonic icon to you at the place of prayer.

All the above, together comprise the process of spiritual mapping. A continent, nation, city, town, village or community many be mapped. It may not always be very intensive; the aim is to let God reveal things directly to you, or enlighten your mind through what you have seen, so you can employ them as a tool for effective spiritual warfare and evangelical breakthrough.

Spiritual mapping is a critical aspect of world evangelism. It will greatly reduce the amount of wasted prayer, off target shots and the number of prayer punches into the air. It will lead groups and individuals to pray with pin-point accuracy and to uncover the skirt of the enemy. Satan thrives and revels on our spiritual ignorance. He operates under the cover of darkness (people's ignorance of him), and would never want any of us to have detailed information about him. Every effort and resource put into spiritual mapping will yield great dividend.

72

TESTED, TRIED AND TRUSTED.

Trials and temptations are part of life. The strength and trustworthiness of anything can be established by its durability under intense pressure. A person's ability to stand firm in the midst of trials and tribulation reflects the 'stuff' they are made of, and the trust they place in God. Your prayer strength will be tested through very difficult circumstances that will require either a 'fight' or 'flight' response from you. If you fight to the end you will emerge victorious, but if you flee before then, you will end up a victim.

Your response to life's problems can impact negatively or positively on your prayer life. If you take things from a positive angle, it will drive you into the hands of God, but if you react negatively to adversity you may be too overwhelmed to pray. As a Christian you will always have crisis and critical moments in life. Some will be orchestrated by Satan, others will be self-made through personal errors, and a few will be part of God's discipline if there is no other way to get your attention. Whatever the source of your trials, you must trust God and never give up. Demonstrate your confidence in God by abandoning yourself in His hands and praying until your situation changes.

Trials or Temptation?

People get confused about whether a problem is a trial or temptation. It is a trial if it comes from the outside of you. A trial is an adversity which God allows your way. It is not meant to destroy you but to bring out the best in you. It should lead to Christian growth and maturity. New lessons may be learned and new dimensions of wisdom and development could be attained. Whereas trials originate externally, temptations have their roots from within. Temptations can lead to spiritual death, and could progress to become sin if not checked. God has nothing to do with this; it springs from within. However, if you fall into temptation, pray and seek God's help and deliverance. When you are vexed and exhausted by trials, do not run from Gods presence, get closer to Him. Whenever life places a demand on you, you must make a demand on God through prayers because, *"If you faint in the day of adversity, your strength is small"* (Proverbs24:10).

Always be ready and be in a state of perpetual armed conflict with the devil. Your response to trials and temptations is one of the measures of your spiritual stamina. You will continue to draw strength from God if you continue to depend on Him.

Discipline, Trials and Temptations

Every child of God will continue to experience divine discipline, trials and temptations- these mean different things. Your understanding of each can influence your response during your experiences. These major forces are broken down here:

	Discipline	Trial	Temptation
Source	God	God, the world and Satan	Satan
Results from	Being Disobedience to God	Being God's Child	Exposure and Lust

How do you know	Deserved	Trial of faith	Outside God's will
Overcoming it	Repentance	Steadfastness	Resist the devil
What not to do	Taking things for granted	Looking back	Yielding to temptations
God's Word for you	You are my child	I am with you	You are walking in the flesh
Outcome	Fear and holiness	Brokenness and divine glory	Sinfulness or victory.

Passing the Test

In 2Corinthians 1:8-11a the apostle Paul paints a picture of how a child of God should respond to trials and temptations:

> "For we would not, brethren, have you ignorant of our trouble which came to us in Asia, that we were pressed out of measure, above strength, insomuch that we despaired even of life: But we had the sentence of death in ourselves, that we should not trust in ourselves, but in God which raiseth the dead: Who delivered us from so great a death, and doth deliver... ye also helping together by prayer for us..."

In this passage Paul gives us a glimpse into the severity of the trials and persecutions he and his team endured in Asia. The predicament notwithstanding, the team placed implicit trust in the Lord. Rather than let their situation push them away from God, they prayed, solicited prayer from other Christians and held on until God granted them deliverance. Paul continued to depend on God as his divine deliverer, availing himself of the preserving power of prayer. He did not only pass the tests he faced, he never failed to rely on God through prayers. He never allowed his plight to pluck him away from the presence of God. Never turn away from your maker in the day of trouble- there is no better time to stay closer to God that when you are facing adversity.

73

TIMING IS CRUCIAL

An hour lost in the morning will never be replaced no matter how desperately you try all day. An opportunity that shows up today may disappear tomorrow. In prayer as in all endeavours it is important to seize every opportunity. In almost every facet of life, success is not necessarily guaranteed to the most powerful, intelligent or skilful. In all cases success is determined by the efficient use of time. Effective praying is the result of effective use of time. As in money making, efficient use of time is a deciding factor in successful praying. *"To everything there is a season, a time for every purpose under heaven"* (Ecclesiastes 3:1).

A particular study revealed that, at seventy years of age an average man has utilised:

> Twenty-four years in sleep.
> Fourteen years in work.
> Eight years in enjoyments.
> Six years at the dinner table.
> Five years commuting.
> Four years talking to others.
> Three years in Education.
> Two years studying and reading.
> Four years in miscellaneous.
> -Unknown source

The question is, do people really spend enough time talking to their maker in their life time? The amount of time you spend with God will determine how much God will do in, through and for you. To maintain a healthy spiritual life you will need a minimum of one hour prayer every day. This can be split into a few minutes at different times of the day for those who cannot do it at once. Some prayer burden God gives you are for an appointed time. Also, certain visions, dreams and revelations God gives you carry a time factor. If you fail to pray at the right time, things may become too late. Most missed prayer opportunities emanate from carelessness and busyness.

Pray well ahead of major events. Do not wait till the last minute. As a pastor, I am aware that I can suddenly be called upon to speak. I strive to make myself always prayer ready. It does not matter what subject I have to speak on, all I will need to do is get my notes ready as quickly as possible, because I make it a point of duty to pray well ahead of time for my speaking engagements.

On a particular occasion I was invited by a close senior colleague to preach in one of their annual conferences. I did not receive the invitation until a few hours before the engagement, although somebody was asked to contact me much earlier. I had very limited time to arrive at the conference venue, and had no time to pray, or prepare my notes. I got to the venue just in time for my session. Throughout my ministration God so visited His people with great grace and unction my hostess refused to believe later that I had no time to prepare. There was no need to convince her, because the glory belonged to God.

No Time to Pray?

Find time to pray. People get so busy they have no time to pray – so they claim. We always have time for things that matter most to us. Keep a record of, or think about how you spend your time on a daily basis. You will discover that more time is allocated to things that are of top priority to you. For many people, time allotted to prayer is very insignificant and yet prayer is the most important of all- the most powerful force on earth. Here are a few suggestions for creating time to pray:

Find More Time for Prayers

1. Plan each day, week and month ahead and set aside specific times for prayers.
2. Avoid procrastinating with prayer. If possible set particular prayer times in stone. It is worth it.
3. Pray smarter. Take prayer walks. Utilise your break times (or part of it) for prayers. Use your waiting time, where possible, to pray. Pray while waiting for your spouse, friend or child in the car.
4. Pray while driving. I do a lot more of praying in the car than listening to tapes or music. This might be distractive for some drivers, so be careful and only do this if you can manage it properly. It is not suitable for everyone, so I make no general recommendation.
5. Use a prayer list. Pray part of it in the morning, afternoon and evening, if this will help.
6. Get away to pray as soon as you have the urge to pray. You do not have to understand why. Just make room for it. It will save you an awful amount of time which you will need if a situation goes out of hand.
7. Do not wait to have all the time to pray. I used to wait until I could pray at least an hour before I pray at all. Now I use every available time. Five, ten, twenty, thirty minutes. When I can, I pray for several hours at a time. Every little helps.
8. Consider the best or most suitable time of the day. You can pray at any time, but decide what time is most productive for you.
9. Deliberately make time to pray. What if you reduced the time spent daily on watching the TV, making phone calls, talking to friends, searching the web, reading and sending e-mails, worrying about things you cannot change- each by ten minutes?

You would have saved about an hour for prayers. Praise God! This takes discipline and determination, but all things are possible.

You cannot maximise the benefits of prayer unless you understand the relationship between time and prayers. Some prayers build up overtime before you can see the impact; unless you make that time available you will not have noticeable success. Missed times of prayer can result in missed opportunities, reduced momentum and loss of ground to the enemy.

74

UNDERSTAND HOW GOD ANSWERS PRAYERS

God answers all prayers no matter how and why you prayed. However, God seldom answers prayers the way we expect Him to. The uninformed Christian gets frustrated and discouraged if God answers prayers in ways beyond their comprehension. Knowledge and understanding are central to everything we do. When you understand that God reserves the right to answer prayers the way He chooses, you will be more relaxed and hopeful during your waiting times. When you pray, God can answer in any of the following ways:

Yes

- Sometimes when God says yes, you may receive a prompt answer to your prayers. This was the case with the syro-phoenician woman whose daughter was severely demon possessed (Matthew 15:22). She got a speedy answer after she persisted.
- Some other times God says yes but gives you a better option, which you may not like because of your limited understanding. God's answers are always the best. The issue here is your prayer received answers which were different from your expectation, you therefore failed to recognise this because you anticipated answers in the wrong direction.

- At other times your prayer will get answered, but the results may be concealed. Anything could be responsible for this. The answer could be right next to you or within your reach, and all you simply need is for God to open your eyes or spirit to discover it.

No

God has a right to say no when anyone prays. This will usually be the case if a person harbours sins in their lives: *"If I regard iniquity in my heart, The Lord will not hear..."* (Psalm 66:18). Having a wrong altitude to God and His Kingdom can also result in unanswered prayers. A Pharisee once had a boastful, arrogant attitude compared to a particular Publican (hated tax collector) at the place of prayer. The Pharisee's prayer went unanswered, but God heard the prayer of the Publican (Luke 18:9-15). God does not answer selfish prayers (James 4:3). Neither has He regard for prayer made as an outward show (Matthew 6:5). God does not solve problems we should or can solve by ourselves (James 2:14-16); and when people do not pray at all, or fail to pray in faith, God has nothing to respond to. The answers to all of these scenarios would be most likely, 'no'.

Wait

In a fast paced hasty world, patience has become a 'scarce commodity'. Everything has got to be ready made, quick and instantaneous. Society is getting increasingly short of patience. Nobody wants to wait for anything. As Christians our Lord is the ancient of days. He is the high and lofty One who inhabits eternity (Isaiah 57: 15).

> *"But, beloved, be not ignorant of this one thing, that one day is with the Lord as a thousand years, and a thousand years as one day"* (2Peter 3:8).

God is not bound by time, neither does He run out of it. If you ask Him to work twelve miracles in your life within a year, one for each month,

He can choose to perform all of them in two months or the very last month. Yet His intervention will not be too late because He is beautiful for all situations, He is a perfect planner, although He may appear slow at fulfilling His promises. For reasons best known to Him (and always in your interest) God could allow you to go through a waiting period before you receive the answers to your prayers. Wait when He says, wait. When God is not ready, you must remain steady and wait for as long as He deems fit.

When you were a child, you probably asked your parents for some ridiculous things, or wanted them to do everything 'right now'. They did not always grant your request because, either they felt it was not safe for you, it would lead to misuse, or it would be illegal for your age. For similar reasons, God may only grant certain requests when the time is right (Romans 8:26-27). The question then, is how does one know whether the timing is wrong? My answer would be to judge all things by the word of God, listen in your heart to what the Holy Spirit is saying to you. If other things or people connected to your request are not ready, this could also cause a delay to your answer.

If you pray for a marriage partner and your 'perfect' match will not be ready in another year, in order to protect you, God may say wait. During your waiting time, do not stay idle or passive, remain active, and try your hands on different things without being trapped by any. You may also need to ask God for the cause of the delay because the devil or your good self may well be the cause.

Something Else

God is not obligated to give what you ask for, all the time. He will answer your prayers in line with His will and purpose. Paul wanted to go to Bithynia to preach. He planned and prepared for that mission. He prayed towards the outreach, but instead God wanted him to go to Macedonia to carry out ministry work. God can override your will and desires when you pray, so be careful not to always insist on what you want, especially in destiny defining situations.

Many years ago, I pastored a church which needed to give birth to a daughter church. We prayed, planned and prepared. In my mind, I had decided which of our current church leaders would be redeployed to pastor the new church. This brother was very humble, loyal and worked quite well with everyone. I thought He was the best choice and everyone probably thought so. On the Sunday morning we were due to pray for and commission him to go and plant the new church, I went before God to pray for the last time to make sure I got things right. For about an hour I sought God's face, and lo, God had a different plan. He chose the most unlikely candidate and I had no choice but to yield to God's will. I later found out why. This brother (God's choice) had begun to sow the seed of division in our church, a fast growing and closely knit congregation. We were a few hundreds, and were growing steadily and happily. Had he remained within us, in no time we would have had a major crisis that could have resulted in divisions and probably a breakup.

After you have prayed, you need to go with the flow of God. This is the only way you can avoid spiritual landmines and painful experiences. God is not limited to answering your prayers in any particular way. If you really trust Him, you will not be afraid of whatever answer you receive, because He will always have your best interest at heart.

75

URGENCY IN PRAYER

Several things in life require speed and urgency. Some things can only happen at a particular point in time, and in nearly all cases the speed at which you are able to do certain things will determine how much edge you will have over your competitors. Prayer opportunities do not last for ever. Some prayers are prayed just too late.

A sense of prayer urgency is a feeling that there is some hazard, impending danger and a prayer job that needs to be completed before it gets too late. This feeling of urgency is very critical to success, and when applied to prayer, you will be *"redeeming the time, because the days are evil."* (Ephesians 5:16). The devil is on rampage, evil is spreading at an alarming proportion, but the church of Christ is simply playing catch up. More than any time in human history, we need to pray more intensely, aggressively and consistently to be able to overrun the enemy.

A Sense of Urgency or a Sense of Emergency

People who lack a sense of urgency at doing things end up reacting to emergencies. Lack of urgency results in fire-fighting, defensiveness and squandered opportunities. If we do not act when we should, we will be forced to act when things are more difficult. It is better to deliberately create an atmosphere of urgency into whatever we do. Treating everything in life with a sense of hurry protects you from serious and unexpected negative situations. When Christians 'sleep' instead of praying, Satan will continue to gain the upper hand. God's kingdom need people who are quick to respond to events around them before things have time to escalate, it takes more time and resources to manage a crisis than to plan and steadily prevent one. The apostle Paul always exhibited a sense of urgency in carrying out God's work:

1. He told the Romans Christians: *"For God is my witness, whom I serve with my spirit in the gospel of His Son, that without ceasing, I make mention of you always in my prayers..."* (Romans 1:9).

2. To the Ephesian Christians, he said I *"Ceased not to give thanks for you, making mention of you in my prayers..."* (Ephesians 1:16).

3. He prayed with intensity for the Thessalonian Christians *"... night and day...praying most earnestly that we may see your face, and may complete what is lacking in your faith"* (1Thessalonians 3:10).

4. Paul constantly remembered Timothy in prayer night and day. (2Timothy 1:3)

5. Paul never stopped praying for the Colossian brethren. (Colossians 1:3.9)

People with a sense of prayer immediacy never slow down or give up in their praying. They are driven daily by prayer need and the prayer passion they possess.

Delay Is Dangerous

Some of the crises society and individuals face today are because of the absence of compelling and strategic prayer action by God's people. Satan and his cohorts are operating at an astronomically faster rate than the Church. *"To everything there is a season and a time for every purpose under heaven."* Christians must strive to match and exceed the speed at which the devil is carrying out his heinous activities. Prayer is a major instrument for confronting and confounding the devil (Ecclesiastes 3:1). He is actively carrying out his plans, while the Church is passively marking time. The only thing that can stop him is active and rapid prayer activities, in addition to persistent practical steps.

Jesus Himself cautioned in Luke13:25:

> *"when once the master of the house is risen up and hath shut the door, and you begin to stand without and to knock at the door saying, Lord, Lord open unto us; and He shall answer and say unto you, I know you not whence you are."*

Why wait until it is too late. All around us we have critical situations that require quick prayer intervention on a daily basis. The world is full of life-and-death situations which 'cry' continually for intercession from God's people. Whether you are listening to news, reading the papers or listening to conversations in public places, you will find compelling reasons to constantly communicate with the Lord on behalf of the Land. Millions of disasters like war, hunger, economic meltdown, political failure- name them, are mainly man-made. But a great many of them could have been prevented had somebody taken the pain to pray for divine intervention.

Now is the time to wake out of spiritual slumber and take the demonic bull by its horns and invoke God's power upon the land and our loved ones. Do not put off prayer until another day as today's prayer opportunity may never show up again.

1. God's business requires haste (1 Samuel 21:8).
2. God has raised you for such a time as this (Esther 4:13-17).
3. Keep pressing in prayers until heaven pours down the blessings. (Psalm70).
4. God says He will hasten His word to perform it (Jeremiah 1:12).
5. God says not to be slothful in business, but redeeming the time (1 Corinthians 7: 29-31), for the days are evil.

If we all prayed when we should and at the right pace, many challenges we encounter today would have been dealt with before they had time to hatch. God would have moved swiftly into our circumstances and make the story completely different. Jesus has given us His name, so that when we pray, we can change the game. We live in dire times, and prayer must be given the highest priority. Prayer must be carried out as a matter of urgency and intensity. God has delegated His ability to curb the enemy to the church- you and I. If we do not exercise this authority, all creation will continue to be at the mercy of evil forces. It is time to rise up and pray, and pray without delay.

76

UNCOMMON PRAYERS FOR UNCOMMON SITUATIONS

Uncommon problems necessitate uncommon solutions. Desperate situations require desperate prayers. Unique problems deserve unique prayers, and long-standing problems demand long-standing prayers. All problems are not equal. Some problems do not need more than a minute or five minutes' prayers. Certain situations can only be changed by special dimensions of prayers. True, it is the same God, and what God can do in one hour, He can equally do in one second. What He can do within three months of prayer, He can also do in three seconds or three minutes of prayers. Nevertheless, some types of situations call for unusual breadth and depth of prayer input, and we see this demonstrated all through the bible, even by Jesus.

The Early Church

When the early church faced unprecedented persecution, the disciples had unusual negative experiences with the leaders of the day. It was new for them to face beatings, threats, bullying and imprisonment of the highest dimensions. They had always found solace in the arms of Jesus. He answered all their questions, fed them, taught them how to behave and shielded them from frightening situations. Now Jesus had gone, they had to preach and do everything for themselves. The chief priests and elders of that period forbade them to preach, beat them up and even committed peter to prison to be killed afterwards.

The church was stirred up to pray day and night with persistence, and a relentlessness that was beyond the norm. They were used to sleeping when Jesus stayed awake or rose early to pray. Now it was their turn to step into deep waters. God heard their prayers, and an angel came to the prison and miraculously delivered Peter. Prayer-as-usual could never have done that. Day and night, non-stop prayer did it. Not prayer request distributed to others. Not waiting for the pastor to do it. The question is how big is your problem? Is it big enough to keep you awake praying all night for seven consecutive days? Is the magnitude of your challenge enough to drive you into a personal retreat- praying alone with God, in fasting, worship and for a whole week? Does your problem upset you enough to warrant you praying for twenty one days, two hours each day? Are you burdened enough about lost souls to embark on a twenty-four hour weekly fast, to ask God for the salvation of lost souls? Desperate prayers are needed for desperate times.

Jesus Prayed Desperately

Jesus was aware the weight of the world rested on His shoulders, that He had an overwhelming mission that He could only accomplish with the help of the Father. Before commencing His earthly ministry He fasted forty days and forty nights because the great commission required great intercession. Jesus would rise a great while before daylight to pray. He also prayed all night because the task ahead was enormous. How gripping is your situation? How absorbed are you by your state? Extreme situations call for extreme measures. Even in His final moments on earth, Jesus, "...*being in an agony He prayed more earnestly: and His sweat was as it were great drops of blood falling down to the ground*" (Luke 22:44).

Going to the Cross was a trying time for the Lord, He prayed differently at the garden of Gethsemane because He was faced with a critical moment. Life-changing problems should be handled with life-changing prayers, nothing less will do.

Jacob

Jacob was in exile, on the run from his brother Esau who threatened to kill him for robbing him of his birth right. Jacob knew he was in a dangerous situation, and that critical times demand once-in-a-life-time kind of prayer. Whilst escaping for his life he had a life transforming encounter with God. It was a do or die moment for Jacob, no time for comfort or procrastination because there was so much at stake. He held unto the angel` and prayed, "Unless you bless me, I will not let you go." Jacob refused to let go, he did not want to risk extermination, but wanted to live; he wanted to prosper. He would not let go of God. God heard, blessed and protected him. His life changed forever. Although he was physically disabled for life as a result of the encounter, Jacob had something to show for his fight. As a result of the prayer, His angry brother was appeased and reunited lovingly with Jacob. His life was no longer in danger. He was saved from almost certain death. His brother had sought to kill him for many years for earlier supplanting and stripping him of his birth right.

Seek God's face until you find Him, until He reveals Himself in that problem. You have an invitation from God to seek Him:

> *"I have not spoken in secret, in a dark place of the earth; I said not unto the seed of Jacob, 'seek ye Me in vain.' I, the LORD speak righteousness; I declare things that are right"* (Isaiah 45:19).

Have you found yourself in peculiar problems? Then separate yourself unto God for uncommon times of prayer. If you are hit with big problems, you must hit back with corresponding amounts of prayers.

The Man at the Pool of Bethesda

A man laid in his bed at the same time, the same place every year by the same pool (the pool of Bethesda). He was known as the impotent man. He could not help himself, but pinned his hope on God. Each year the angel of the Lord came once to stir the water of the pool. Whoever got first into the pool was healed of every ailment – no matter what it was. This man was always too slow. Many people were smarter and faster and got into the pool even before the impotent man could attempt to get in. This went on year on year. It was a painful and disappointing circle of agony for this man, but he had no options. This was his only hope.

He stayed there at the pool year after year until Jesus came to the rescue. Jesus saw his desperation and need, and moved to heal him once and for all. Had the man become discouraged, abandoned his attempts and given up, we would never read of his story.

Too often, too many people give up without putting up enough fight. The question remains: are they really desperate? Are they in a dire situation? If their situation was truly critical, if it was acute; if their condition was extreme and they had no options, they would act exactly like this man. They would stay with God until it all happened. Put God to the test today. Seize the momentum. Grab the situation, it is all there in the bible, written for you and I. Whenever people reached their limit and turned to God, He never failed them. If you consider your problem to be too big for you, then go to the God who is bigger than your problems.

77

VOW AND KEEP YOUR VOWS

What has a vow got to do with prayer? A vow is a promise or an undertaking to do something. It could also be a pledge to abstain from taking an action. God considers a vow to be a serious matter, and expects us to always keep our vows. You can challenge God to do something for you, by making a vow. It is a form of prayer in which you call on God to do something for you in return for something else-usually very tangible and beyond the ordinary. *"When thou vowest a vow unto God, defer not to pay it; for He hath no pleasure in fools: pay that which thou vowest"* (Ecclesiastes 5:4).

Making a vow is not a way of bribing God. It is no short cut for getting God to answer prayers. However, a vow is an act of faith, exercised in situations of desperate need and times of solemn commitment. You can make a vow to God to go into a fast, to pray on particular days, time or durations, you can also do so to challenge God for a particular miracle you want in your life. Vows give you a sense of commitment, drive, and the feeling that you may have stirred God to work on your behalf. This feeling can enhance your faith and keep you motivated when you pray.

God Honours Our Vows

Jacob understood the power of a vow. He had cheated his brother of his birth right and was facing the risk of death as Esau went after his life. He was really in trouble- big trouble. He ran for his life and made a vow during his flight from his brother.

> "And Jacob vowed a Vow, saying, if God will be with me, and will keep me in this way that I go, and will give me bread to eat, and raiment to put on, so that I come again to my father's house in peace, then shall the Lord be my God: And this stone, which I have set for a pillar, shall be God's house: and of all that thou shalt give me I will surely give the tenth unto thee" (Gen 18:20-22).

I have listened to many of God's children testify to the power of vows. They made vows (promises) to do something if God delivered them from a particular situation, and God honoured their vows. Vows are so powerful that you do not need to pray for ages, just tell God what you want to do if He gave you victory in a certain area. Be careful though, not to make foolish vows. You will still have to fulfil biblical conditions for answered prayers, in addition to your vows. God paid attention to and had respect for Jacob's vow. In Jacob's vow he:

- Committed to making the Lord his God if God protected him, preserved his life and prospered his ways.
- Undertook to sacrifice on the stone which served as his pillow when he slept out in the open as he fled from Esau, his brother.
- Promised to honour God with a tenth of all that God would bless him with. In Haran God prospered and blessed Jacob indeed with a large family, abundant wealth and protected him from Laban (his oppressive uncle), from every evil and from the wrath of Esau, his brother, on his return home after many years in exile.

Vows are not the easiest form of prayers because you cannot expect to get away with not fulfilling them. God will act on your behalf in response to your promise but you must keep your part of the commitment.

Jacob probably forgot the vows he made, but God reminded him. God attaches great importance to vows. Jacob returned to his homeland after been on the run for several years. Then God spoke to him, *"Arise, go up to Bethel and dwell there, and make an altar there to God, who appeared to you when you fled from the face of Esau your brother"* (Genesis 35:1).

A vow is a serious business with God. He wants us to keep our commitments, because He will always fulfil His part of the agreement:

> *"When thou vowest a vow unto God, defer not to pay it; for he hath no pleasure in fools: pay that which thou hast vowed. Better is it that thou shouldest not vow, than that thou shouldest vow and not pay. Suffer not thy mouth to cause thy flesh to sin; neither say thou before the angel, that it was an error: wherefore should God be angry at thy voice, and destroy the work of thine hands?"* (Ecclesiastes 5:4-6).

Keep Your Vows to God

Many Christians make vows to God which are never kept. This is unacceptable to Him and can stand in the way of answered prayers. Failing to make vows will not stop God from answering your prayers, but not keeping them can hinder you from getting God's attention. So think very well before you make a vow, they are just as powerful in obstructing your prayers as they are in enhancing them. *"When thou shalt vow a vow unto the LORD thy God, thou shalt not slack to pay it: for the LORD thy God will surely require it of thee; and it would be sin in thee"* (Deuteronomy 23:21).

As we have already examined in Genesis 28:20-22, Jacob made a vow to God. God was moved by the vow and blessed Jacob, and delivered him from impending disaster. Never make foolish vows like Jephthah did in Judges 11:30-31. Jephthah made a foolish vow that cost him the life of his daughter; it was a rash one which should have been avoided. So think twice before you make that promise to God, as you will have to fulfil your obligation. God honoured His part of the commitment, by giving Jephthah victory over his enemies, so did Jephthah- although it was a very difficult one for him. You must only promise God that which you are capable of delivering. Never make a vow in a hurry. Once again, making a vow cannot twist the arm of God to do the unusual on your behalf. Spiritual laws will still apply, faith must be exercised and the will of God will still remain a critical factor.

78

WATCH AND PRAY

The apostle Peter made a stark warning to God's children to:

> *"Be sober, be vigilant; because your adversary the devil, as a roaring lion, walketh about, seeking whom he may devour"* (1 Peter 5:8).

Many of the battles we fight could easily be avoided by simply being vigilant and on the look-out for the adversary's tricks. We can repel (with less effort) demonic encroachments by being observant and guarding against their ploys. In Matthew 26:14, Jesus told His disciples, *"Watch and pray, that ye enter not into temptation: the spirit indeed is willing, but the flesh is weak."* On three separate occasions the phrase "watch and pray" was used in the gospels (Matthew 26:41; Mark 13:13; Mark 14:38). A lot of people are very good at praying but bad at watching; therefore they pray a lot more than they should. Two similar but different Greek words are used for "watch" in the New Testament:

GREGOPEO, used in Matthew 26:41 and Mark 14:38; it means "to be vigilant," "to keep awake," "to be on the alert," and "to keep one's eyes open."

AGRYPNEO, used in Mark 13:33; it means "to be sleepless," or "to keep oneself awake for the purpose of watching." Although both words are similar, the later word draws more attention to sleep. God wants his children to both be vigilant and stay awake. Awake, not just physically, but in every one of our faculties. Jesus rebuked His disciples for sleeping when they should have been wide awake. *"And He cometh unto the disciples, and findeth them asleep, and saith unto Peter, What, could ye not watch with me an hour"* (Matthew 26:40).

Jesus has a reason for asking us to watch and pray. On its own, praying is a great act, but if you fail to be vigilant, the enemy can undo the results of your prayer and create a myriad of problems for you. Watch what you say after you have prayed. Watch for the enemy's tactics and antics. Watch to see what direction God is leading you before and after you have prayed.

Old Testament Watchmen

In Isaiah 62:6 God says,

> *"I have set watchmen upon thy walls, O Jerusalem, which shall never hold their peace day nor night: ye that make mention of the LORD, keep not silence…"*

1. The Old Testament watchman was on duty day and night-nonstop vigilance (Isaiah 62:6).
2. The Old Testament watchman performed the duties of a guard over the house of the Lord (2kings 11:4-8).
3. God has given us the privilege to watch in prayer and be vigilant over His house and His people (2 chronicles 23:6-8).
4. The Old Testament watchman delivered God's word to his people (Ezekiel 33:7-8). We have the same responsibility.
5. The Old Testament watchman needed to see clearly (2 Samuel 18:24); therefore, they needed to be on a tower or elevated surfaces.
6. Faithfulness was required of the Old Testament watchman so he could truly represent God and man. (2 Sammuel18:24-27). God requires faithfulness from us as intercessors in carrying out our spiritual duties of watching and praying.

Why Watch And Pray?

A watchful person is spiritually awake and aware of environmental realities. They pay attention to the things happening around them on a continuous basis. Watchful people make God's word their standard and never get carried away by secular opinions and ideologies. A vigilant Christian keeps both their physical and spiritual eyes open, knowing that Satan is still out and about to corner God's people into sin and disobedience in the most subtle way possible. A watchful person never takes anything for granted because of the knowledge that the enemy is relentlessly deploying his schemes and forces against God's children.

Watch every hour for the coming of the Lord. It is no use praying, fasting and getting engaged in spiritual activities, only to miss the coming of the Lord. Watch the unfolding local, national and global events for signs of the Lord's coming. He has warned that no one knows the hour of His coming, yet many Christians live like life begins and ends here. Jesus cautions us to watch out for deceptions, wars and rumours of war, famines and pestilences, persecutions, earthquakes, offence and betrayals, abundance of iniquity, and false prophecies. Keep watching and praying about all these issues and anything else God reveals to you.

We live in very hostile times. There is an ever growing hostility towards the gospel and everything that our faith stands for. Some of these hostilities are so subtle that you will hardly recognise them. The only way you can escape the enemy's trap is to both watch and pray. Pray about everything you observe. Take action about everything God impresses on your heart. The most effective weapons against the enemy are to watch and pray, so you must continue to be sharp-eyed and defend yourself and God's kingdom against every demonic aggression.

79

WORK AND PRAY

"God is not obligated to bless people who don't work hard."
Sunday Adelaja

Jesus admonished us to watch and pray. He equally wants us to work and pray. All praying without work is an attempt to make God a magician, which He is not, similarly all work and no prayer removes the divine touch from human affairs. Prayer alone with little or no work is irresponsible living. Jesus worked very hard on earth to achieve His goals. He also prayed very hard so the father can take full control.

God Blesses Hard Work

God does not want His people to conceal their laziness and fear of hard work under the pretext of prayer. It is an abdication of responsibility to be:

Praying instead of evangelising.

Knocking on heaven's doors instead of knocking on people's doors.

Praying instead of studying for exams.

Praying when you should be working harder on your relationship.

Praying and waiting when you should be training and working

Jesus is our great example of hard work. Once He said,

"I must work the works of Him that sent me, while it is day: the night comes, when no man can work." (John 9:4). This was His response when His disciples wanted Him to take a break from the day's work and have a meal. Food, clothing, fame, position, and other things people crave were the least of His priorities. This is not to imply that we should not take breaks or eat, it means He focused all His energies where it really mattered- work, hard work, soul winning and restoration of the Kingdom. On another occasion He said, *"My Father worketh hitherto, and I work"* (John 5:17).

By this Jesus meant that His Father continues to work, and He is doing exactly what the Father is doing- work at reconciliation, restoration, healing and deliverance. He threw everything at it. Jesus worked tirelessly; He prayed hard- sometimes praying all night. He worked hard probably working all day. He left us an example; that through much prayer and much work the kingdom would be advanced. Jesus lived by and performed miracles. He also worked harder than anyone around Him. His life was a combination of both miracles (answered prayers) and conscientiousness.

The Protestant Work Ethic

At the root of modern capitalism is what was once known as the Protestant Work Ethic. Max Weber (1864-1920) is credited to be the source of this concept. The concept emphasises hard work, diligence and frugality as an authentic display of salvation and the Christian faith, in contrast with mere religious piety and profession of faith. Max Weber noted that Protestants were successful because they believed that work was good, and it glorified God. Wealth was therefore seen as a sign of God's grace, although it was not to be spent on pleasure but reinvested. Over the years the protestant work ethic evolved into what Weber referred to as the 'Spirit of Capitalism'. Capitalism is the idea that it is morally good to work for the purpose of profit. The bible endorses working for profit:

"In every labour there is profit: but the talk of the lips tendeth only to penury" (Proverbs 14:23). In the early stages of European capitalism the protestant ethic was pivotal to the economic success of protestant organisations which pursued and interpreted worldly success as an indication of eternal salvation. There may have been some extremes to this belief, however it is this philosophy that later became the platform for the prosperity enjoyed by western economies for several generations. The idea was that Christians owed God a duty to effectively utilise God –given gifts and resources for economic and societal advancement. Jesus taught hard work through His personal life. Paul also wrote,

> *"I have shewed all things, how that so labouring ye ought to support the weak, and to remember the words of the Lord Jesus, how He said, It is more blessed to give than to receive."* (Acts 20:35).

The Christian faith is not all about spiritualising things. It is also about thrift and sweat. A lot of Christians would rather 'pray' the price, when they should be paying the price. God will never take over our responsibility; He will always play His part, and expect us to play our part.

Pray persistently, but also work with intensity. Prayer will be more effective if Christians pray earnestly, work enthusiastically and give themselves doggedly to productive work. God wants us to lean on Him, but He also cautions that, *"By much slothfulness the building decayeth; and through idleness of the hands the house droppeth through."* (Ecclesiastes 10:18).

Prayer is an aid to hard work. Prayer waters the seed you have sown. It protects the efforts you have applied and works with the actions that you have set in motion. Miracles are not for every day, work is for every day. That is the way God designed things. Miracles only happen when they are really needed, not when people shirk their God-given responsibilities to plough, plant and prune. Hardworking people enjoy both self-respect and earned respect. A studious life leads to self-efficacy and self-sufficiency. God only blesses the works of our hands. The psalmist prayed,

> "... And let the beauty of the LORD our God be upon us, and establish thou the work of our hands for us; yes, establish the work of our hands." (Psalm 90:17).

Prayer does not work in a vacuum. Pray, yes. Work a lot more than you pray. Sometimes you will find that prayer may not be needed in most cases at all. Prayer 'lubricates', supports and multiplies your efforts. It never replaces physical activity. So, work and pray; add a lot more work to prayer.

80

WISDOM FOR PRAYERS

Knowledge, discernment and perception are fertile grounds for effective praying. If you pray incorrectly, you will end up where you do not expect. When I listen to some people pray, I get the impression that their prayer is uninformed, unorganised and too generalised. I become tempted to think that they may have to pray for a very long time with little or no result for their efforts, because their prayers seem to lack clarity, direction and inspiration. Wisdom will lead you to pray with precision, and with good progress. It is a good idea to pray hard; but praying smart is more important; and this takes wisdom.

God's Word on Wisdom

The bible has so much to say about wisdom: The fear of the LORD is the beginning of wisdom (Proverbs 9:10). Wisdom belongs to God (Job 12:13). If you lack wisdom you should ask God who gives it generously (James 12:13). The mouth of the righteous utters wisdom (Psalm 37:30-31). God gives pure wisdom to His people (James 3:17). Wisdom delivers a person from wicked or evil people (Proverbs 2:12). We must obtain wisdom at every cost (Proverbs 4:7). It is foolish to trust in yourself (Proverbs 28:26) instead of depending on God (Proverbs 3:7). Wisdom is better than money and everything else we may desire to have (Proverbs 8:11).

Wisdom is sometimes used interchangeably with understanding. Wisdom acts as a catalyst for successful praying. Divine wisdom is the ability to perceive things God's own way, based on the knowledge and understanding of His word. This can make a world of difference to how you pray, and the impact your prayer makes. Knowledge, understanding and wisdom are sometimes used interchangeably in the bible. Other times they are used in different and distinct ways. Knowledge relates to facts. Understanding relates to getting meaning from the facts. Wisdom is the ability to take the next step based on facts and understanding.

In prayer, you may have all the facts, have a thorough understanding of the situation and still lack the ability to apply them when praying about a particular situation. How well or accurately you phrase a prayer request can determine the effectiveness of your prayer. You need wisdom to communicate the right words to people. You also need wisdom to communicate correctly with God. It is true that God understands our hearts desire, and will accept us at our level of communication. Wisdom will lead to precision and accuracy in crafting your prayer. Precision praying will help you to hit your prayer target with exactness without having to ramble or vacillate.

Knowledge	Understanding	Wisdom
Facts	Meaning	Next steps to take
Information	What are the principles?	How do I apply them?
Memory	Reason	Action
Scholars	Teachers	Prophets

Impact of Wisdom on Prayers

Wisdom gives insights on how to pray. The accuracy and all-inclusiveness of your communication in prayer will depend substantially on the application of wisdom. Wisdom can save you time and energy in prayer. One prayer point wisely designed may be all you need instead of multiple prayer items which will require more time and energy to carry through.

Wisdom will enable you to discern which situation requires spiritual warfare, which ones will need you to simply worship God, and which ones will be better dealt with by other forms of prayer. What if you are carrying out the prayer of intercession for someone when the person actually needs a personal prayer of consecration? Would the results not be completely different? What if you were confessing sins when you should be confessing God's word? Would that not change the dynamics? Wisdom is the principal key in talking to God about what you want Him to do.

Sometimes I come before God with pre-meditated, pre-planned and well itemised prayer points, only for God to inspire me to pray about something else. On many occasions He impresses on me to worship instead of praying. Several times I had planned to pray about something for a specific amount of time, however God redirects my attention to something else- in nearly all the cases, He lays in my heart to pray over the issue for at least double my originally intended duration. This is divine wisdom in action. God even changes the wordings of my prayer many times when I pray, because they are not the way He wants them to be.

It is common for people to ask us to pray for them. They may have a lot of skeletons in their cupboards; may have been living in perpetual disobedience to God's word, and probably live double lives. Wisdom will save you from wasting time on them, guiding you on whether to pray, or how to pray for them. Wisdom will save you from wasted hours of prayer because God is not likely to answer you until they turn from their sinful ways.

When you spend money prudently, relate with people circumspectly, communicate sensibly with others, you will make fewer mistakes and encounter less problems; as a result you will have less praying to do because the application of wisdom has preserved you from self-made setbacks. The exercise of wisdom in daily life will protect you from most of the pains and troubles that drive people into emergency and unplanned prayers.

81

WORRY DRAINS PRAYER ENERGY

One of the greatest enemies of prayers is worry. Worry is the agitated feeling that something might happen. It is a demonstration of fear, concern or anxiety which keeps many people awake at night, drain their energy, cause them to make mistakes and doubt God. People who worry too much can expose themselves to satanic attacks and find it too difficult to pray.

> *"Be anxious for nothing, but in every thing by prayer and supplication, with thanksgiving, let your requests be made known to God; and the peace of God, which surpasses all understanding, will guard your hearts and minds through Jesus Christ"* (Philippians 4:6-7).

Leave your cares at the feet of Jesus. Worry never makes any situation better. It simply complicates the problem by sapping you of strength and making you more vulnerable to the enemy.

Unbelief in Disguise

Anxiety over problems is usually a veiled form of unbelief. It is unbelief putting up a mask, a lack of faith in God and His word. Unbelief is a sin because God has promised to help us in times of trouble.

Apprehension demonstrates our lack of faith in God and His word. There are occasional moments when every one gets caught in the web of panic, but some people are habitual worriers. This robs them of the confidence and power needed for meaningful praying. Even when they attempt to pray, their words are laced with fear and anxiety until they become too weak and unsettled to pray with results. *"It is vain for you to rise up early, to sit up late, to eat the bread of sorrows; for so He gives His beloved sleep"* (Psalm 126:2).

Leave your problems in God's hands as you pray. Approach His throne with unwavering faith. Talk to Him as your father and go to sleep, rest assured that your trouble is in His hands. I consider worrying a double tragedy, because you already carry the weight of a problem, getting absorbed in it increases the severity of the situation. The longer you accommodate fear, the better chance Satan has to ruffle and keep you from praying.

Costly Mistakes

Worry can lead to deadly mistakes and aggravate situations. Moses sent out twelve people to spy out the (promised) land which God would later give to His people to inherit. On their return from the spy mission, they reported (as matter of fact) that there were giants in the land. The evidence proved that there were giants in the land, but ten out of the twelve spies blew the problem out of proportion because they were overwhelmed by the weight of what they saw. Worry makes people see a problem bigger than it truly is. Their bad report threw the congregation into panic:

> *"And all the congregation lifted up their voice, and cried; and the people wept that night. And all the children of Israel murmured against Moses and against Aaron: and the whole congregation said unto them, Would God that we had died in the land of Egypt! or would God we had died in this wilderness! And wherefore hath the* LORD *brought us unto this land, to fall by*

the sword, that our wives and our children should be a prey?
were it not better for us to return into Egypt? And they said one
to another, Let us make a captain, and let us return into Egypt"
(Numbers 14:4).

The result of this disastrous mistake was that God caused them to complete the journey of 40 days in 40 years. Worrying can cause very expensive set-backs; it will keep you longer in a problem state because you will have lost creativity and the ability to apply common sense, both of which are needed for prayers, and in dealing with a crisis situation.

Worry Harms Your Health

Becoming apprehensive can be detrimental to both your spiritual and physical health. If you let agitation rule your life during difficult times, it could be injurious to your physical health. Your blood pressure may go over the roof causing heart problems, colds, stomach ulcers and headaches among others. The spiritual implication is that you might become so destabilised and lose interest in prayers and other spiritual activities. The more you worry the less you are likely to pray, and vice versa. Put all your energies into prayer and do not feed your worries.

You Can Be Free From Worry

Get rid of every form of gloom, panic and unease. Cast your burden upon Jesus. 'That sounds familiar', you may say. People rarely sincerely cast their burdens upon Jesus. When God is allowed to take full control of a problem, you will never feel like you are still carrying the weight. It is completely off your heart and your shoulders.

Cultivate God's presence through fasting, worship, personal study of God's word, group fellowship and praying in tongues. Also listen to motivational and inspiring tapes- they all have their place. In every trial there is a hidden testimony. Discover it. There is gain hidden underneath every pain. Find it. Do not be habitually panicky, be a spiritual warrior. Rid yourself of every form of tension and demonic pressures.

Worry is bad for your physical health. It is also bad for your spiritual health. Prayer and worry cannot mix properly. Stop worrying. Start praying. Do not let it rob you of the energy and faith to pray.

82

WALK WITH GOD

The word 'Walk' in the bible denotes conduct in life, general disposition and deportment. Enoch "walked with God" (Genesis 5:24). It means he had a conduct and lifestyle that centred on God. His conduct and courses of action completely reflected God. God was his focus. Everything else was secondary. A man's prayer life will never amount to much unless he learns to walk with God in the complete sense of it. Walking with God and talking to Him go hand in hand. The bible talks about walking in darkness (1John 1:6), walking in the light (1John 1:7), walking by faith (2Corinthians 5:7), walking by the Spirit (Galatians 5:16) and walking in all the ways of the Lord (Deuteronomy 5:33).

Walking with God brings us into a closer relationship with Him which forms the basis of our daily prayers. Walking closely with God brings the Christian into better understanding of His ways and a greater manifestation of His power in our lives. God commanded Abraham to walk before Him (Genesis 17:1). When you walk with and talk to Him you will constantly bask in his power. Then prayer will no longer become a drag, but a delight. The prophet Micah made a call to the people of Israel:

> *"He has shown you, O man, what is good; and what does the LORD require of you, but to do justly, to love mercy, and to walk humbly with your God?" (Micah 6:8)* NKJV

You cannot successfully work with God until you are truly walking with Him. Proximity to God gives you prosperity in prayers.

What it means To Walk with The Lord

Some people walk ahead of God, so they lose divine direction, fall into traps and stumble in their ways. An individual that walks with God patiently follows Him, neither too fast nor too slow. They keep pace with God, following every one of His instructions on a timely basis. They are not moved by what they see, but by what God says. Walking constantly beside God keeps your prayer fire steadily burning

It is also dangerous to walk behind God. Finding and doing God's will in God's time is the best favour any Christian can do to themselves. Do not allow your attention to be diverted from God. Instead, stay closely connected to Him. Never walk ahead of God or behind Him. Keep pace with, and stay abreast of Him. This is what it takes to walk with God. The prophet Amos once asked this salient question, *"Can two walk together, except they be agreed?"* (Amos 3:3). You cannot talk to God from a distance- by this I mean when your heart is far from Him, and your relationship with Him is broken. When you make God your walk companion, He will make you a worthy champion.

How to Walk With God

A closer walk with God will give you a level of intimacy that will open the secrets and treasures of heaven to you at the place of prayer. You will be able to understand the heart-beat of God, and when He speaks you will hear Him loud and clear. As a result of your nearness to Him, when He smiles, winks, frowns or sighs, you will quickly understand Him. This will take your prayer to a marvellous stage because your spirit is constantly infused with the life of God.

The bible tells us of so many ways to walk with God: walk in all the ways which the Lord your God has commanded you. (Deuteronomy 5:53); walk worthy of your calling and of the Lord. (Ephesians 4:1, Colossians 1:10; 2:6) walk in love and as children of light. (Ephesians 5:2, 8); walk in the fear or reverence of God. (Nehemiah 5:9; Acts 9:31); let your walk reflect the Christ you have received. (Colossians 2:6). God also wants His people to walk uprightly and by faith (Proverbs 10:19; 2Corinthians 5:7). Walking apart from God could remove the touch of divinity from your prayer, making it a mechanical and powerless experience.

Steps in the Right Direction

People who fail to walk with the Lord will spend more efforts and time on prayer because they will find themselves in the wrong direction. It is better to mark time with the Lord (as it may seems sometimes) than to run faster than Him. God is a master programmer, and He will always be on time. In many places in the bible we are told the importance of ordering our steps in God's footprint.

When Saul continued to hunt for David's life in his (Saul's) backslidden days, David wisely stayed within the boundaries God allowed him to walk, and one day David lamented to Jonathan son of Saul,

> *"... thy father certainly knoweth that I have found grace in thine eyes; and he saith, Let not Jonathan know this, lest he be grieved: but truly as the LORD liveth, and as thy soul liveth, there is but a step between me and death"* (1Samuel 20:3).

We need God to direct our steps all the time. It reduces the amount of unnecessary prayers we pray because we receive God's help to step away from all sorts of dangers. When you walk side by side with God, He will enlarge your steps so you do not slide (Psalm 18:36) and get hurt. You will constantly draw energy from your closeness to Him, and in the unlikely event that you try to stumble, quickly raise your voice to Him (not long prayers) and you will be able to reach out quickly for God's hand just as Peter did during a storm in the sea.

83

WARFARE IN THREE DIMENSIONS

The three dimensions of man are increasingly engaged in spiritual warfare. Understanding how this warfare relates to every aspect of an individual can be the deciding factor in winning spiritual battles. The bible differentiates between three compartments of man – Spirit, Soul, and Body. These three form the centre of every spiritual warfare. To have total victory over the enemy you must continue to fight and win in all three levels.

The body is prone to sickness, feebleness, disease, pain and other physical afflictions which can weaken your ability to pray. The soul can be attacked by mental illness, emotional crisis and a broken will. This again can have a ripple effect on your prayer life. When your spirit feels empty, hopeless, isolated and lost you cannot have a fruitful spiritual relationship (including in prayer) with God. So, you must make every effort to promote soundness in these three areas so you can enjoy awesome fellowship with your heavenly Father in prayer.

How God Designed Us

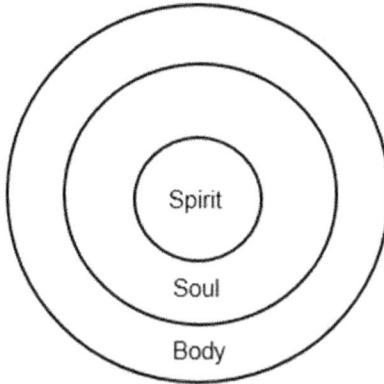

Spirit

Soul

Body

Now may the God of peace himself
sanctify you completely, and may your
whole spirit and soul and body be kept
blameless at the coming of our Lord Jesus
Christ.
1 Thessalonians 5:23

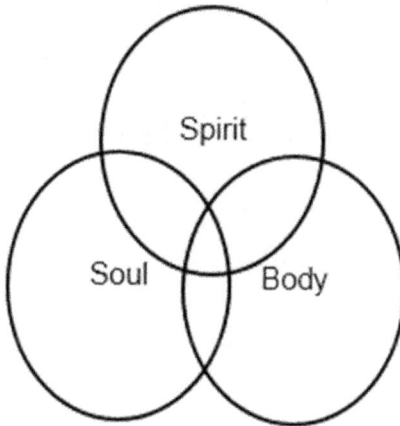

Spirit

Soul   Body

Until a person dies or until a Christian is caught up to meet with the
Master in the air, there remains a permanent link between the three
compartments of man. Whatever affects one easily impacts on the other.

Spirit

The human spirit is the part that knows God, and relates with the spiritual realm. If a person has not encountered or developed a personal relationship with God, they will be unable to communicate with Him. The only prayer they can pray successfully at this point is that of repentance and forgiveness from sin. Some of the things that take place in the faculty of the spirit include faith, hope, prayer and worship. The life of God in you connects you with the power of God. The life of God transmitted to your spirit at the new birth is the powerhouse for prayer, so an unsaved person is completely detached from the Spirit of God and cannot truly encounter God in prayers.

The human spirit plays a critical role in prayers because:

1. The spirit of man is the lamp of the Lord, searching all his innermost parts (Proverbs 20:27).
2. The Holy Spirit bears witness with our spirit that we are the children of God (Romans 8:16).
3. God is spirit, and those who worship Him must do so in spirit and truth. (John 4:24).
4. If Christ is in you, although the body is dead because of sin, the spirit is life because of righteousness.
5. Your spirit is the breath of God. It is the only place which can interact with Him (Genesis 2:7).

A healthy spirit is the foundation for all prayers. A heavy spirit will have difficulties praying with vigour and interest. Always keep your spirit in good shape, because that is the place where God meets with you in prayer. Feed it constantly. Fix it quickly whenever something is not quite right.

Soul

The soul consists of the mind, will and emotions. At salvation the spirit is renewed and reborn, but the soul remains unchanged. Whereas salvation of the spirit is instantaneous, the soul is progressively changed in a continuous process. The soul is the source of feelings, thoughts, desires, reasoning and personality. Your emotions can be easily influenced by the things that happen outside you (Proverbs 25:28), and this can influence your prayer life either positively or negatively. To pray effectively, you need a healthy soul. You will have to constantly win the battles within this region to continue to experience breakthroughs in prayer.

Renew your soul every day by the Word of God (Colossians 3:16). No matter how much you pray, you will never dwell in victory unless your mind accepts that God has made provisions for your sickness, rejection, poverty, failure, barrenness, defeat and everything else that you bring before God. Your soul must agree with your spirit, your body will then walk in the blessings attracted by your spirit and soul. Poor self-image, temptations, guilt, defeat, discouragement, depression and many other weapons of the enemy become effective when this aspect of you is weakened by the enemy. When your will power is weakened or overcome there is little your spirit and body can do to get you to engage with God in prayer.

Body

The body or flesh is the outward, unchanged part of us with which we interact with the physical world through the physical senses. Paul says in 1 Corinthians 9:27

> "But I keep under my body, and bring it unto subjection: lest that by any means, when I have preached to others, I myself should become a castaway." Paul further stressed in Romans 12:1, "I beseech you therefore, brethren, by the mercies of God, that ye present your bodies a living sacrifice, holy, acceptable unto God, which is your reasonable service"

Subjecting the body to the total influence of the Holy Spirit is mandatory if you want to be at your spiritual best. "And the very God of peace sanctify *you wholly; and I pray God your whole spirit and soul and body be preserved blameless unto the coming of our Lord Jesus Christ"* (1Thessalonians 5:28).

Tiredness, sickness, ungodly pleasures and different forms of vanities can be used by Satan to distract the flesh from focusing on a powerful and purposeful prayer life. Self-centred prayers are the product of a life dominated by the flesh. Prayer demands your entire being. Any defects in any of the realms of your spirit, soul or body can weigh down your prayer life.

84

WORLDS OF PRAYER

During His Sermon on the Mount Jesus taught His disciples to ask, seek and knock. Dr Lester Sumrall refers to these as the three worlds of prayer. These three levels are widely viewed as an ascending level of prayer stages. Jesus said, *"Ask and it will be given to you, Seek and you will find; Knock and the door will be opened to you. For everyone who asks receives; the one who seeks finds; and to the one who knocks, the door will be opened"* (Matthew 7:7-8). NIV

I believe the main focus of Jesus in this teaching is to underscore the need for perseverance in prayers: "Continue to ask", "continue to seek", "continue to knock", He seems to be saying. "Keep doing these until I show up". The question is why would God want His children to keep asking, keep seeking or keep knocking when He could simply and very easily give us everything we need even without praying? The bottom line is that God is not merely interested in 'dishing out' things to us. He sometimes uses prayers as a tool to train and develop His children to trust Him and become rugged to withstand difficulties.

Prayer World One: ASK

God only does things in response to prayers. *"Ye have not because ye ask not"*, James says (4:2). Jesus said, *"Ask and ye shall receive."* (7:7). If you do not ask, you will not receive. This is an invitation to bring your requests before God. There are uncountable number of things that God wants to give you, but until you ask, you are not likely to receive. 'But God knows our needs'. True. Yet, God wants you to ask. Most people will not value things they do not ask for, neither would they appreciate things for which they have made no sacrifices. Not only should we ask, we must keep asking until we have received. Leave nothing to fate, ask and you will receive. It sounds easy to do, but many people do not really ask, instead they complain and get discouraged.

The early stage of the three levels is to Ask. Some things we ask for we receive immediately. Few Christians go beyond this level. If they do not receive soon after they have asked, they lose hope, and may stop praying altogether. You can depend on God because His word is true and He cannot lie (Hebrews 6:18). If you ask in accordance with His will and in faith persistently, He has promised to answer you (1John 5:14-15); James 1:6-8).

Prayer World Two: SEEK

When we seek for something it means we are doing everything we can to find it. We seek things by going after and hunting for them. It requires endurance and vigilance to seek and find things that are not clearly within sight. Sometimes I ask my children to help look for miss-laid items in the house. Too often a child comes back to me to say they are unable to find an item, when in fact they had not put sufficient efforts into their search. In most cases I leave what ever I am doing, go to the very spot they have checked, and with a little more concentration and patience I come out with the same thing they could not find. It is for these same reasons that some of God's children seek and find the desires of their heart, and others never receive answers to their prayers. The business of prayer is easier for those who are patient and persistent.

Seeking involves both asking and taking action. Seeking can sometimes entail finding out God's will on a matter. To seek suggests that something is not readily available – but you must find it nevertheless. You will have to try, strive and make repeated attempts until you find. It could involve fasting for short and prolonged times, but you must keep seeking because God has promised that you will find. Hunters who seek games have to walk large expanses of land until they find their target. They do not give up their search and retire to their homes just because the task is cumbersome. In prayer never stop seeking until you find, sometimes victory may just be around the corner.

Prayer World Three: KNOCK

The third world of prayer is knocking. You ask, seek and then knock. An example of knocking: You have decided to visit a friend in another part of your city, and have agreed to meet the person at home. The first thing you do is to get the person's address, then use a map or navigator to locate where they live. The next thing you do is to find the door and knock on it with the expectation to receive an answer. You are very optimistic that your friend who gave you the appointment and the location address will be there to open the door. You simply knock for as long as it will take for the friend to emerge through the open door. If your friend takes too long to open the door you may take a break or a walk, and return to the door because you have a promise that he or she would be in and nothing has changed since your friend made that promise. God's promise to you is to knock until the door is opened. No matter the delay you should knock on heaven's door until you face an open door.

You have God's address, promises and permission to knock until the door is open. Yes, God is not dead, never sleeps and is never on break. But He says we should knock – that means we must knock until something happens. Knocking can progress from the casual level to the point where you will have to bang, pound, beat or 'hammer'. In the parable of the friend at midnight who needed help from another friend, Jesus tells us that a friend may not respond to the dire needs of another friend in the middle of the night. Jesus says,

"But I tell you this – though he won't do it for friendship's sake, if you keep knocking long enough, he will get up and give you whatever you need because of your shameless persistence" (Luke 11:8) NLT.

You must move from asking to seeking, and then to knocking until the door is wide open to you. When God says ask, seek and knock, He means every bit of what He says. He can never go back on His word to you.

85

WAIT ON THE LORD

Nobody likes being asked to wait, especially if they have to wait for a long time. Although this is a necessary part of life, it is still one of the most uncomfortable things we have to do. It is not one of those things that people can endure regardless of age, experience or background. The word 'wait' easily reminds me of queues at the post office, the bank and the Doctor's practice. I personally cannot bear traffic queues; I can wait patiently for hours anywhere but the traffic queues. Notwithstanding, I have accepted the fact that waiting in a line of traffic is unavoidable if I must drive. If you must pray, you will also need to go through the discipline of waiting (if need be) until your prayers are answered.

What It Means To Wait Upon the Lord

The bible says:

> *"Wait on the LORD: be of good courage, and He shall strengthen thine heart: wait, I say, on the LORD"* (Psalm 27:14).

The most commonly used words in the Old Testament for 'wait' are:

- Qavah - "to bind together", "look patiently", "tarry or wait", "hope, expect".
- Yachal - "to wait", "hope, wait expectantly", "and trust".

- Damam - "to be dumb, grow silent, be still", "wait tarry, rest".
- Chakah -"to wait, tarry" "long for".

The Old Testament context suggests dependence on God in the face of challenges. The New Testament mainly uses the word, *prosdechomai*- in the context of waiting for the coming of the LORD.

The bible says we should wait patiently (Psalm 37:7, Habakkuk 3: 16); expectantly (Psalm 123:2, Micah-7:7.); with faith (Psalm 130:5); quietly (Lamentations 3:26); eagerly (Romans 8:19-23) and prayerfully (Psalm 25: 4-5). Waiting on God does not mean 'dumping' our responsibilities on God. G. Campbell Morgan asserts:

> "Waiting for God is not laziness. Waiting for God is not going to sleep. Waiting for God is not the abandonment of effort. Waiting for God means, first, activity under command; second, readiness for any new command that may come; third, the ability to do nothing until the command is given."

Why Wait Upon The Lord?

Learning to wait has many advantages for us; inability to wait, or doing so in the wrong way could have unpleasant consequences.

Opportunity to Seek God's Face

Continue to seek the Lord while you wait. Keep studying God's Word, ask Him questions and get further directions from Him. Wait actively, instead of crossing arms doing nothing. Waiting can be passive and frustrating if you stop taking action. Continue to pray, fast and seek the Lord's face until you celebrate your victory. If there comes a moment when God says to you to stop praying, do just that, but until then never stop praying while you are waiting.

Opportunity to Learn and Do More

Waiting time is an opportunity for further learning. Find out more about your situation and keep the lesson for life. Is there something you failed to do which may have caused you some delay? Go back and work on it; make amendments, and if there is still need to pray, then keep up praying. Develop new skills and knowledge. This could make your prayers unnecessary. Continue to prepare and develop yourself along the path of your prayer requests, and do something that may bring you closer to victory while you continue to wait.

A Chance to Be Still Before God

Waiting time is not for you to carry unnecessary weights. If you have turned things over to the Lord, you must leave them with Him. Waiting is a chance to be still before God. He says, *"Be Still and know that I am the Lord"* (Psalm 46:10); when you stay still (unruffled, strong, courageous, and in charge) before God, the Bible says, *"The Lord will fight for you, and you shall hold your peace"* (Ex 14:14).

Perfection of God's Timing

Although waiting does not mean folding arms endlessly, hoping something will happen someday, it is noteworthy that God has a perfect time for everything (Ecclesiastes 3 : 1-8). He knows what, and when is best for you. Therefore, *"... let us not lose heart in doing good, for in due time we shall reap if we do not grow weary"*. Relax in God's arms and He will keep you until the right time. Your heavenly Father is never in as much hurry as you, therefore, do not go ahead of Him.

Character Moulding

Waiting period is a time for God to make and mould our character. Some people breakdown and give up at this time. God is all powerful and all knowing; when we pray, we are often in a hurry, but waiting is an act of faith and you must hold on till the very end. Anyone who understands God will agree with me that waiting time is not wasted time. God also uses this time to build up your character and strength.

People who have no patience to wait usually miss their place in the queue. They either have to start all over, or forfeit their purpose of being in the line. God can use your waiting to recover and restructure your destiny. So wait patiently and let Him work on you. Sometimes people pray and then continue to wait endlessly for God, when in fact, all the while God has been waiting for them- either to step out, or change course altogether. Having to wait is crucial, but learning to wait correctly is very important.

God Knows the Best

We must never forget that our knowledge of ourselves and our lives is extremely limited compared with the omniscience of God. He knows the end of a thing even from its beginning (Isaiah 46:10). He may refuse or delay to answer prayers in our own interest. Sometimes Christians think they know their own best interests and with that limited knowledge they cry unto God in prayer. Jesus asked God to let the Cup pass over Him. If that prayer had been answered, will there be Christianity today? The child wants candy twenty times a day if possible, but the mother knows it is a short cut to sickness and discomfort (Jeremiah 29: 11-13). That is the reason why we must learn not only submission, but also obedience, in our prayer attitude. Trust and obey.

86

WRONG PRAYERS PRODUCE WRONG ANSWERS

Even when people do things with the best intentions, right motives and in good faith, they can still go wrong when the right things are done in the wrong way. One of the reasons why many prayers are unsuccessful is because they have been prayed in the wrong ways, and may be, for the wrong reasons. For Him to answer our prayers God has laid down guidelines that must govern our praying. If a person fasts and prays for 100 days, in the wrong way, he or she will end up with the wrong answers.

In first Chronicles chapter thirteen, David selected priests and Levites from across the land to return the ark of God which had been captured several years back, to Jerusalem. God wanted him to do it. It was the right thing to do and he had the backing of God and the people. Yet God was unhappy with David. Although God wanted the ark back in Jerusalem, David did not follow God's instruction regarding the transportation of the ark. With great excitement David and his people made a new cart for the conveyance of the ark to Jerusalem. This was contrary to God's previous instructions to Israel that the ark must only be carried by the Levites on two poles (Numb 4:5-6). As the journey continued back to Jerusalem, the ark wobbled and threatened to fall. The Bible says a man name Uzza put out his hand to hold the ark, but God struck Uzza dead.

What went wrong? David failed to follow God's instructions for moving the ark. The ark represented God's presence. When we come into God's presence in prayer, we must follow the rules. It is only the prayers carried out in line with God's prescription and standards that will command His attention. There are operating principles for everything in life; God also has His own principles that govern prayers. If will follow them, we will have His ears, if we do not, prayer will remain a struggle.

Wrong Ways to Pray

There are many examples of wrong prayers made by people in the Bible. I will examine just a few of them:

Selfish Prayers (James 4:3)

Christians that continue to make themselves the focus of daily prayers will not enjoy many testimonies of answered prayers. There is so much God wants us to pray about- our leaders, the church, unreached countries, and the needs of other people. This is authentic, unselfish praying. It is more blessed to give than to receive.

Unoffered Prayers (James 4:2)

James says *"Ye lust, and have not: Ye kill, and desire to have, and cannot obtain: Ye fight and war, yet ye have not, because ye ask not."*

It is baseless expecting God to answer the prayers we have not prayed. Occasionally, God grants the desire of our heart, or even work ahead on our behalf; I can testify to countless numbers of such experiences. However, the normal thing is to ask, seek, and knock. Laziness, apathy, discouragement and overconfidence, are just some of the reasons why people may not pray and yet, hope God will arise on their behalf. God cannot answer a prayer that has not been prayed.

'Micro – Wave' Praying (Luke 18:1-8)

In a fast paced world, everyone seems to be in short supply of the virtues of patience and endurance. People want prayer answered even before they say a word. It is not the standard way God works with His children. The instruction is to ask. Luke chapter eighteen teaches the need to persist patiently in prayers. Keep praying, keep pushing. I have discussed this in an earlier section. Hit and run is not God's preferred method of praying.

Vain Repetition (Matthew 6:7)

This should not be confused with the prayer of importunity as encouraged by Jesus. The problem here is not the repetition. It is the word "vain". Repetitive prayer is vain when it is futile, pointless and insincere. It is vain repetition when prayer is simply prayed to fulfil all righteousness with no expectation for answer, not from the heart, without faith and without love for the subject of prayer. Simply chanting prayers a number of times a day, is also vain repetition. I believe that until God leads otherwise, you can pray over a situation as many times as necessary until you gain victory in that area, so long as your prayer is rightly motivated and in keeping with God's word.

Wavering in Prayers (James 1:6-7)

We must ask in faith. There are different levels of faith. It is only by faith that you can please God, and He expects us to always pray and act with the confidence that He will not disappoint. When you pray with a wavering heart you are praying wrongly. The storm may rage, the battle may be intense many times after you have prayed, but keep holding onto the Word of God until you achieve your prayer objective.

Generalized Prayers

When prayers are too generalised they will lack focus. They will be neither here nor there. You need to be specific about what you want

God to do. Prayers with clear goals are the right kind of prayers. Simply asking God to bless you is not enough; in what ways do you want God to bless you? If you want to count your blessings one by one, you must name your requests one by one. It is alright to pray in tongues, but you will miss out on many things if that is all you do. Be specific in your prayer, if you want to receive specific answers.

Because You Ask Amiss

"Ye ask and receive not because ye ask amiss" (James 4:3)

Amiss means: not quite right; inappropriate or out of place; incorrect; improper; astray.

Many prayers go unanswered, many cries go unheard because they do not comply with God's standard. Look back to those times, days and years when you have had no result in your prayers. Could something have been be wrong? I am not making a judgement (I do not have the right to). If you keep asking God to kill your enemies, give you what you refused to work for or change His mind on an issue, you might be asking Him to do the impossible. If you refuse to forgive an offender or harbour iniquity in your heart, you will almost certainly be praying amiss.

Look within you today and find out how you may have been praying in the wrong way. If you keep praying according to God's rules, then you can look to Him to reward your pray times. God is merciful but He will not bend His rules for anyone.

87

'X-RAY' YOUR SPIRITUAL LIFE

An X-ray is an electromagnetic wave which can pass through solids. It takes the image of the internal structure of an object. Diagnostic X-rays penetrate the structure inside the body, producing images on photographic film or fluorescent screen. X-rays are vital in detecting abnormalities within the body and revealing problems such as broken bones, dental decays, tumours and the presence of 'foreign bodies'. The technologist helps the patient into an appropriate position, while the X-ray beam is focused on the part of the body to be examined.

The physician is able to (without intrusion) visualise what is wrong with your body without having to make an incision. On an ongoing basis every one of us needs to be X-rayed by the Holy Spirit, so we can know what aspect of our lives require adjustment or spiritual treatment. Spiritual sickness, especially tricky ones can only be revealed when we expose ourselves to the light of the Holy Spirit. Then we can ask God to restore our spiritual health based on what His Spirit has exposed. An unsolved spiritual problem can constitute a barrier to prayers.

Spiritual Examination

Just like medical practitioners use X-rays and similar devices to examine our health and well-being, God expects us to constantly carry out spiritual self- examination. We can do it by ourselves, but more importantly we should go before God frequently, asking him to shine his light upon us and reveal where we need healing, cleansing and refreshing. Scriptures tell us:

"Examine yourselves, whether ye be in the faith; prove your own selves. Know ye not your own selves, how that Jesus Christ is in you, except ye be reprobates?" (2 Corinthians 13:5).

You must always carry out self-scrutiny to ensure you remain in good spiritual condition. Often people are unable to determine why they find prayer unsavoury, boring and challenging. When you put yourself under the full beam of God's light (the Holy Spirit and the word) He will reveal accurately, where you need a touch of the master physician-Jesus Christ; He will expose things to you which must be eradicated in order for you to freely fellowship with your Father in heaven.

The Spirit and the Word

God's primary agents for self-examination are His Word and the Holy Spirit:

"For the word of God is quick, and powerful, and sharper than any two edged sword, piercing even to the dividing asunder of soul and spirit, and of the joints and marrow, and is a discerner of the thoughts and intents of the heart" (Hebrews 4:12).

When you deliberately and constantly expose your life to the power of God's Word and the Holy Spirit, God will unveil every spiritual problem within you that is capable of hindering prayer efforts. The Holy Spirit is the true light that can shine in every dark region of a Christian's life- as far as the innermost parts of our lives. He searches the deep and hidden things, so let Him reveal who you truly are to you. Take action on whatever He uncovers. Do something about it without any delay. This is the only way to keep yourself pure, prayerful and powerful. Jesus says,

"These things I have I spoken unto you, while yet abiding with you. But the advocate, even the Holy Spirit, whom the father will send in my name, he shall teach you all things, and bring to your remembrance all that I said unto you" (John14:16, 17;25,26).

The passage emphasizes the revealing power of the Holy Spirit. Invite the Holy Spirit frequently into the very centre of your being, let Him continue to search you and reveal your shortcomings to you on a daily basis. Give the Spirit full control because, *"But as it is written, Eye hath not seen, nor ear heard, neither have entered into the heart of man, the things which God hath prepared for them that love him. But God hath revealed them unto us by his Spirit: for the Spirit searcheth all things, yea, the deep things of God"* (1 Corinthians 2:9-10).

If you do not allow God into the most secret parts of your life, He will not give you access to the deepest secrets of His heart. The Psalmist knew this and prayed:

"Search me, O God, and know my heart: try me, and know my thoughts, And see if there be any wicked way in me, and lead me in the way everlasting" (Psalm 139:23-24).

It is impossible to carry out thorough cleaning in a dark or badly lit room. Light reveals dirt, brings clarity, disinfects, overcomes darkness, provides guidance and reveals truth. Presenting yourself before the light of the Holy Spirit will enlighten and give you direction, enhance your spiritual progress, expose evil and sin and protect you from stumbling in your walk with God. Your prayer life will gain fresh momentum and inspiration each time you lay still and bare before God's spiritual X-ray.

Periodic Check Ups

Akin to physical health, you need to carry out regular spiritual check-ups. Like the physical body the soul can be unwell, or it may have some hidden disease waiting to come to light. When you go bare before God, He will reveal 'diseases' that the enemy has yet to unleash.

You must periodically weigh yourself on God's Spiritual Scale (Job31:6) Are your spiritual eyes growing deem, so deem you cannot seem to visualise God's heart cry for humanity? What about your spiritual ears? Do you hear God speak clearly? Does God or your spiritual leader have to scream before you hear, and when you hear do you respond promptly? How is your mouth (teeth and tongue)? Do they gossip, bless people, preach the gospel or simply complain, murmur and criticise? Do you suffer from spiritual blood diseases? The condition of your blood is critical to the successful functioning of your body organs, because life is in the blood. Ask God to purify every aspect of your spiritual life with the purest and most powerful blood that ever existed- the blood of Jesus.

Always take time away before God for spiritual check-ups. Never be too confident of your state; the healthier you are spiritually, the better you will be able to pray. Make your Spiritual health a matter of priority- over and above Christian service or church attendance.

88

YIELD TO GOD

God stresses in His Word the need for us to submit fully to Him. Anyone who is not totally yielded to God cannot be an effective tool in the ministry of prayers. God wants to channel His grace through you at the place of prayers. Submission does not mean leaving your responsibilities to God. It does not mean waiting needlessly and endlessly for God to act on your behalf when you should be doing more to make things happen. Failing to submit to God's will, can expose God's people to demonic activities which will in turn lead to unnecessary praying. Jesus is an example of absolute surrender to the Father's will:

> *"And He went a little further, and fell on His face, and prayed, saying, O my Father, if it be possible, let this cup pass from me: nevertheless, not as I will, but as thou wilt"* (Matthew 26:39).

Striving with God is simply fighting a losing battle. Problems will not yield to your prayers until you have learned to yield fully to God. It is only as you totally surrender to God that you can enjoy real victory in spiritual warfare. Until you lay it all down at His feet your prayer life will remain at the level of shallow waters, lacking in depth and void of impact.

Why People Find It Difficult To Submit To Authority

Fear.

Fear is a primary reason why people struggle with God. Fear of not being in control. Fear of the unknown and fear of God asking them to do the uncomfortable. The bible says perfect love casts away fear. Surrender your fears to God. Trust Him to give you a good ending.

Pain

It is commonly said that 'No pain, no gain'. Submission sometimes leads to painful experiences. Not a lot of people want that. Jesus knew the pain He would experience on the cross. He defied the pain and shame and yielded totally to the fathers will. The end of it is the redemption of mankind. One man's pain became everyone's gain.

Trust

Submission is usually an outcome of trust. Jesus trusted that if He laid down His life on the altar, that if He died, the father would raise Him up. Trust in the Lord with all your heart, stop struggling with Him and all will be well with you. We pray unnecessarily when we fail to abandon our lives into God's hands.

Submit To the Word of God

God's word is our ultimate authority. Make a choice to receive it, believe it and apply it to every area of your life. The bible tells us that every word of God is pure (proverb30: 5-6); is a lamp to your feet and a light to your path (ps119:105); and that the word of God stands for ever (1peter 1:25).

Submission to your employer or government also amounts to submission to God. (1Peter 2:13). When children submit to parents, it is a sign of being under God's authority. (Ephesians 6: 1-3). Wives are to submit to husbands as a sign of submission to God. (Ephesians 5:22-24). The bible says believers should all submit one to another- that includes husband and wife submitting to one another.

When you are obedient to God, opposing forces and circumstances will bow to you and yield to your demands at the place of prayer.

> *"For the weapons of our warfare are not carnal but mighty in God for pulling down strongholds, casting down arguments and every high thing that exalts itself against the knowledge of God, bringing every thought into captivity to the obedience of Christ, and being ready to punish all disobedience when your obedience is fulfilled"* (2Corinthians 10:4-6). NKJV

If a child of God is disobedient and un-submissive to God, they will experience exactly the same from the devil. Your success in prayer will be in direct proportion to your obedience (in all things) to God. *"Submit yourselves therefore to God. Resist the devil, and he will flee from you"* (James 4:7).

In one of his sermons Charles G. Finney noted that submission to God is:

- To joyfully acquiesce in all the providence of God
- To cordially, joyfully and actually obey all the known will of God
- To practically and joyfully put all that we have at the disposal of God
- To yield ourselves completely to God, to be exhaustively used up by Him to accomplish His best interests in the universe
- To deeply and continually long that the whole will of God be done on earth as it is in heaven
- To refuse to be anxious or agitated by His future dealings with us
- To be pleased with whatever God does with us or with others (www.GospelTruth.net)

Submission to God should be a thing of joy, but if you find yourself struggling with it, you will have to learn it like you do in everything else. God will make His grace available to you. Your prayer life will move to appreciable dimensions, and in the end, you will be glad that you let God completely into your life.

89

ZEAL

Zeal is the enthusiasm and fervour to do or carry things through with a sustained eagerness and earnestness no matter what comes your way. It is a type of unstoppable and unyielding militancy that accommodates no apathy, indifference or passivity.

Sustained enthusiasm is a crucial factor in successful praying. It takes dedication and fervour to pray in the first instance, and to do so continuously and at all cost. Sometimes you may be filled with a burning desire to pray, while at other times there may be a total lack of passion to approach the throne of grace. Zeal and speed are crucial companions of prayer. It takes Zeal to become successful in everything we do.

Not much can be accomplished in prayer in the absence of enthusiasm. Zeal is like an indwelling fire or restlessness that keeps a person going, and stopping at nothing to accomplish an aim or goal. A fervent spirit will pray with intensity and will esteem being in God's presence more than comfort, rest and other things that lure from God. An apathetic spirit will wait for times of severe hardships before taking hold of God in prayer. Most prayers carried out when a disaster hits are usually less effective.

Be On Fire for God

The Christian's Zeal must be centred on God. A cold and lukewarm Christian life will reflect in the way we pray. To the Laodicean Christians Jesus said,

"So then because thou art lukewarm, and neither cold nor hot, I will spew thee out of my mouth" (Rev 3:16). To the Colossian Christians Paul wrote: *"If ye then be risen with Christ, seek those things which are above, where Christ sitteth on the right hand of God. Set your affection on the things above. Not on things on the earth. For ye are dead, and your life is hid with Christ in God"* (Colossians 3:1-3).

A zealous Christian is moved by the things that move God, touched by the things that touch God and vexed by the things that vex God. We fail to harness the benefits of prayer not because we cannot pray, neither is it because God cannot save, but because we would not pray intentionally and consistently.

A Life Void of Zeal

It is easy to recognise people who have Zeal for God – whether for prayer, soul-winning, financial giving or simply loving other people. True enthusiasm for God is founded on knowledge and conviction, not just emotions. Zeal is not mere fanaticism. People who lack passion for God and the things of God:

- Live an average Christian life.
- Are indifferent towards the suffering of other people.
- Are unwilling to make sacrifices to advance the gospel of Christ.
- Fail to use their potential to accomplish great things for God.
- Are spiritually blind and cannot perceive things from God's own perspective.
- Make unremarkable or run-of-the mill achievements.

For the above reasons people fall far short of doing great things for God, at the level He expects. Imagine the early church being unmoved when Peter was awaiting death in prison (Acts 12:5). What if they failed to sell what they owned (Act 2:42-47) to meet the needs of the brethren and the gospel, the inspiring testimonies we read in the book of Acts would not be there. These people gave and prayed fervently so God made the lame to walk and the blind to see; He raised the dead and opened prison doors. People prayed all night for days. They banded together and prayed until the gates of the enemy gave way.

Zealous For God

On their way to the Promised Land Israel was experiencing a period of falsehood, ungodliness and moral erosion. God was very displeased with them and meted out severe punishment to His people. Whilst they had yet to recover from the consequences of divine judgment, an Israelite man brought into the camp and into his tent a Midianite woman (an act forbidden by God). A man called Phinehas was provoked by this evil because he had great zeal for God. He wasted no time, but moved swiftly to prevent the judgement of God:

> "Now when Phinehas the son of Eleazar, the son of Aaron the priest, saw it, he rose from among the congregation and took a javelin in his hand and he went after the man of Israel into the tent and thrust both of them through, the man of Israel, and the woman through her body. So the plague was stopped among the children of Israel" (Numbers 25:7-9).

This exemplifies how intercessors should act swiftly to prevent the anger of God upon this generation. Phinehas stood between God and the land. He staved off further judgement which the sinful Israelite would have brought upon the congregation by bringing a Midianite woman into the presence of God. God had previously warned against association with the Midianites because they were an idolatrous people.

If Phinehas was cold and indifferent to the things of God, there would have been calamity upon the people. Unresponsiveness by God's people and their failure to pray and appease God for the land will always lead to spiritual crisis. Satan's role is to lure people, leadership and entire communities to do things that displease and invite God's judgement, but men and woman who are addicted to God will make themselves channels of God's mercy and power and bring the blessings of intercession to bear upon the land.

We must all behave like Phinehas- not by physically killing people, but by appeasing God for our land and people through prayers. God needs zealous people like David who will look Goliath in the eye and risk their lives to bring deliverance and freedom to God's people; people like Daniel who will be prepared to risk being thrown into the lion's den in order to do the will of God, and people like Queen Esther who will be willing to perish so that their fellow citizens will be saved. It takes zeal to fast and pray- to do mighty things for God without expecting personal reward. It takes zeal to take risks on behalf of God and His people.

90

ZEPHANIAH 3:17

A lot about prayers can be learned from the book of Zephaniah 3:17. Zephaniah is a bible name meaning, 'the Lord is my secret'. The Hebrew meaning of Zephaniah is, 'the Lord has concealed' or 'the Lord has protected'. God holds the deepest secrets of our lives and the universe. We must be completely reliant on Him to shed light in all our ways. The secret things belong to God. Meditating on and praying with Zephaniah 3:17 can give a fresh touch to your prayer. The passage says, *"The LORD thy God in the midst of thee is mighty; He will save, He will rejoice over thee with joy; He will rest in His love, He will joy over thee with singing"*

What a comfort, encouragement and reassurance this passage provides for God's children in times of difficulties? This scripture should cheer the heart of every believer. Let us examine the different parts of this passage and their relevance to effective prayer.

"The Lord your God Is In Your Midst"

Moses said to God, *"If thy presence go not with me, carry us not up hence."* (Exodus 33:15). God's presence means much more than gold to his children. Have you ever gone into the place of prayer and then feel God was not present there? What a frightening position to be! Occasionally you may feel empty and fatigued at the time of prayer; but it is never about your feelings but God's assurances. If you do not feel His presence at the place of prayer, you must claim His presence. Every aspect of our daily walk with God is by faith. You were saved by faith, so you must pray by faith. Feelings or no feelings, the Lord is always there with you. He is always in our midst.

"The Mighty One Will Save"

God's power is the life behind your faith and the force behind your prayer. Prayer is never by human strength. Samson did great things through God's power. David killed Goliath through the same power. Moses took Israel out of Egypt by the mighty hand of God. Joshua divided the Promised Land by the power of God. Jesus did incredible miracles through the mighty hand of the Father. The Apostles performed miracles, signs and wonders by the might of God.

No matter what you face God is mighty to save. He saves from sin. He will save from poverty, sickness, emotional crisis and every form of demonic entrapment and harassment. He is able to save to the very end everything and everyone committed to His trust. If you cannot trust in God's ability to deliver you or whoever you are praying for, what is the point of praying?

"He Will Rejoice Over You with Gladness and Singing"

God takes great delight in us, the bible says: *"Let the Lord be magnified who takes pleasure in the prosperity of his servant"* (Psalm 35:27). He is happy to see you prosper. He is eager to hear you pray because your progress gives Him pleasure. God gives you audience because He enjoys your presence.

- He takes pleasure in the prosperity of His people (Psalm 35:27)
- He is thrilled by the praise of His people (Psalm 69:30-31)
- He is delighted in the prayer of the upright (Proverbs 15:8)

- He is pleased when you come to Him, full of faith (Hebrews 11:6)

Yes, God is thrilled over us. Our prayer is a sweet smelling savour to Him. We were created for his presence. Revelation 5:8 states: *"And when he had taken the book, the four beasts and four and twenty elders fell down before the Lamb, having every one of them harps, and golden vials full of odours, which are the prayers of the saints."*

To God prayer means relationship, fellowship, communion and taking time out with His children.

He Will Quiet You

Jesus is the Prince of peace. He died so that we might be saved and enjoy God's perfect peace. No matter the turbulence you face your peace is guaranteed in Jesus.

If you find it difficult to have a restful mind, a surrendered will and a hopeful heart, take time out with God and ask Him to fill you with peace that surpasses all comprehension. Jesus has given you an invitation to bring your troubles before Him:

> *"Come to me, all you who labour and are heavy laden, and I will give you rest. Take my yoke upon you and learn from me, for I am gentle and lowly in heart and you will find rest for your souls"* (Matthew 11:28-29). NKJV

You need peace to enjoy all that God has for you. You need a peaceful heart to pray effectively. God has made provisions for you to enjoy His peace in its fullest measure.

"With His Love"

We are the redeemed of the Lord, purchased by the blood of Christ- the delight and chosen of God. The Church is the bride of Christ- purified, protected and 'patented' by Him. You are God's precious possession. His love for His children exceeds all understanding- the kind that made Jesus lay down His life on the cross. Our humanity and frailty never dilute God's love for us. This love cannot be quantified, neither can it be fully explained. In and outside of the prayer closet, you must continue to see God's love around you. Every answered prayer is a product of God's love for us.

Always remember in your closet that: The Lord your God is in your midst; He will save; He will rejoice over you with gladness; He will quiet you with his love and He will rejoice over you with singing.

CONCLUSION

I hope your trip through this book or parts of it has been both inspiring and instructive. One of the focuses of this book was to give the reader an insight into numerous aspects of prayer, especially those not frequently addressed in Christian meetings and Christian organisations, which are nevertheless, crucial to an effective prayer life.

Prayer is a journey, not an event. Prayer is a process that takes place within the closet. Prayer has many interconnected aspects which if neglected or ignored, can remove the steam from its practice and speed from its wheels. Although you do not necessarily have to be perfect in all the issues addressed in this book, a disregard for them can squeeze the life out of your relationship with God, and constitute stumbling blocks to your prayer path.

Anyone can pray but very few can pay the price needed to pray certain dimensions of prayer. Prayer can bring about real change and usher in awesome dimensions of divine intervention. Anything that is worth doing is worth doing very well. Every prayer that is worth praying should be given all that it requires to make it productive. Many Christians agree that prayer is truly the master key to victorious Christian living, yet not everyone will go the extra mile to pay the price for effective prayers.

Your prayer must change you before it can change anything or anyone else. If your prayer cannot transform your life, it will hardly alter anything else. Prayer is designed by God to overhaul destinies, bring about revolution and rebuild that which the enemy has broken down.

I hope that at least one session of this book has blessed your life. I therefore encourage you to take steps to put into practice whatever God has ministered to you from its pages. I have prayed, and will continue to pray for everyone who picks up this book; I believe that something new will be born out of your prayer life as a result reading the message communicated through the book.

BIBLIOGRAPHY

Caballeros H, (2001). Victorious Warfare: Discovering your Rightful Place in God's Kingdom. Thomas Nelson

Freedman D. N, (2000). Eerdmans Dictionary of the Bible. Grand Rapids, Wm. B. Eerdmans Publishing Co.

Hickey M, (2000). Breaking Generational Curses: Overcoming the Legacy of Sin in Your Family. Tulsa, Harrison House

Hunt J, (2008). Counselling through Your Bible Handbook. Eugene, Harves House Publishers

Marshall T, (2003). Explaining Covenants. Tonbridge, Sovereign World.

Mulinde J. & Daniel M; (2010). Awakening the Church. Orlando, World Trumpet Mission

Munroe M, (2004). Rediscovering the Kingdom. Shippensburg, Destiny Image

Phillips K. (1999). Discovering Truth. Aurora Publications

Sumrall L; (1999). Prayer. South Bend, Sumrall Publishing

Unger M.F; (2005). The New Unger's Bible Dictionary. Oxford, Lion Hudson PLC

Zuck R.B (1997). The Speaker's Quote Book. Grand Rapids, Kregel Publications.

The Guardian (1 August 2006). MoD admits body armour would have saved tank commander. http://www.the guardian.com/uk/2006/aug/01/military.iraq
(Accessed: 21st December, 2014).

www.ingramcontent.com/pod-product-compliance
Lightning Source LLC
LaVergne TN
LVHW051620080426
835511LV00016B/2090